The
Fast Forward
MBA in Marketing

D1370248

THE FAST FORWARD MBA SERIES

The Fast Forward MBA Series provides time-pressed business professionals and students with concise, one-stop information to help them solve business problems and make smart, informed business decisions. All of the volumes, written by industry leaders, contain "tough ideas made easy." The published books in this series are:

The Fast Forward MBA in Business
(0-471-14660-9)
by Virginia O'Brien

The Fast Forward MBA in Finance
(0-471-10930-4)
by John Tracy

The Fast Forward MBA Pocket Reference
(0-471-14595-5)
by Paul A. Argenti

The
Fast Forward
MBA in Marketing

DALLAS MURPHY

John Wiley & Sons, Inc.

New York • Chichester • Weinheim • Brisbane • Singapore • Toronto

Copyright © 1997 by Dallas Murphy
Published by John Wiley & Sons, Inc.

Library of Congress Cataloging-in-Publication Data:
Murphy, Dallas.
    The fast forward MBA in marketing / Dallas Murphy.
        p.   cm.
    Includes index.
    ISBN 0-471-16616-2 (alk. paper)
    1. Marketing—Handbooks, manuals, etc.   I. Title.
HF5415.M834   1997
658.8—dc21   96-40005
                                                            CIP

Printed in the United States of America

10 9 8 7 6 5 4 3 2

Dallas Murphy is a freelance writer specializing in business and marine topics. He is also a novelist, author of *Lover Man, Apparent Wind, Lush Life,* and *Don't Explain.* He lives in New York City.

ACKNOWLEDGMENTS

All my thanks for their generous assistance to: Janet Coleman, Carl Dec, Stuart Dworeck, Jim Heddleston, Robert Hogan, Mary Hogan, David Langhorne, Eugenia Leftwich, Wade Leftwich, Jonathan Russo, and Bob O'Sullivan.

CONTENTS

I am pleased to include at the close of most chapters a section called *Fast Forward to the Real World.* There you will find selected articles from *Marketing Tools* magazine, a publication by American Demographics, Inc., a Dow Jones Company. In each article, leading practitioners of and thinkers about marketing apply the concepts contained in the preceding chapter to the actual world of professional marketing. Their experience and practical advice will prove useful to students, teachers, and working marketers alike.

I am grateful, also, to American Demographics, publisher Wade Leftwich, and Peter Francese, author of *Marketing Know-How,* for supplying "Sources of Marketing Information" which appears as an appendix to this volume.

The Marketing Concept and the Marketing Mix

There are no products. There are only customers.
—*Peter Drucker*

Once, not long ago, there was manufacturing—they made the widget—and there was marketing—they sold the widget. The two functions were separate. Marketing had little influence over manufacturing, and manufacturing had little interest in marketing. Marketing didn't even enter the mix until manufacturing was complete. Marketers thus had to take the product as a given. Their task was to create a demand for the widget, package and price it, and establish a physical network to carry the product to its potential customers. Manufacturing naturally wanted marketing to sell the product, but manufacturers didn't want marketers wandering around the shop floor telling them what kind of widgets to make and fouling their coattails in the widget machine. Marketing and manufacturing converged somewhere around the bottom line, but by then, as we shall see, it was often too late.

A new view has largely superseded that old separation between the two functions. Called *the marketing concept,* it was institutionalized around 1948, when the American Marketing Association offered its *official* definition of marketing: "The performance of business activities directed toward, and incident to, the flow of goods and services to customer or user." This heralded a shift in focus from sales orientation to customer/market orientation. The shift did not happen quickly, universally, or painlessly. Many former powerhouses of American business—IBM, Sears, General Motors, and the Chrysler Corporation—lost significant market share through their unwillingness or inability to adjust their marketing strategies to the changing marketplace.

Consider the impending plight of the American automobile manufacturers in 1962 when Volkswagen bugs began to proliferate on the nation's highways. Detroit's Big Three ridiculed the thing—it was tiny, definitely homely, and its design never changed—and went on blithely producing the same kind of cars that had, after all, made them the Big Three. They tweaked a tail fin here and there, but the cars were fundamentally still flashy, heavy, and uneconomical. Big Three marketing departments continued dutifully to sell the products they were given by adjusting their promotion pitches. They spent bundles on advertising, sales gimmicks, rebates, and sweet financing deals. But sales of American cars continued to plummet as tsunamis of Japanese imports broke over West Coast ports, and Germans stormed ashore on the East Coast.

Once fat and happy, Chrysler, Ford, and GM were starving to death. What had changed? Well, the market had changed. Customers in overwhelming numbers were buying smaller, more economical cars because gas prices had soared and tastes had changed. And then there was the quality issue. People in droves were buying foreign cars because they were better than American cars. When, in the halcyon days, Americans bought new cars every year, declining quality didn't matter significantly. But now people wanted their cars to run better longer. American cars seemed to spend more time in the shop than on the road.

Why, we might well ask, did these giant companies allow this to happen? Why didn't they know what the public clearly knew? It didn't take a market analyst with a Harvard MBA to count the foreign cars in the shopping-mall parking lot. And if the Big Three knew, why didn't they act? Seemingly blindly, they continued to produce cars that their customers didn't want. Auto-industry historians point out that marketing people beseeched their bosses to address offshore competition by building smaller cars. So did their dealerships, from the front lines of failure. Management replied, "We don't know how to build small cars. We've always built big cars."

Then came the Clean Air Act and the 1974 gas shortage. Only when at death's door did automakers produce compact cars, but they did so in a panic, and the results—the Corvair and the Pinto, for instance—were rushed, ill-planned, and shoddy. Partly as a result of Ralph Nader's *Unsafe at Any Speed,* which called the Pinto a firebomb waiting for a light, Congress passed the Motor Vehicle Safety Act. In 1978, the Big Three recalled more cars than they produced. Instead of looking their own management failures squarely in the eye, the Big Three squealed about unfair competition and high domestic-labor costs. Detroit, once the embodiment of the American dream, turned into a ghost town.

CONCEPT

The Big Three had forgotten the marketing concept. Simply put, the marketing concept holds that business activity is the process of creating a satisfied customer (i.e., making a market) and that profit is the reward for doing so. Moreover, the product is not an inflexible given, but variable according to customers' changing wants and needs. Marketing, then, becomes a core business function, a matter of keeping everyone in the entire organization focused on the customer even before manufacturing fires up its first machine. If you have it on reliable evidence that more and more customers want long, slim widgets, you don't go on producing short, squat ones, even if your company was founded on and hitherto profited from the production of short, squat widgets. Today, marketing is part of everyone's job description.

CONCEPT

"INSIDE OUT" VERSUS "OUTSIDE IN"

While many companies—Procter & Gamble, Marriott, Disney, to cite only a few—adhere to the marketing concept in every move they make, others—like the Big Three—gravitate back to the "selling concept." In other words, sell the thing you make rather than what the customer wants. The focus here is on short-term transactions rather than long-term customer satisfaction. The selling concept tends by definition to view customers as conquests. For a brief upward spike in sales volume, companies are willing to risk losing customers. All marketing studies demonstrate that customers who have been burned tell their friends about the experience in much greater numbers than do satisfied customers.

The selling concept takes an inside-out view, since it starts with its own factory and existing products. "In contrast, the marketing concept takes an outside-in perspective. It starts with a well-defined market, focuses on customer needs, coordinates all the marketing activities affecting customers, and makes profits by creating long-term customer satisfaction."[1]

In the June 8, 1992, issue of *Marketing News,* Thomas E. Caruso put the principle this way: "The shortest definition of marketing I know is 'meeting needs profitably.' The purpose of marketing is to generate customer value. You've got to generate more value for the consumer but not give away the house. It's a very delicate balance."[2]

This book will examine the broad subject of marketing from the perspective of the marketing concept. Modern marketing holds that managers actively *implement* strategies to supply value to the customer. How does the marketer implement his or her strategy?

To begin to answer this question, we will turn first to the fundamental aspects of marketing—the so-called marketing mix. Traditionally, marketing texts and courses have referred to the components of the marketing mix as "the four Ps": Product, Price, Place (meaning distribution, but that doesn't start with a "P"), and Promotion.

Certain modern thinkers about the subject view "the four Ps" as old-fashioned, because they don't focus enough on the customer. These marketers contend that customer service demands as much attention as product, price, place, and promotion, and we will examine that notion in Chapter 5, "Customers." But for our purposes now, the four Ps serve as a way into the fundamentals of marketing. We will examine each "P" in turn.

Fast
Forward to the Real World

Outclassing the Competition

Bradley T. Gale

Ever since the oil crisis of the 1970s ended an era of almost effortless prosperity, Western businesses have been struggling to deal strategically with a new world in which markets experienced little or no real growth. Many firms responded by experimenting with schemes to "restructure," "find synergy," "feed the stars." Few of these popular nostrums worked, and far too many of the organizations that tried them are no longer around.

Companies that did well, on the other hand, were those that tended to employ simple strategies: they identified real customers and gave those customers what they wanted to buy. These firms recognized that customers choose one product or service over another for a very simple reason: they believe it's a better value than they could expect to get from the alternative. Entrepreneurs like Frank Perdue understood this line of reasoning perfectly. As we will shortly demonstrate, Perdue elevated the humble uncooked chicken from a commodity to a premium product—and made a lot of money in the process—by responding to his customer's notions about value.

Unfortunately, most efforts to plan business strategy neglect this simple truth. And by failing to ensure that their product or service will be a value leader, businesses set themselves up for failure.

Businesses follow generally accepted accounting principles (GAAP) in financial management. As a result, everyone can agree on financial goals, understand how they'll be measured, and work together to achieve them.

But companies have lacked generally accepted strategic principles (GASP) that would define the customer value metrics at the heart of a company's strategic navigation system. There has been little agreement on how the components of competitive advantage should be pursued or how to measure progress. This has made it hard for people in organizations to work together to achieve competitive success.

The basis of GASP should be a simple idea: companies succeed by providing superior customer value. And value is simply quality, however the customer defines it, offered at the right price.

valve = quality + price   *(Continued)*

5

(Continued)

While this strategic principle is simple, it's also very powerful. Superior customer value is the best leading indicator of market share and competitiveness. And market share and competitiveness in turn drive the achievement of long-term financial goals such as profitability, growth, and shareholder value.

These facts are not only supported by common sense; they're also supported by rigorous research. AT&T, for example, has found that changes in real, technically measured quality of its products are followed only about three months later by changes in the customers' perception of the quality of those products. Changes in perceived quality, on the other hand, are followed a mere two months afterward by changes in market share. *perceived vs real*

Customers: What Goes on in Their Minds?

The first step in achieving leadership in market-perceived quality and value is to understand what causes customers in your targeted market to make their decisions—to decide that one product offers better value than another. Understanding that is the most central objective of a customer value analysis.

Figure I.1 summarizes how customers make purchase decisions. The factors that contribute to quality in the customer's mind need not be

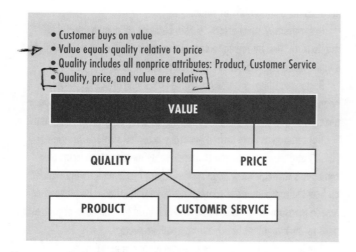

- Customer buys on value
- Value equals quality relative to price
- Quality includes all nonprice attributes: Product, Customer Service
- Quality, price, and value are relative

VALUE

QUALITY   **PRICE**

PRODUCT   **CUSTOMER SERVICE**

FIGURE I.1 *How customers choose between competing suppliers. (Source:* Managing Customer Value, *by Bradley T. Gale; copyright © 1994 by The Free Press.)*

(Continued)

(Continued)

mysterious. Customers will gladly tell you what they are. A customer value analysis uses information from customers to show how customers make decisions in your marketplace. And in giving you that information, it suggests what you need to change to ensure that more of them will buy from you.

The simplest customer value analysis consists of two parts. First, you create a customer value profile that compares your organization's performance with that of one or more competitors. This customer value profile itself usually has two elements:

- A market-perceived quality profile
- A market-perceived price profile

Second, once you have created the customer value profile, you draw a customer value map.

Of the elements of a customer value analysis, the single most important is the market-perceived quality profile. That's because it summarizes the aspects of the marketplace that are usually easiest to change to improve your business. In many markets, price is an even greater driver of customer decisions than market-perceived quality. But cutting prices won't usually improve your bottom line.

The market-perceived quality profile is a chart that does three things:

1. It identifies what quality really is to customers in your marketplace.

2. It tells you which competitors are performing best on each aspect of quality.

3. It gives you overall quality performance measures based on the definition of quality that customers actually use in making their purchase decisions.

The process of creating a market-perceived quality profile is relatively simple, though it's time consuming to do it well:

1. Ask people in the targeted market—both your customers and your competitors—to list the factors that are important in their purchase decisions. You can ask them in forums such as focus groups.

2. Establish how the various quality attributes are weighted in the customer's decision. One way to do this is through sophisticated statistical analysis of customers' statements about their overall quality rating and performance ratings on the individual quality attributes. But in most cases, it's almost as good—and much easier and cheaper— simply to ask customers how they weight the various factors. Ask

(Continued)

(Continued)

them to distribute 100 points of "decision weight" among all the high-level factors they listed in the previous round of research.

3. Ask customers to rate, on a scale of, say, 1 to 10, the performance of each business on each competing factor. Then multiply each business's score on each factor by the weight of that factor, and add the results to get an overall customer satisfaction score.

Customer Value Analysis: Playing Chicken

To understand customer value analysis, let's look at the case of Perdue Farms, which has in the last 20 years become the dominant brand of uncooked chicken on the eastern seaboard of the United States.

In the early 1980s, I had a chance to speak before the members of the Southeast Egg and Poultry Association, a group of Perdue's competitors. I asked them how consumers compared Perdue's chicken with their own. I've often used the results to demonstrate how to create a market-perceived quality profile—and to illustrate its power by showing how and why Frank Perdue changed the chicken market and became a very rich man.

Many of the members of the association remembered the days before Perdue inherited his chicken business from his father Arthur. In that era, chickens were a commodity—as they had been for generations. The customer generally ignored the brand names that some companies put on their chickens and bought principally on price.

Figure I.2 shows a simple market-perceived quality profile describing the chicken business in Perdue's father's day—before the consumer perceived any significant differences among chicken producers. This profile and the one that follows were created by a panel of Southeast Egg and Poultry Association members under my guidance.

First, I asked the panel to list the key characteristics (other than price) that affected buying decisions. They are shown in the first column of Figure I.2. Second, I asked them the relative weight of these issues in Perdue's father's day. These appear in the second column. In those days, "availability" represented an overwhelming share of the nonprice factors in chicken purchases—people usually bought whatever was on the shelves. Third, the panel estimated customers' opinions of Perdue's father's performance and the performance of the rest of the industry for each criterion, on a scale of 1 to 10. Not surprisingly, there were no differences. In the old days, the ratings of Arthur Perdue's chickens and those of the rest of industry were identical. The last column of Figure I.2

(Continued)

(Continued)

Quality attributes	Importance weights	Perdue	Performance scores: Others	Ratio
Yellow bird	5	7	7	1.0
Meat-to-bone	10	6	6	1.0
No pin feathers	15	5	5	1.0
Fresh	15	7	7	1.0
Availability	55	8	8	1.0
Brand image	0	6	6	1.0
	100			
Customer satisfaction score:		7.15	7.15	
Market-perceived quality ratio:				1.0

FIGURE I.2 *The quality profile indicates that before Frank Perdue launched his poultry improvement project, there were no perceived differences between chicken producers. (Source:* Managing Customer Value, *by Bradley T. Gale; copyright © 1994 by The Free Press. Adapted from the* PIMS Principles, *by Robert D. Buzzell & Bradley T. Gale; copyright © 1987 by The Free Press.)*

is the ratio of Perdue's performance to his competitors'. Naturally, because the Perdue performance and the performance of the industry were the same, all of the ratios are 1.0. The overall market-perceived quality ratio is also 1.0—indicating (of course) no significant difference.

Next, we analyzed the market situation under Frank Perdue. This provides a good example of how a market-perceived quality profile helps explain a typical market.

Frank started his work by learning what customers wanted in their chickens, and then he learned how to deliver it. That changed the chicken market forever.

The market-perceived quality profile based on the Southeast Egg and Poultry Association panel's report on the chicken market under Frank Perdue appears in Figure I.3.

We used the same quality attributes for the analysis of today's markets as we used for the analysis of the market in Perdue's father's day. I started by asking the panel to estimate the weighting of the different nonprice purchase criteria in customer decisions today. As the second column of Figure I.3 shows, Perdue's better chickens had caused customers to change their decision-making dramatically. The weight on "availability" fell from 55 percent to 10 percent as consumers began to place more weight on attributes where Perdue had pulled ahead ("meat-to-bone," "no pin-feathers," and "brand image").

(Continued)

(Continued)

Quality attributes	Weight	Perdue	Avg. comp.	Ratio	Weight times ratio
1	2	3	4	5 = 3/4	6 = 2 × 5
Yellow bird	10	8.1	7.2	1.13	11.3
Meat-to-bone	20	9.0	7.3	1.23	24.6
No pin feathers	20	9.2	6.5	1.42	28.4
Fresh	15	8.0	8.0	1.00	15.0
Availability	10	8.0	8.0	1.00	10.0
Brand image	25	9.4	6.4	1.47	36.8
	100				
Customer satisfaction:		8.8	7.1		
Market-perceived quality ratio:					126.1

FIGURE I.3 *As this quality profile shows, Perdue's campaign to build a better chicken had a noticeable impact on customer perceptions. (Source:* Managing Customer Value, *by Bradley T. Gale; copyright © 1994 by The Free Press. Adapted from the* PIMS Principles, *by Robert D. Buzzell & Bradley T. Gale; copyright © 1987 by The Free Press.)*

Next, I asked the panel to estimate, on a scale of 1 to 10, customers' ratings of the quality of Perdue chickens on those quality attributes versus customers' ratings of average chickens (i.e., the chickens sold by other members of the association). These figures appear in the next two columns.

From this information, we can calculate customer satisfaction scores for both Perdue chicken and the rest of the industry. These scores, created by multiplying the performance ratings for each purchase criterion by the estimated relative weighting of that criterion, appear in the "customer satisfaction" row under the ratings of Perdue chicken and the ratings of the average competitor's chicken.

By themselves, the individual customer satisfaction ratings are not very meaningful. Any researcher who tells you, "You should be really excited because you scored an 8.8 in customer satisfaction" is misleading you. The 8.8 is meaningful only in relation to how other people score.

Thus, what is truly meaningful in this chart are the ratios of the ratings customers give the different competitors. The "ratio" column of the chart shows ratios between ratings given Perdue for each quality attribute and the ratings given his competitors.

We can also calculate an overall market-perceived quality score for Perdue chicken versus the rest of the industry. Assigning a weight from

(Continued)

(Continued)

column 2 to each number in the "Ratio" column, we get the numbers in the "Weight times ratio" column. Adding these together, we get a market-perceived quality score of 126.1.

If you want to produce a weighted ratio of Perdue's scores to his competitors' scores, you can simply divide this market-perceived quality score by 100. The result is the market-perceived quality ratio. It is a strongly favorable 1.26. Either way, Frank Perdue had produced a market-perceived quality rating 26 percent higher than his father's.

Comparing column 6 with column 2 also allows you to pinpoint why Perdue is so far ahead. Of Perdue's 26.1-point lead, 1.3 comes from "yellower bird," 4.6 comes from "meatier chicken," 8.4 comes from "fewer bruises or pinfeathers," and 11.8 comes from superior "brand image."

Creating a Value Map

In the chicken business, retailers buy from chicken producers and then list the retail price per pound in their advertisements. Customers, therefore, can make a simple decision, and there is no need for a complex analysis of how consumers understand the price of the product. We don't have to create a market-perceived price profile. If Perdue chickens cost 69 cents a pound this week and Brand X costs 59 cents a pound, we can produce a customer value map like that shown in Figure I.4.

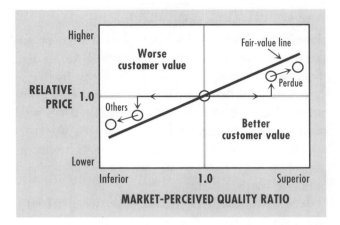

FIGURE I.4 *A customer value map of the chicken business finds Perdue's product is in the best possible position in relation to the competition. (Source:* Managing Customer Value, *by Bradley T. Gale; copyright © 1994 by The Free Press.)*

(Continued)

(Continued)

Running from the upper right of the customer value map to the lower left is the "fair-value line," which indicates where quality is balanced against price. The fair-value line should be the line of points at which a competitor would neither gain nor lose market share. That is usually difficult to calculate with precision, but ordinarily we can approximate it simply by asking customers how much weight they put on quality and how much weight they put on price. Then we plot a line with a slope equal to the percentage of the decision that the average customer says is based on quality divided by the percentage of the decision the average customer says is based on price. Anyone below and to the right is in a strong, share-gaining position. Anyone above and to the left is in a share-losing position.

Before Frank Perdue took over the business and began to make pull-ahead moves on different quality attributes, all competitors plotted more or less at the center of the value map with the same perceived quality and price. As Frank made his moves, Perdue Farms moved to the right into the "grow and prosper zone," and competitors were pushed to the left. Unable to quickly match or offset Perdue's quality improvements, competitors then cut prices, which increased Perdue's price relative to theirs. A succession of customer value maps over time would allow one to track these changes in relative perceived price and quality. Here, the same progress over time is indicated by two different sets of points. The dark point indicates where Perdue was when he first started to advertise his chickens. The lighter point above and to the right indicates the position he achieved after his brand name was more established.

We have drawn this map on the assumption that chicken buyers place two-thirds of the weight of their buying decisions on price and one-third on quality. (Despite the Perdue revolution in the chicken market, chicken buyers remain highly price sensitive.) Nonetheless, Frank Perdue remained on the share-gaining side of the line for an extended time period. And he earned better margins than the producers of lower-priced chickens, too. Frank Perdue was in the best position on the value map, below the fair-value line, but in the upper right corner. His organization was producing a higher-priced, premium product and yet still offering better value than his competitors.

As this analysis shows, Frank Perdue's competitors recognized that his product was superior to ordinary chickens on almost every nonprice criterion.

This success wasn't surprising: Perdue had started his efforts to create his brand with research to learn just what customers wanted in their

(Continued)

(Continued)

chickens. He began from a position where consumers perceived all chickens to be more or less equal, as we showed in Figure I.2. But he invested in careful breeding and improved feed to give customers what his surveys showed they wanted: meatier, yellower chickens. Finally, Perdue invested heavily in advertising and promotion to tell customers what he had done. In recent years, under Frank Perdue's son Jim, the company has even begun improving its once-uneven labor relations. The result: a product that dominates its competitors in what was previously a "commodity" market.

You Can Do It, Too

If Frank Perdue's competitors really want to challenge him, Figure I.3 provides the right place for them to start. The competitors should, of course, check the impressions of the experts by surveying real consumers to learn if this is an accurate picture of how they make their decisions. When they do that, they'll encounter at least a few minor complexities. Customers probably won't all agree on a neat list of quality attributes such as we've shown in Figures I.2 and I.3. Some will refer to "yellow bird," others will refer to "good color," still others to "a fresh-looking bird." Researchers must work out a short, "clean" list of nonoverlapping attributes that accurately represents what the customers are saying.

If customers list numerous attributes (as they probably will), it's good to summarize them in a list of a few "high-level" attributes—major issues, which in this case might be items such as "appearance," "brand image," and perhaps "the eating experience." The rating on the high-level attribute "appearance" would be a summary of performance on sub-attributes such as "yellowness," "no pinfeathers," and whatever other appearance issues the customer says are important.

In other businesses, the high-level attributes might be issues such as "customer service," "quality of sales staff," and "product quality." For each, you'd produce a list of sub-attributes—attributes that contribute to determining whether the organization has achieved quality on the main attributes. For example, for the quality attribute "customer service," subattributes might include "friendly personnel," "knowledgeable personnel," and "promptness." This produces a hierarchy of attributes.

Once Perdue's competitors had generated a list of attributes and sub-attributes from customers, they could ask customers how they weighted them. Then they could ask how the customers rated each competitor. A properly researched market-perceived quality profile from real customers

(Continued)

(Continued)

would give them the data they needed to decide how to meet Perdue's challenge by matching his strong points and developing their own strong points.

You can conduct a customer value analysis of any products in any market. Indeed, if you can't afford expensive scientific research, you can still gain some insights by informally surveying customers you'd talk to anyway. Start by writing down how you think customers make decisions. Then ask them.

To do a customer value analysis right, be sure to include all the most important competitors—which means the two or three largest competitors, the fastest-growing competitors, and any competitor with new or unusual technology. (Be sure you don't leave out any new competitors from the rapidly growing ranks in Asian countries.)

Customer value analysis is especially powerful if you conduct separate customer value analyses for various segments of your market and for different customers in your distribution chain.

If you discover that poor relative performance on one or more criteria is hurting you, you should probably try to design a leap-frogging move. (Japanese automakers did that when they went from producing cars known as "tinny rustbuckets" in the 1960s to cars that provided the kind of transportation customers wanted—and couldn't get from U.S. manufacturers—in the 1970s.)

Try experimenting with a market-perceived quality profile right now, using the customer value profile form shown in Figure I.5. Better yet, make copies of the form and have several people in your organization complete it. Then compare how you each understand customer decision-making today.

Note that there is nothing "subjective" about a customer value analysis, when it is properly conducted. Any market research firm should be able to determine, objectively, whether or not the opinions of the panel of Southeast Egg and Poultry Association members were correct. If market researchers do their jobs well and the definition of the market served is held constant, then a market-perceived quality profile and a customer value map produced by one research firm will be essentially the same as a market-perceived quality profile and customer value map produced by another. Thus, a properly calculated market-perceived quality profile provides an objective, impersonal measure of how the customers in any given marketplace really judge and select products.

Of course, we could imagine minor changes in methodology that might have led to minor changes in results. We could have used different

(Continued)

(Continued)

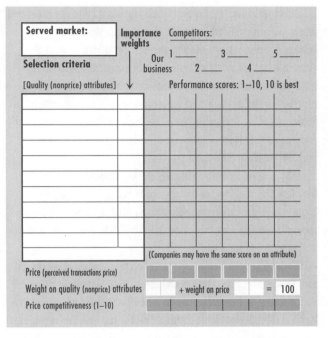

FIGURE I.5 *Try experimenting with a market-perceived quality profile for your own business, using this customer value profile form. (Source:* Managing Customer Value, *by Bradley T. Gale; copyright © 1994 by The Free Press.)*

rating scales, for instance, and that might have affected the size of Perdue's favorable ratios. If we had asked for customer's ratings on a scale of 1 to 7 instead of 1 to 10, the final ratios might have come out slightly different. But that's just like saying you can measure the distance between New York and Washington in either miles or kilometers, and you'll get different numbers. The distance between New York and Washington is real and unchanging. Who does the measuring and what scale is used are ultimately unimportant, as long as he or she is objective.

Why Satisfied Customers Leave Anyway

You can easily see why this analysis is more useful than traditional customer satisfaction measurements. An old-line chicken producer's customer may give their chicken a rating of 8 out of a possible 10, and that may translate to "highly satisfied." But they'll nonetheless switch to Perdue if Perdue's innovations make them even more satisfied. A customer value analysis, on the other hand, can provide early warning of what is happening and give the competitor insights into how to prevent it.

(Continued)

(Continued)

Market-perceived quality profiles also highlight other key issues that simple customer satisfaction studies obscure. Take the case of AT&T's General Business Systems division, the U.S. market leader in small-business telephone switching systems. The strength of telephone-switching-system manufacturers varies from region to region because customer service plays an even bigger role in customer satisfaction than hardware quality. And service varies depending on the performance of each region's managers. Moreover, different promotional strategies work differently in different regions.

AT&T General Business Systems (GBS) had always been strong in New York City. And that seemed strange to headquarters executives because customer-satisfaction data showed AT&T customers were more dissatisfied in New York than elsewhere. Could it be that customer satisfaction wasn't so important?

When GBS began conducting market-perceived quality analyses in each region, executives came to understand their markets in a new and profound way. In New York, they learned what studies had hidden: New York is a difficult place to do business, and the customers of almost all brands of switching equipment were more dissatisfied in New York than in other parts of the country.

So even though AT&T's New York customers showed more dissatisfaction than customers elsewhere, satisfaction relative to competition in New York significantly exceeded customer satisfaction relative to competition in other regions. A plot of two of GBS's 26 regional operating units ranked by customer satisfaction and relative perceived quality reveals how the New York City unit differs from a region where customers are easier to satisfy. Prior to the new approach, many managers were more focused on competition with other regions than on beating real live competitors in their own regions. At GBS, the focus on relative market-perceived quality shifted managers to competing knowledgeably in the real world.

Using a Market-Perceived Price Profile

Price plays a powerful role in most buying decisions, but usually it cannot be mapped as simply as in the chicken business. The customer's perception of how much a product costs is often a composite of several different factors.

One simple way to study price is to ask customers how satisfied they are with the price of the product, on the same scale you ask them their satisfaction with the quality attributes. The ratio of the customers' satisfaction with prices of the average competitor to customers' satisfaction

(Continued)

(Continued)

with prices of the firm being analyzed can then be used on the price side of the value map.

But that doesn't give you a deep understanding of the price side of the equation. It's a somewhat slippery issue. For example, automakers are notorious for departing from list price. And some automakers depart from list price much more than others. Some make more use of aggressive financing packages. A better approach for many businesses is to create a market-perceived price profile, analogous to the market-perceived quality profile.

Figure I.6 shows a market-perceived price profile comparing the price of the Honda Acura Legend with prices of other luxury cars. For automobiles, the price attributes customers consider include the perceived purchase price, the expected trade-in allowance, the probable resale price, and finance rates.

Knowing your market-perceived price profile can help you to decide how best to improve your price competitiveness score without just cutting the purchase price across the board. For example, one AT&T equipment business found that its price competitiveness was perceived to be worse than competitors'. AT&T's analysis showed that labor rates for installation services had been set nationally and thus upset customers in low-labor-cost regions. Rather than cutting equipment prices, AT&T gave regional managers the flexibility to set installation rates at levels that customers perceived to be more reasonable.

Price attributes	Importance weights	Acura	Satisfaction scores: Others	Ratio
1	2	3	4	5 = 4/3*
Purchase price	60	9	7	0.78
Trade-in allowance	20	6	6	1.00
Resale price	10	9	8	0.89
Finance rates	10	7	7	1.00
	100			
Price satisfaction score:		**8.3**	**7.0**	
Relative price ratio:*				**0.86**

*If customers score you better on "price satsifaction," they score you lower on "relative price" vs. competition.

FIGURE I.6 *A market-perceived price profile comparing the price of a Honda Acura Legend with the prices of other luxury cars. (Source:* Managing Customer Value, *by Bradley T. Gale; copyright © 1994 by The Free Press.)*

(Continued)

(Continued)

Using relative price ratios calculated as in Figure I.6 and relative performance data from Consumer Reports, we can create a customer value map, Figure I.7.

The "fair-value line," which indicates where quality is balanced against price, is more steeply sloped in the luxury-car market, especially at the upper end, than in the chicken market. It takes a small difference in quality to compensate for a large difference in price in luxury cars.

Overall, Lexus has achieved the position furthest below the fair-value line. Its quality is perceived as superior to any competitor, with a market-perceived price that is only slightly above the other cars. It's not surprising that Lexus has been running away with this segment of the luxury-car market.

To conduct a competitive strategy analysis of the luxury-car market, one wouldn't take the data from Consumer Reports but would gather perceptions from a large number of real customers (both customers of the sponsoring company and of its rivals) to obtain accurate estimates about market-perceived quality and relative price for the overall luxury-car market and for customer and market segments. A complete study would reveal how quality profiles based on Cadillac customers differ from the quality profiles based on BMW or Lexus customers. These data from customers could then be compared with objective data on relative quality and price, to reveal where the sponsoring company had the most opportunity to improve its market position.

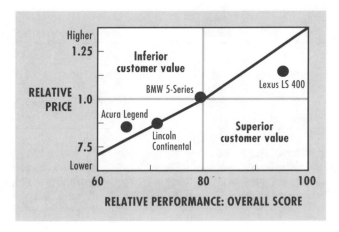

FIGURE I.7 *Lexus has been running away with its segment of the luxury-car market. This customer value map help explain why. (Source:* Managing Customer Value, *by Bradley T. Gale; copyright © 1994 by The Free Press. Information for relative performance based on Consumer Reports ratings, April 1993.)*

(Continued)

(Continued)

Intuition versus Information

Very few companies have market-perceived quality profiles, and fewer still have customer value maps. But executives often argue that most operating managers have an "implicit model" in their heads. Managers have a "feel" for who their competitors are, for what is important to purchases, and for how their company performs versus competitors.

Sometimes in organizations with exceptionally good leadership, these implicit models work well and are truly aligned to the real needs of customers. But you can easily check whether that's true in your organization. Simply ask each top-ranking member of the business-unit team to produce, individually, his or her picture of the customer value profile for the business and its key competitors. Use a one-page quality profile template, like the one shown in Figure I.5, so that you can easily summarize and contrast their opinions about customers' perceptions.

If, when you do this, you find that all top managers have similar opinions, there's a reasonable chance that the implicit models in their heads are accurate. This is particularly true if several members of the top-management team spend most of their time with customers.

But check managers' perceptions carefully. Are all of their purchase-selection criteria, weights, and relative performance scores beautifully aligned within the management group—and with customers in the targeted market?

Most organizations find that when they make this implicit model check, the alignment within the organization is much worse than the management team imagined. And if managers can't even agree among themselves about the customers' desires, it's unlikely they can achieve rapid progress toward fulfilling them.

Likewise, an organization that bases its business strategy on GAAP (generally accepted accounting principles) alone is hamstringing its own efforts. An income statement is a financial history: It tells you the components of sales and costs, and tells the amount of resulting profit. But it won't tell you much about why your sales are growing or shrinking.

By contrast, the customer value map shows you where you are competitive in the marketplace. And the market-perceived quality profile shows you why customers rank you higher or lower than your competitors. An income statement looks at the past. Customer value maps and market-perceived quality profiles look to the future.

Source: Marketing Tools (September/October 1994).

F ast orward to the Real World

TQM: Taking the Next Step

Theresa A. Flanagan

Total Quality Management (TQM), the pet economic nostrum of the 1980s, seems to be falling out of favor everywhere you look these days. It's not because TQM is simply ineffective: Quality management programs have demonstrably improved the overall value of U.S. products by focusing the attention of the work force on producing better goods and services. The trouble is, many companies that have implemented these programs are hard put to show a positive impact on the bottom line.

It's easy to see why former proponents are suffering a certain disillusionment. Under the old doctrine of TQM, once a company achieved the desirable level of quality, financial success would surely follow. In practice, however, many companies that implemented TQM have not experienced the financial success they expected. Even the companies that did show financial improvement have no models or tools for demonstrating how improved quality contributed to the company's success.

The result is that many businesses are ready to abandon TQM. They are forced to bow to the economic pressures of today's business environment and stockholders' demands for quick profits. Unfortunately, they are overlooking the root of the problem.

Instead of giving up on TQM, business executives should be asking these questions: What's wrong with TQM as it has been implemented in the U.S.? Why hasn't improved quality generated a windfall for all those companies that invested the time and money to design and implement a quality management program?

The answer is simple: *Quality should be defined by the customer.* Before hurrying off to alter this and change that, someone should have asked the customers which improvements would make them loyal to the product, or buy more of it, or pay more for it. Instead, in many cases, decisions about which areas needed quality improvement—even the decision as to what constitutes "quality" in the first place—were made internally, with the "buy in" of all employees.

But you can't expect internal perceptions of what customers want to be accurate, at least not all the time. Measuring the customer-perceived quality of your product or service is the best gauge for determining what customers like or dislike and, consequently, what needs improvement.

(Continued)

(Continued)

Companies that have created a quality management program based only on internal perceptions needn't simply abandon their efforts. They can leverage their investment in TQM by implementing a customer-perceived quality management process designed to build customer loyalty. In this approach, research is used to identify what the customer considers important and what the company needs to do to retain existing customers and attract new ones.

Customer Loyalty Management is a way to focus the quality management process on those issues that are critical to the customer, but it still requires the involvement and support of the entire company. Those companies that have a quality-conscious work force have already paved the way for this enhanced approach to quality management.

TQM in Today's Economic Climate

Improved financial performance was not necessarily an original goal of TQM—just a very desirable side effect. But the economic climate has changed since the late 1980s. Managers and shareholders now demand to know the results of their investment in quality. And despite its renewing effect on much of American industry, and the product and service improvements that have resulted from the process, TQM has not always lived up to expectations of increased market share, sales, and profits.

For one thing, it is difficult to correlate TQM with those benefits. While the notion of increasing sales by offering high-quality products and services seemed reasonable, no models were developed within TQM to determine what effect, if any, improved product quality had on sales.

Even when companies did collect vast quantities of customer satisfaction data, the information was not always brought to bear on the quality improvement process. In some cases, marketing data that were collected were unreliable or could not be developed into actionable quality programs. Often, research activities became an end in themselves. There was frequently a lack of coordination among diverse research efforts and a failure to integrate the quality group's research with the marketing function.

TQM was also plagued by problems of focus. Many TQM programs were simply not implemented in those areas that would yield results. Invalid conclusions were often being made because improvement priorities were driven by internal assumptions rather than external feedback. Because companies were not integrating effective customer satisfaction research into the TQM process, managers were not identifying customers' expectations or weighing their priorities. The intangible factors

(Continued)

(Continued)

that influenced a purchase decision often went unnoticed, as quality improvement was largely focused on the product.

Today, an increasing number of companies are realizing that customer-perceived value involves more than guaranteeing zero defects. A good example of this shift in attitude occurred at a leading manufacturer of microprocessors. The company worked diligently in order to reduce product defects. After reaching its quality milestones, executives realized that the company needed to go one step further to ensure quality, and has since embarked on a customer-value-based quality management program.

The company used advanced research methods to assess customer priorities so that its quality programs would reflect those priorities accurately. By identifying customer needs, weighing the importance of tangible and intangible product/service factors that influence purchase decisions, and measuring customers' perceptions of how the company performed relative to the competition, the manufacturer was able to pinpoint the product and service weaknesses that needed immediate attention. Many of these came as a surprise to management.

What Do the Customers Think?

Customer Loyalty Management is a strategic tool that companies can use to determine which product/service attributes are important to their customers. They can then use that information in planning and product development. Companies use customer input to drive internal processes, and rely on the customer to establish the benchmark by which a company can judge its performance.

A customer-driven quality management process has many short-term and long-term benefits. Just asking customers what they think can have an immediate impact on customer relations—if the customers believe that their ideas will be considered and acted upon within a reasonable time.

Querying customers about their level of satisfaction can help a company identify unhappy customers, possibly preventing them from defecting to a competitor. This is an especially beneficial technique for companies that have a small number of very large customers. Customer research can also better define the purchasing process within a client company, so that those individuals who actually influence the purchasing can be identified and targeted for sales.

In the long run, improving customer-perceived value provides financial rewards through increased customer retention and market share.

(Continued)

(Continued)

Customer satisfaction-based quality improvement programs also save companies money, because efforts are focused on those things that are important to the customer. Resources can be targeted to those areas that are significant to the customer, and first to those areas of greatest significance.

An increasing number of U.S. companies that have implemented traditional TQM programs with little net gain are switching to a Customer Loyalty Management process. They recognize that their previous efforts to implement TQM have produced a work force that has a 'quality mindset,' and is willing to support a customer-driven quality management program; and they take advantage of that commitment. These companies are employing models that demonstrate the positive effect of this type of quality management on the company's bottom line, and are measuring the contribution of quality to sales and profits. And many of these companies are beginning to see a quantifiable return on their new investment in customer-driven quality management.

U.S. business executives are becoming more savvy when it comes to quality management. They recognize that quality is not an end in and of itself, that quality is defined by the customer, and that a customer-driven quality management process ensures that customers are satisfied. Most important, they understand that satisfied customers are the surest way to financial success.

Source: *Marketing Tools* (September 1995).

F ast **orward to the Real World**

Meeting of the Minds

Vincent P. Barabba

The foundation of a market-based enterprise is neither its physical assets nor the shape of its organizational chart. Its foundation is an open information system that allows a free flow of knowledge between individual employees across functions. At its core, it is a network of market-based decisions that take place in an environment that encourages and rewards the sharing of knowledge. This "core competence" is what gives the enterprise its competitive edge in product development, pricing, and so forth.

What does a truly market-based enterprise look like? What is its form and what are its behaviors? And what are some examples of enterprises that use market-based decision making to satisfy customers on a consistent basis?

The Vertical Organization

To answer the first question, we need to discuss the structure of the enterprise. In the classic command-and-control organization, decisions and activities are controlled hierarchically, both within the individual departments and collectively through top management's control of all functions. The result is sometimes referred to as the "silo problem," a situation in which employees with specific interests and responsibilities are organized into narrow, vertically structured functions. Each silo tends to become absorbed in its own specialties, reporting to top management but never to each other. The silo problem is one of particularism versus globalism.

From the customer viewpoint, the silo enterprise too often ends up being a creature with many faces and uncoordinated voices. The outward results may be minor irritants, such as the U.S. Postal Service's priority mail envelope, which is made of a high-finish paperboard to which the Postal Service's own postage stamps do not stick well. Or they can be major aggravations, like the nonsmoking woman's car with a factory-installed cigarette lighter and ashtray but no place to put a purse.

What is lacking in these examples is the definition of "product integrity." In a cross-national study of manufacturing firms, Kim B. Clark

(Continued)

(Continued)

and Takahiro Fujimoto concluded that product integrity characterizes the more successful firms; and that product integrity has both an internal and external dimension. Internal integrity refers to the consistency between a product's function and its structure: the parts fit smoothly, the components match and work well together, the layout maximizes available space. Organizationally, internal integrity is achieved mainly through cross-functional coordination with the company and its suppliers. External integrity refers to the consistency between a product's performance and customer expectations—a largely unexplored and unexploited territory.

More often than not, lack of integrity in an enterprise stems from the fact that one group of people determines what customers want; another group designs the product; other groups do the engineering, manufacturing, and promotion; and still other groups have individual responsibility for selling, for servicing, and for determining the terms of trade. Too few of these people talk to each other in a systematic way in the classic silo enterprise. And the fault for this lack of communication has less to do with individual employees than with the structure of the organization and the way work processes link people together.

The late W. Edwards Deming was among the first to teach manufacturers that the problem of quality had much less to do with people than with processes—the way work was structured. Inferior product quality, in his view, was not so much the fault of uncaring workers as it was the fault of processes designed without adequate care. Manufacturers should spend less time managing people, he told them, and more time managing and honing their processes. This important idea virtually revolutionized the world of manufacturing, which quickly discovered that the same workers who had turned out second-rate goods for years could produce top-quality goods once their work processes were changed and managed as if quality mattered.

Deming's injunction to manage the process and not the people is as important to the production of services as it is to manufactured goods. The current movement of business "reengineering" is a direct descendent of this fundamental idea.

The Horizontal Organization

Many companies are trying to eliminate the problems of the vertical structure by redrawing the organizational chart. Organization pundits have prescribed many new architectures for the post-hierarchical

(Continued)

(Continued)

enterprise, chief among them the virtual corporation, the modular organization, and the horizontal organization. Each is seen as having important advantages for competitive success in the Information Age. It is the horizontal organization that has the greatest relevance to this discussion.

Unlike the vertical, hierarchical organization structured around functions or departments, the horizontal organization is rebuilt around a handful of "core processes," such as product development, sales, fulfillment, customer support, and administration. According to its advocates, the horizontal organization has a number of important benefits: the elimination of non-value-added activities; reduced supervision responsibilities; less money and energy spent on maintenance of the vertical, multidepartmental edifice; elimination of the "disconnects" that occur when work moves from one functional area to another; and closer contact between customers and decision makers in the enterprise. [T]he horizontal enterprise may be subject to the same coordination problems that afflict its vertical counterpart.

The horizontal organization is the kind of structure that the apostles of business reengineering have been working so mightily to create. Reengineering is a direct descendent of the many Japanese programs that were developed to improve work processes. "Reengineering is a natural outgrowth of the quality movement that began in the 1970s," according to Fred Adair of Mercer Management Consulting. "That movement encouraged companies to think about customers and to focus on how work was accomplished. What reengineering added was, first, an understanding that customers and processes were the most important aspects of the quality movement, and second, a recognition that quantum leap improvements in the way business was done [were] both possible and necessary. It's the magnitude of these improvements, and their necessity, that has made reengineering so popular."

Working back from the customer, determining which activities directly serve that customer, and then organizing those activities into coherent and efficient processes constitute an organizational method for aligning resources in a very direct way to serve the customer. When properly designed, each process contains all the decision-making capabilities needed to create customer satisfaction, and all the human elements see the customer as the object of their labors.

This new structure has the potential to improve the focus of work on value-adding activities, to eliminate costly bureaucracy, to improve com-

(Continued)

(Continued)

munication between the enterprise and the marketplace, and to enhance communication and decision making within the business. The fact remains, however, that our experience with these new forms is extremely limited. Enterprises that have adopted them wholly tend to be new and small businesses. In fact, organizing around activities instead of formal structures has always been a natural way to begin a new business. When large corporations have used these new forms, they have done so in limited ways—an accounts payable department here, a production facility there. Across-the-board reengineering is not only rare but exceedingly difficult, requiring a level of culture change and top management commitment that few enterprises have been able to demonstrate.

Most providers of reengineering consulting services report implementation failure rates in the 50 to 70 percent range. This is roughly twice the failure rate reported for broad-based quality programs, giving rise to the warning, "If you thought TQM was hard to implement, wait until you try reengineering." Given the high costs associated with this new approach to organizing work on behalf of the customer, most managers will want to think twice about attempting it in any but limited situations.

Source: Marketing Tools (March/April 1996).

Fast Forward to the Real World

Dismantling the Silos

Vincent P. Barabba

The current enthusiasm for these new organizational forms is uncomfortably reminiscent of the great expectations managers held out for similar "panaceas" of the past: management by objectives, synergy through conglomeration, and the "excellence" movement. Each had much to recommend, and many enterprises benefited when these philosophies were thoughtfully applied, but none has proven to be a definitive solution to the endless challenge of creating products and services that satisfy customers.

Speaking of the attractions of horizontal organization in a *Business-Week* interview, management scholar Henry Mintzberg observes that "the danger is that an idea like this can generate too much enthusiasm. It's not for everyone." Unfortunately, the consultants who develop these ideas and beat the drum for them around the country are as guilty of overselling as senior managers are hungry for universal solutions. The two create a dangerous mixture of hype and hope.

Promoters of the current obsession with creating flatter, nonhierarchical organizations fail to recognize that these concepts are not something new; they have a history of their own. According to Robert Eccles and Nitin Nohria, management scholars in the 1920s were writing about practices involving "cross-functioning," the replacement of "vertical authority" with "horizontal authority," and so on. The persistence of the functional, "silo" organization—even in the long presence of alternative forms—suggests that it is not totally wrongheaded and may be with us for some time to come. Although they are criticized as inflexible and inefficient, traditional functions have been instrumental in developing and harboring real depths of practical know-how that horizontally construed organizations have yet to match. The real challenge for top managers is to find mechanisms for capitalizing on the deep know-how of the functions and putting them in the direct service of the customer.

The Hybrid Organization

In the final analysis, the most serious problem of the functionally structured organization is the problem of coordination within and across func-

(Continued)

(Continued)

tions. It is in the gray space between functions on the organizational chart that this coordination must take place. Consider the idea of turning the functional organizational chart on its side, so that finance, marketing, engineering, and so forth are horizontal. Now relabel them as product development and manufacturing, sales and order fulfillment, and so on. The gray space is still there. Instead of silos we have processes, but they are still disconnected. So how much has really changed?

Henry Mintzberg, in his essay "The Innovative Organization," favors a hybrid approach. He would group people with specialized skills in functional units but deploy them in project teams to attack specific tasks. With this arrangement, information and decisions flow informally; coordination becomes the responsibility of these skilled people and not those normally endowed with hierarchical authority. The downside of this arrangement, according to Mintzberg, is the high price paid for frequent communication and coordination. Stanley Slater and John Narver point to studies of high-tech firms that rely on formal organizational structures as a base, with temporary teams drawing from appropriate functional areas to attack new-product projects, strategic assessments, and other tasks requiring cross-functionality. No less an authority than Thomas Davenport, credited by many as being the father of process reengineering, recognizes the continuing importance of strong functions: "I can see shrinking functions, but I can't see getting rid of functional expertise completely. Process management is an important dimension of structure, but it should simply be added to the multidimensional matrices most organizations already have."

By the 1980s, American automakers were learning how to do what Davenport had described. As Clark and Fujimoto discovered in their auto industry study, "even the most resolutely functional development organizations had established formal mechanisms such as coordination committees, engineering liaisons, project managers, matrix structures, and cross-functional teams to improve product development."

A Vision of the Market-Based Enterprise

The previous discussion should make it clear that there is no one way to structure an organization in fulfilling the philosophy of the marketing concept. The new, horizontal structure may be fine for some, particularly smaller enterprises, but there are many examples of enterprises that have retained a strong functional orientation while meeting the definition of being truly market-based in the way they do business. Indeed,

(Continued)

(Continued)

the response to the challenge of becoming market-based is in the process, not in the structure. One of the reasons that command and control no longer works as it once did is that its process is rooted in its hierarchical structure. The process of the market-based enterprise is not limited to one organizational structure.

So if we cannot describe the market-based enterprise by its structure, how can we describe it? Here it is useful to create a vision of what we might agree are the characteristics of a truly market-based enterprise. Visioning can be a powerful and creative tool. A vision is an idealized image of what we hope to create; it offers an ideal pattern against which we can begin building a common vision among relevant team members. An ideal vision of the market-based enterprise . . . could be described as follows:

- An unambiguous sense of direction, relative to developing customer-satisfying products and services, permeates the entire organization. No one needs to be told the mission of the enterprise.

- Strategic and operational plans reinforce each other, and there are no downstream disconnects between activities.

- Decision makers understand how their roles contribute to the total enterprise, and their accountability is clear—all the arrows are aligned.

- Planning and execution recognize the full complexity and uncertainty of the market. There are no simplistic ideas about how customers or competitors will respond to the actions of the enterprise.

- There is empowerment throughout the enterprise. Direction is clear, resources necessary to meet the objectives are allocated with the decision to proceed, accountability is well-defined, guidelines for implementation are clear, and there is no micromanagement from above.

- Conflict and differences of opinion are not suppressed. When they surface, they are channeled into a process that seeks win-win solutions.

- Market knowledge results in a steady stream of innovative and customer-satisfying products and services that leverage the capabilities and resources of the enterprise.

This ideal company has formed itself in such a way that the customer sees and recognizes one face and hears a familiar and consistent voice. Every point of customer contact—from printed material to products to

(Continued)

(Continued)

after-sale service—must present the customer with a clear and harmonious impression of the company, its products, and its services. And this unified outward image is a reflection of the company's internal consistency. In this sense, the market-based enterprise meets the test of external and internal integrity, as defined earlier. Underlying this integrity is a high level of cross-functional coordination between the many parts of the enterprise and its suppliers.

Besides uncovering the value of product integrity and its two dimensions, Clark and Fujimoto also identify an important unifying organizational philosophy, which underscores the value of the market-based decision-making network: "We found a handful of companies that consistently created products with integrity. What set these companies apart was their *seamless pattern of organization and management* [emphasis added]. The way people did their jobs, the way decisions were made . . . everything cohered and supported company strategy."

Fundamental to this seamless form of enterprise—be it organized horizontally or vertically—is an understanding of industries, customers, and community based on decision-making networks informed by knowledge developed from listening, learning, and leading. This knowledge and the decision-making networks it supports are the ties that bind the otherwise disconnected pieces of the enterprise. It is a dynamic set of activities that enriches the enterprise when performed well, and defines the enterprise as one that is truly market based.

Source: Marketing Tools (March/April 1996).

CHAPTER 1

Product

CONCEPT

The *product* is a tangible object (a car, a boat, a bag of nacho chips) or service (auto repair, boat storage, carpet cleaning to remove fallen nacho chips) for which the customer pays money. [The product is the pivotal ingredient in the marketing mix.] Without it, there would be nothing to price, place, or promote.

Some wrinkles on that definition. Marketing planners and managers think of the product as existing on three levels:

1. *Core product.* The basic benefit(s) or performance characteristics that define the product. While the core product might be the physical object—what Theodore Levitt calls "the thing you can drop on your foot"—no one buys that.

2. *Expected product.* Customers buy the expected product. Sometimes called the *actual* or *generic* product, this includes all the supporting qualities and services the customer routinely expects, such as speedy delivery and guaranteed replacement should the product fail.

   A firm recently established a water-transportation service to Yankee Stadium. Called the *Yankee Clipper* after Joe DiMaggio, the boat runs from South Street Seaport up the East and Harlem Rivers to the stadium; this—the trip itself—is the core service. However, the customers expect certain additional features: They expect that safety equipment such as life preservers for all are on board and that fire extinguishers are available. They expect shelter from the elements, and they expect to land somewhere near the ticket gate. They expect that reservations can be easily made by phone and will be reliably honored.

3. *Augmented product.* This includes the additional features and services appended to the expected product. With product augmentation, the marketer seeks to "delight," not merely to satisfy the customer's expectations.

Say a computer company sells a home computer as a package, including CPU, monitor, and keyboard, and then throws in a preinstalled up-to-the-minute word-processing program and two popular games. To its customers, the company is saying, "We want to do something special for you."

Similarly, the *Yankee Clipper* might augment its safe, timely ride to the game with complimentary refreshments or even a tour guide, who might point out the remains of the hospital on Roosevelt Island where Typhoid Mary was interned or the riverfront homes on Sutton Place, the most exclusive address in New York.

In today's market, most products are augmented, and most competition centers on the nature and degree of augmentation. Not surprisingly, augmentation increases costs to the producer. Sometimes marketers gain a strategic advantage by eliminating all augmentation and returning to the expected, or generic, product and cutting the price. Such advantages are often temporary, because competitors will tend to respond in kind.

The trouble with such distinctions between core, expected, and augmented products is that they imply an unchanging market. In fact, the customer and his or her notion of value is for the marketer a moving target. The computer customer comes to expect throw-ins such as installed software and technical support because your competitors have imitated your "something-special" gesture, and thus the augmented product reverts to the expected product. What is the marketer to do?

The marketer must continue to "lead" his or her target market to focus on a product's *potential,* which includes all the creative opportunities for improvement and innovation the marketer can conceive of. This can be thought of as the marketing imagination, and the companywide management of innovation thus becomes a pivotal aspect of the marketing concept. Paul Allaire, CEO of Xerox, puts it this way: "We're never going to outdiscipline the Japanese on quality. To win, we need to find ways to capture the creative and innovative spirit of the American worker. That's the real organizational challenge."[1]

DESIGN

Design should be distinguished from style. Style is superficial, while design is intrinsic. Design is related to performance. Braun, the German manufacturer of small household electrical appliances such as coffee grinders, electric razors, and hair dryers, among other similar products, is noted for its sleek and functional designs. So are Black & Decker's cordless electric hand tools. There is a maxim in the sailing world that holds that if a product looks good, it usually is good.

Design is also a means of differentiating, or positioning, a product. Automobiles like the Miata and the Taurus have profited from their cutting-edge designs. Today everything must be designed. Given a choice between two products that perform equally well, the customer will choose the one that is more pleasingly designed. Good design can improve performance (or will at least suggest better performance to the customer who takes it in hand), attract attention, and cut production costs, as well as make the product more competitive.

PRODUCT LIFE CYCLE

A pet principle of marketing holds that products, like living organisms, progress through four stages, from birth to growth to maturity, thence to decline and death. Yet some contemporary thinkers about marketing reject the whole notion of life cycles. Listen to Theodore Levitt[2]:

> *Every major industry was once a growth industry. . . . In every case, the reason growth is threatened, slowed, or stopped is not because the market is saturated. It is because there has been a failure of management. In truth, there is no such thing as a growth industry, I believe. There are only companies organized and operated to create and capitalize on growth opportunities.*

Speaking as a true believer in the marketing concept, Levitt rejects the determinism of birth-growth-death because it lets the marketing manager off the hook. However, because the product life cycle is useful as a model and as an introduction to the subject, we include it here (see Figure 1.1).

PRODUCT DEVELOPMENT

The central question, as always, is how the product relates to the customer, not how it relates to the rest of the firm. Just because a company can make a thing doesn't necessarily mean that it should. This notion is particularly apt in high-tech fields, where product development is speedy and the market unpredictable.

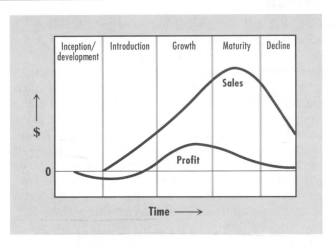

FIGURE 1.1 *Product life cycle. (Source: Hiam and Schewe, p. 236.)*

Innovation remains the backbone of American industrial success, but innovation just because it is technologically possible or because engineers find it fun is only accidentally profitable. Paul Cook, CEO of Raychem, an electronics and fiber-optics producer, puts it this way: "Raychem's mission is to creatively interpret our core technologies to serve the marketplace. That means we don't want to be innovators in all technologies. We restrict our charter . . . to niches that can sponsor huge growth over a long period of time and in which we can be pioneers, the first and best in the world."

Stages of Product Development

Some companies hand new-product development to a single product or brand manager who manages existing as well as new products within his or her area, say, skin and beauty products at a conglomerate such as Avon. Other companies judge this to be too large a job for one person, and they pass all new products to a separate manager. Still others establish temporary or permanent committees to manage new products, depending on the extent of the company's new-product activity.

"A newer approach is the venture team. At larger companies such as Dow Chemical, Monsanto, and Westinghouse, groups of managers, each a specialist in a certain area, are given the task of bringing a specific new product to market. The team combines needed resources and expertise, such as product design, engineering, capital management, market analysis, accounting, and marketing. To promote creativity, members . . . are usually excused from regular duties and report directly to top management."[4]

While the in-company mechanisms for generating new products vary, most marketers agree that product development typically progresses through six stages.

Stage 1. Generating Ideas

Sometimes new product ideas originate with the customer. Some companies offer cash bonuses or other prizes to employees who come up with successful ideas, and, of course, research and development divisions exist to formulate new products and ideas. "At 3M," Hiam and Schewe relate, "one story has it that a fired scientist kept sneaking back into the lab to develop an improved asphalt shingle and eventually won a promotion to vice president."[5]

Some companies hold regularly scheduled brainstorming sessions to generate new ideas. These can be rather rigidly structured around goals or entirely freeform, depending on the proclivities of upper management, but to encourage creativity, most managers try to remove the element of criticism from these sessions. "Most changes don't come from listening to the customer. Most major innovations come from 'crazy people' in the organization who have an idea for something that will work and add value."[6]

However, other managers point to the growing trend to involve customers directly in the very early stage of idea generation. Focus groups and new-product testing labs ask customers to respond to proposed products and even to help refine them for market.

Stage 2. Screening Ideas

Out of your brainstorming sessions might come 20 ideas. Since ideas should be uncritically received, there will inevitably be too many of them, and they won't all be good or they won't fit the financial, managerial, or technical capabilities of the company. The list needs to be mined for the gems it might contain.

Marketers try to establish a set of criteria for screening ideas. Criteria can—*must*—be tailored to fit individual companies, but marketers believe that four broad aspects cannot be ignored:

1. *Item:* Performance, salability, defensibility, marketing

2. *Company:* Technology, production, marketing

3. *Environment:* Competition, suppliers, government

4. *Venture:* Support, investment, strategy.

Some marketers will use alternative language for these criteria, but the general points will remain clear. So will the purpose: to cull the losers before they go to market.

Stage 3. Testing the Idea

At this stage, general concepts need to be refined into a form that can be tested. Hiam and Schewe suggest that

$3\ ?'s$

marketers should be asking themselves three questions: (1) Who will buy the product? (2) What is the primary benefit of the new product? (3) Under what circumstances will the new product be used?

A clever new product has arisen to serve the growing ranks of mountain bikers. Called the Camelback, it is a water bladder similar to a wineskin and set inside a form-fitting backpack. Because mountain bikers often can't safely take their hands off the grips, the Camelback has a tube running from the bladder up over the cyclist's shoulder. The biker may take a drink simply by turning his or her head slightly and drawing on the tube.

You know who will buy the Camelback; you can easily determine the number of mountain bikers in the country and key the potential product growth to that of the mountain-bike industry. You know the product's primary benefits, and you know under what circumstances the Camelback will be used. Now you want to test it before you spend too much more money.

A product like the Camelback is fairly easy to test. You might hire a market sample of mountain bikers based, say, on how much time they devote to their recreation, ranging from the casual, sometime biker to the hard-core cyclist for whom mountain biking is a lifestyle. This sample testing could be done in-house or hired out to a company that specializes in new-product testing.

KEY CONCEPT Companies must seek to manage innovation just as other business functions must be managed. It is best to treat new ideas with flexibility and openness at the early stages, but with cool-eyed business sense in the later, more expensive stages. Campbell Soup has lost millions of dollars in what Anthony J. Adams, vice president of marketing research, has called "mindless line extensions."

Stage 4. Business Analysis

Marketers must determine projected costs, profits, return on investment, and cash flow in a realistic, detailed manner. Fixed and variable costs need to be considered along with the economies of scale and experience. Marketing plans need to be laid and their attendant costs analyzed. Our Camelback example is a fairly simple one in that it is marketed to a specific, determinable, special-interest group. (The producer might consider which other sports enthusiasts would be interested in this "water delivery system.") However, business analysis would be more difficult for the large packaged-food producer thinking about a line of bottled pasta sauce, because the market is so much bigger and less distinguishable and the risk potentially greater.

As always, [some balance must be sought between wild risk taking and a too-conservative approach] If inflexible company policy says that all new products must be proved profitable by the first year after introduction, then product innovation will suffer. Conversely, if you have to retool or acquire new heavy machinery to produce the product, then you'd better be certain about your financial projections.

Stage 5. Producing a Prototype

If the business figures check out, the next stage requires that the product take tangible form in a prototype. Computer technology in some industries has made prototyping unnecessary. Until very recently, airplane manufacturers had to build one or two fully operating airplanes to demonstrate to potential customers, but more critically to be sure they'd actually fly. Boeing's 777 was produced entirely by computer simulation. However, the Camelback would probably need a prototype.

At this stage, marketing commentators run up a caution flag: Don't let your new product get bogged down in corporate hierarchy and interdepartmental rivalry. A product that proceeds from research and development to engineering, thence to design and packaging, on to manufacturing, and from there to marketing is in danger from the very system that creates it. Again, marketing as a *management* function can help circumvent delays, shoddy manufacturing, and bad communications. The Japanese have proven themselves masters at "fast-cycling" new products by using a team approach, now being copied worldwide.

Stage 6. Test Marketing

Often test markets are geographical. The firm advertises, prices, and distributes the product to a limited market just as it would if the product were being marketed nationally. By this means, the producer can glean reactions to the product from distributors, retailers, and customers at relatively limited risk.

Despite the risks inherent in a headlong plunge to market, there is today a growing trend away from test marketing because it can be slow, expensive, and vulnerable to corporate spying. For example, Hiam and Schewe refer to General Foods' test-marketing foray for new frozen baby food. The test was ruined when Gerber, Heinz, and Libby bought up all the product in the test market.

PRODUCT INTRODUCTION

After the product is first placed before the public, sales, according to the model, start slowly as potential customers grow aware of the product's existence. Production costs will be high at this stage due to inexperience.

A Product Introduction:
The Melges 30—
Story of a Racing Boat

In 1995, Melges Performance Sailboats introduced a light, sleek, stripped-down, and wildly overpowered 30-foot sailboat called the Melges 30. Before hull number one touched water for the first time, experienced sailors were talking about it.

Its pedigree was impeccable. Buddy Melges, the builder and marketer, is one of the world's most respected racing sailors; some people say he's the best helmsman ever. Richel-Pugh, the designers, have an international reputation for drafting fast racing boats. The Melges 24, introduced in 1994, had swept the market. Ninety Melges 24s hit the starting line at Key West Race Week in 1995. Only 24 feet long, carrying a huge sail area, the boat demanded young, fit sailors.

The Melges 30 was to be a drawn-out version of the 24, giving older sailors with iffy knees the same speed thrills without the stringent physical demands. The 30-footer would also be very expensive for a single-purpose (day-racing) boat—$92,000 before sails and electronics, about $150,000 race ready.

Two boats debuted on Long Island Sound for the fall 1995 race series. On Saturday, in wind of about 25 knots, one boat lost the bulb, an essential stabilizer, at the foot of her keel. The bulb simply fell off, sank like the chunk of lead that it is, and the boat turned turtle, mast pointing toward the bottom of Long Island Sound. On Sunday, the other Melges 30 lost its bulb and capsized. This was the worst-case scenario, the marketer's feverish nightmare. The best that could be said about the debut was that nobody drowned . . . wasn't it?

Well, no. The boat became a huge success. As of March 1996, Melges had sold 29 hulls, and the sailing season for much of the market hadn't even begun. How could that be, given its inauspicious introduction? Because Buddy Melges built a brilliantly conceived and designed product, and he keenly understood his customers.

They represented a niche within a niche. Racing boats are a segment of the sailing market, itself a part of the boating market, in which an estimated 76,828,000 people participate nationwide. "Sport boats," in which category the Melges 30 firmly fits, is a segment of the racing-boat market. Sport boats, purpose-built racers with no compromises and no frills, exist to excite and sometimes frighten their crews. Since weight is the mortal enemy of speed in sailboats, they are built very light—space-age carbon composites make sport boats possible. "However," says Hans Melges, marketing director, "we didn't mean to fit into an existing [market]. We meant to make our own."

(Continued)

(Continued)

And so these very public breakdowns on Long Island Sound didn't matter. In fact, they showed that Melges and his collaborators were serious. They were building right at the edge. Okay, they erred a little to one side in their keel-to-bulb connections, but they'd get it right. (Melges gave the owners new boats.) Buddy Melges understood that only one thing mattered to his potential customers—that the boat be a rocket ship.

Mass marketing is usually necessary because marketers are often unsure of the new product's targeted market, unless it has been clearly defined.

However, there is a "news" aspect to new-product introduction (e.g., the hype that accompanied Windows 95) that might make promotion easier. Yet at this stage, the new product's life is in great danger. Over 15,000 products were introduced in 1991. Today, most are gone.

GROWTH

If the product satisfies its customers, it will grow. New buyers will follow the leaders. New competitors will also follow, adding new features to the product, causing the market to expand.

Prices will remain generally the same or fall somewhat as producers gain experience, but promotion spending, a function now of competition as well as customer education, will tend to increase.

Profits will increase with volume and decreased unit costs. Producers strive to sustain growth by developing and refining products and by opening new markets. However, competitors will be nipping at their heels. To capture a commanding lead, a producer must continue to spend money on product improvement, promotion, and distribution. We are talking, remember, about the marketing "mix."

Strategies During the Growth Stage

There are only two ways to capture market share: You can take customers away from your competitors, or you can earn new ones who've never used the product. The first way can be very expensive, often leading to the "battle of the ad agencies," a fight that has more to do with advertising than product. The "Yes I can, No you can't" ads by AT&T and its competitors exemplify that trend.

It is easier to keep a customer than to usurp one. This fact tempts marketers to rush a product to market, under the so-called first-mover concept. If you let a first mover cover the market with a new product, then you're left with no alternative but to try to seize market share from that person.

On the other hand, brand loyalty, like the old horse in the song, "ain't what she used to be." Brand loyalty, everyone agrees, has been eroded by a proliferation of products and price-cutting promotions, but not every- one agrees on the extent of the erosion. The lucrative sports-shoe market can claim a certain brand loyalty, mostly due to expensive endorsements by megastars such as Michael Jordan, but most of the high-end shoes are as good as, but not better than, their competitors. To a certain extent, brand loyalty is a matter of fad and fashion, not customer decisions about quality.

Competition grows rapidly during the growth stage because new producers realize that if they delay prod- uct introduction, they risk losing share to the first mover and thus fighting an uphill battle against brand loyalty. The slow-to-market producer not only faces competition for customers, but also for distribution channels. Competition engenders market segmenta- tion, as producers try to differentiate their products in the consumers' minds or to find new users for old products. At this stage, marketers who can't find any other way to differentiate their products do so on the basis of price, another kind of segmentation. During the introductory stage, promotion was used to build demand; during the growth stage it is used to build brand loyalty.

Full-Line Strategy

Product lines tend to expand during the growth cycle, so most companies in a position to strategize own mul- tiline products. Wild expansion, as we've said, is not the answer; careful management is. Full-line strategies can be more flexible in response to changing forces in the market.

Yet the old trade-offs still come into play. Multiline products run the risk of losing focus by management. Multiline advantages, such as increased customer recognition, higher demand, and promotional effective- ness can be lost if they result in the expansion of prod- ucts people don't need.

Line-Filling Strategy

Under this strategy, marketers seek to fill gaps in the market. These gaps might have opened because nobody noticed them or because consumer tastes changed. For example, Hiam and Schewe point to Cuisinart's food processor. Cuisinart introduced the machine in 1973. Introduction-stage sales were slow,

Compact Discs

Compact discs (CDs) were introduced to Europe and Japan in 1982, and to the U.S. market in 1983. At the time, many industry experts predicted that consumers would refuse to discard their records and tapes, and their turntables and tape players, for the uncertain benefit of digital recordings on compact discs. Some experts saw it differently, remembering that the history of the recorded music industry is one of new standards displacing old with superior sound. An oft-quoted commentary by the editor of a trade magazine comes from 1949, when 33⅓-rpm (revolutions-per-minute) plastic records were first introduced to a market dominated by shellac 78-rpm records: "I ask readers if they want to feel that their collections of records are obsolete, if they really want to spend money on buying discs that will save them the trouble of getting up to change them, and if they really want to wait years for a repertory as good as what is available now to them?" Much to the expert's surprise, consumers answered yes to these questions, both when long-playing records (LPs) were introduced in 1949 and when CDs were introduced in 1983.

Sales of CD players in the United States started at 35,000 in 1983, a decent showing for the introductory stage of the life cycle. In 1984, sales grew dramatically, to 208,000 units. Although this represents 494-percent growth, the percentage is not particularly important because the base was so small. The next year's growth rate of 188 percent, however, was striking because it represents growth on a fairly large base. This growth brought industry sales of CD players to 600,000 units by 1985, and put the product onto the classic accelerating growth curve characteristic of the first half of the growth stage of the product life cycle. Interestingly, CD players were introduced by several companies at roughly the same time, including the original innovators, Sony and Philips. No single company could claim to have a significant time-lead advantage in this market, although, as the innovators, Sony and Philips turned out to have some advantages that allowed them to hold onto a strong position.

CD players on their own are of no more value than CDs are on their own. The consumer generally will buy neither a CD until he or she has a CD player, nor a CD player without being convinced that CDs are a desirable purchase. Thus, the growth of the CD market is dependent on the growth of the CD player market; their life cycles are linked. In 1983, total unit sales of CDs was 443,320. This is a pretty good showing for the first year in the U.S. market, and it represents about a dozen CDs per CD player. CDs cost consumers about $20 each at the time, so the

(Continued)

(Continued)

average owner of a CD player invested about $240 in CDs during 1983. From these statistics, we can also compute that the total sales of CDs was almost $9 million—nothing to sneeze at for an introductory-stage product. Nevertheless, unit shipments of all forms of prerecorded music totaled about 600 million in 1983, which means that CDs accounted for less than one-thousandth of the total market for prerecorded music! The bulk of sales was accounted for by 33⅓-rpm LPs, which accounted for 45 percent of unit sales; by 45-rpm singles, with 20 percent of sales; and by cassette tapes, with a little over 30 percent of sales. Eight-track tapes held only a few percentage points of market share, as cassette tapes had largely displaced them by 1982.

Since 1983, CD unit sales have grown much as the product life cycle might have predicted. Figure 1.2 shows CD sales plotted over time. Exactly when the product moved from introduction to growth is difficult to say—the definition of life cycle stage is based on judgment as much as anything—but it looks like the curve shifted upward in 1985, making this the first year of the growth phase. It is worth noting that the total market for prerecorded music did not grow at all during this time period; it has stayed fairly constant and even declined at times in recent decades, as is typical of a mature market.

A difficult strategic issue for the innovators in this case was how to capture a leading position in the CD market that their innovation had spawned. The innovators were Philips, which developed CD technology

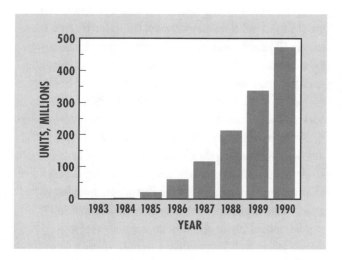

FIGURE 1.2 *Compact disc unit sales, U.S.*

(Continued)

(Continued)

for video applications in the 1970s, and Sony, with which Philips entered into a joint venture for the purpose of developing and introducing CDs for prerecorded music. Although these companies focused on developing and marketing the CD players, not the CDs, they also had an active interest in CDs via Philips's record-producing subsidiary, Polygram, and via Sony's acquisition of CBS records. In other words, the joint developers of the CD technology stood to profit handsomely if their record-company subsidiaries could, between them, gain a preeminent position in the market for CDs. Although the companies could have prevented other companies from producing CDs, this would have ensured that the new technology would *not* become an industry standard.

The CD technology had to be adopted throughout the industry to provide consumers an extensive repertoire of music and to make the new product a viable competitor against the LP standard. In fact, Philips and Sony joined forces specifically to ensure that they would not create competing standards. It was essential to disseminate the new technology widely and encourage record producers to make the new CDs through generous licensing agreements. The necessity of creating an industry standard pushed the innovators to give their technology away, but the desire to profit from CD sales pushed them to maximize their shares of this new market. Further complicating this difficult situation was the fact that CD production capacity must be added in large, expensive increments. Building a new factory is no small investment. Yet Philips and Sony did not know how successful the new CD standard would be, and thus were not eager to invest in excess capacity. They could have preempted the market by building a huge factory, but they would have lost heavily on this investment had the market not grown as it did. What happened?

but afterward, during the late 1970s and 1980s, sales grew rapidly, and trailed off almost as quickly.

Sunbeam studied the food-processor market in 1984 and learned that most Cuisinarts languished unused on kitchen shelves. Cuisinarts were complex, hard to clean, and expensive. Yet the company was reluctant to dilute the product's quality by offering a simpler, cheaper model. Sunbeam, having no such qualms, introduced the Oskar in 1985. It filled a market gap by offering a small, easy-to-clean, and simple food processor. Cuisinart failed to respond to this competitive foray by Sunbeam, and Cuisinart went bankrupt in 1990.

We might well ask why a company with complete access to marketing research didn't notice its vulnerability to line-filling competition. The blunder was probably not due to dull-wittedness. Companies have the same foibles as people, since people make marketing decisions on what they think is best for the company. Also, the world is always clearer in retrospect. Sometimes, however, decision makers are just dead wrong. Remember Apple's refusal to license its operating system and the Big Three automakers' refusal to respond to changing tastes among American motorists until it was almost too late.

Line- and Brand-Extension Strategies

Brand extensions take the brand name of one product and extend it to another. *The Portable MBA in Marketing* gives us Armor All as an example. Armor All made a lot of money selling its product to car owners who used it to clean dashboards and tires. In the late 1980s, Armor All's parent, the McKesson Corporation, expanded the product line to include waxes, cleaners, and other protectants. The original Armor All is directly related to its extensions—they're all car-care products.

Remember, in this stage of a product's life, the market, due to competition, separates into segments. Price is one kind of segmentation. If you can make an expensive, mid-priced, and cheap version of your product, you can expand your market coverage—but not without risk.

Bicycle manufacturers typically offer a wide range of quality and price, and everybody knows that they get what they pay for. Kmart, successful as a mass-market discounter, recently "traded up" by refurbishing its merchandising and adding higher-end products. This may have been a successful piece of stretching, but it came at enormous cost to the company, and some watchers don't see much physical change in the stores. Plus, Wal-Mart is answering with its own trade-up.

When companies "trade down," they seek to expand the market toward customers who want the name but can't afford the original. The trouble is, the new low-end model can damage the reputation of the older high-end model. This happened to Jaguar. Nobody wanted a cheap Jaguar, and the company finally withdrew the low-end model at a significant loss. A similar thing happened to Tiffany when Avon bought it and tried to trade down. Tiffany had traded on its identity, which Avon blurred.

Brand names have some elasticity, but according to present marketing wisdom, not much.

Repositioning Strategies

Products get repositioned when marketers try to change the consumer's perception of a brand or product. Repositioning requires advertising and promotion to establish the new identity.

Fifteen years ago, the National Basketball Association was nearly moribund. Through some sensible labor-relations agreements, shrewd marketing moves to invigorate old rivalries between teams, and perhaps most visibly the brilliant play and personalities of Michael Jordan, Larry Byrd, and Magic Johnson, the game and the association have climbed out of the dark hole to megastardom.

Planned Obsolescence Strategies

Planned obsolescence gives marketers and manufacturers a bad name. Thorstein Veblen was among the first to use the phrase in his critique of capitalism, *The Theory of the Leisure Class* (1899), and today planned obsolescence flies in the face of the marketing concept. Obsolescence takes four different forms:

1. *Technological obsolescence* occurs naturally, not necessarily as a marketing ploy, in high-tech industries like electronics. If you keep your old computer long enough for the monitor to die, you might have difficulty finding a replacement compatible with your old system. This encourages you to buy a whole new system.

2. *Planned obsolescence* takes advantage of the consumer by withholding new technological developments until demand for the old product declines. Gillette, for example, withheld its new Teflon-coated blades until sales of chromium blades flattened.

3. *Physical obsolescence* is the production of products meant to last only a short time. We're used to this with lightbulbs, batteries, and socks, but it became particularly egregious in the American auto industry.

    Let's combine items 1 and 2 in a hypothetical example. Let's pretend that the research and development arm of a major battery producer comes up with batteries that will last ten times longer than the present ones. The company, already making a tidy profit on replacements, chooses not to market the long-lasting battery—at least not until one of its competitors makes a move in that direction. We can understand the logic, but the effect of that decision leaves customer choice out of the equation, not to mention the company's disregard for the environment.

4. *Style obsolescence* is often criticized because it dictates buying decisions to the consumer. It changes a product only superficially but markets the product as if it were new. Women's hemlines bounce around not necessarily because customers want them to, but because style changes profit the fashion industry.

Though the party-line response to planned obsolescence, particularly in style, says that change is one of the attributes of a product consumers want most, the customer generally feels cheated when things fall out of style too fast. Planned obsolescence degrades the customer–company relationship to a state of suspicion.

MATURITY AND DECLINE

Many marketers who should know better make the mistake of thinking that growth will last forever, and they are caught flat-footed when sales begin to decline or even plummet. If the product life cycle were more precise (and the market less mercurial), it would be possible to forecast when one stage would end and the next begin.

However, once sales decline, the model shows that sales will become vulnerable to economic shifts, and cost cutting will prove necessary to sustain any profits. But costs can be cut only so far before something else must be done.

Marketers are left with two separate choices at the maturity stage: an *offensive* or a *defensive* strategy.

The defensive strategy tries to keep market share up by cutting costs and eliminating weaknesses in the product itself. The marketer might make changes in the marketing mix by changing or improving packaging and promotion. The marketer might change the focus of promotion from the customer to the distributor by offering distributors discounts or other price incentives.

Offensive strategies focus on finding new markets for declining products. Sometimes marketers "relaunch" improved products. This is particularly true with home-cleaning products where, for instance, the same old dishwashing liquid might be augmented with a lemon scent and relaunched as something new. Dunkin Donuts bought expensive time during the Atlanta Olympics to announce that it was now offering *iced* coffee!

If these two strategies don't stanch bleeding sales, then the company must consider deleting weak products. There are three ways to cut products from a line (they're also called *strategies*):

1. *Continuation strategy.* Here the marketer sticks with the same market plan until the product is discontinued.

2. *Milking strategy.* This cuts marketing and other costs to get as much revenue as possible from the product before it dies.

3. *Concentrated strategy.* Here marketers aim all their efforts at the product's strongest segment, letting the others wither.

CRITICISM OF THE PRODUCT-LIFE-CYCLE MODEL

A vocal body of marketing opinion holds that adherence to the product-life-cycle model *causes* the decline and death of products. Here's why. At the introductory stage, the marketer is customer-focused. This must be so, because new-product development is fueled by the marketer's perception of customer needs. The product is tested on this basis, then modified and improved according to the results of these tests. Sure, costs need to be considered at this stage, and so do distribution and price, but the company is thinking mainly about delivering value to the customer. And then the company begins to change its focus.

Hiam and Schewe say that the introductory stage begins "the fall from grace."[7] Now, when the product has progressed from an idea to a thing on the shelf, its producer begins to turn inward, concentrating on the practical demands of manufacturing, distributing, and supporting the product. Management searches for a way to cut costs, increase volume, and fiddle with distribution channels.

This shift of focus away from the customer accelerates as the product matures. As sales level off (according to the model, it is inevitable that they must), producers are loath to increase spending, and innovation seems a case of throwing good money after bad. Marketers stop seeking information about customers, and they cut back on promotion spending, their main means of communicating with their customers.

By the decline stage, this inward turning is nearly complete. The company is hustling to defend itself against loss or to gain as many sales as possible before dropping the product. In the decline stage, marketers don't make many changes to the product or its packaging. Efficiency, not innovation or customer need, becomes the company watchword. "When the product enters decline, it is already dead in the sense that the life force provided by the initial consumer focus is gone.[8]

In *Waiting for Godot,* Vladimir says, "There's man all over for you, blaming on his boots the faults of his feet." This is rather the way new thinkers like Hiam and Schewe and Theodore Levitt, whom we quoted earlier in this chapter, view management's relationship to the product life cycle. "In fact," say Hiam and Schewe, "we suspect that this gradual shift in focus is what makes products mortal. It is something inherent in the way companies manage products, not in the products themselves."[9]

So what is the alternative for managers? When this century was young, Henry Ford pointed the way: "The man who will use his skill and constructive imagination to see how much he can give for a dollar, instead of how *little* he can give for a dollar, is bound to succeed." Hiam and Schewe hold that all successful innovation is predicated on giving value to the customer. "This is what being customer-oriented really boils down to. And as the customer focus is displaced by concern for competitors, and finally, in the decline stage, concern for the company itself, the emphasis shifts to seeing how little one can give for the dollar."[10]

BRANDS

A *brand* is a name, symbol, sign, or design identifying the product or service of an individual producer. The efficacy of and loyalty to brand names have become a matter of some controversy in modern marketing, and we'll have more to say about "branding" in a later chapter. While branding may not carry the same clout with consumers as it did a decade ago, it will not, at least foreseeably, go extinct.

Because developing a brand name takes time and money for advertising, promotion, and packaging, marketers protect brand names ferociously. Brands still command *consumer franchise,* a technical term for loyalty, even when reasonable substitutes are offered at lower prices. Anxious, first-time tourists to New York City, a town world renowned for excellent restaurants in all price ranges and ethnicities, often gravitate to Beefsteak Charlie's or the Olive Garden because they know what to expect.

Marketing-textbook authors identify four levels of brand awareness:

1. *Attributes.* These are usually adjective phrases that, through promotion, get attached to a product: "The pause that refreshes," "Quality is job one," "Designed like no other car in the world."

2. *Benefits.* One marketing guru pointed out that people don't buy ¾-inch drill bits, they buy ¾-inch holes. Attributes must provide functional benefits. Volvo focuses its advertising messages on the cars' crash-

What is the most widely understood word in the world? "Okay." What is the second most widely understood word in the world? "Coca-Cola."

Ten Most Powerful Brand Names in the United States

Coca-Cola	NBC
Campbell	Black & Decker
Disney	Kellogg
Pepsi-Cola	McDonald's
Kodak	Hershey

Source: *American Demographics and John Wiley & Sons.*

worthiness. People who buy Volvos are buying safety as part of the cars' benefit package.

3. *Values.* This does not mean monetary value; rather it refers to the lifestyle values of the consumer. People buy Rolex watches because, as well as being excellent timepieces, they say something about the buyer's self-image. It is the marketer's job to determine products' values and find the customers whose values match.

4. *Personality.* Brands reflect personality. Among motorcyclists, Harley-Davidson reflects a personality different from that of a BMW touring bike. People tend to choose products that match their perceptions of their own personalities.

Brand Equity

Brand equity is the marketing term for a brand's value in terms of awareness and perceived quality—in other words, its power to draw and keep customers.

While equity is hard to measure and compare across the market, it carries some clear-cut marketing advantages. Promotion costs can be decreased because customers already know about products with high equity. Because customers expect to find high-equity products on the shelf, these products hold more clout among members of the distribution channels. Since most brand names have earned customer trust, their producers can more credibly launch brand extensions. Moreover, powerful brand equity offers the producer a certain protection against price-cutting by competitors. People pay more for a Mercedes, which, incidentally, came third on the lists for the most powerful brand names in Germany and Japan, while Mercedes's competitors advertise that their vehicles give all the same value at a fraction of the cost.

Marketers must constantly manage their brand names. Some companies have installed "brand equity

BRAND LOYALTY

Product	Percentage of Brand-Loyal Users
Cigarettes	71
Mayonnaise	65
Toothpaste	61
Coffee	58
Headache remedy	56
Film	56
Laundry detergent	48
Beer	48
Automobiles	47
Shampoo	44
Soft drinks	44
Underwear	36
Television	35
Batteries	29
Athletic shoes	27
Garbage bags	23

managers" to watchdog their brands' quality, promotion image, and associations in the short term and the long. In fact, some companies see brands as their major assets; thus a company's major marketing function is to keep customers for life. Brand equity and customer equity are directly related, if not the same thing.

PACKAGING

Among most marketers, packaging is considered part of product strategy, not promotion. As a verb, *packaging* refers to designing and making a container for a product. Labeling is a part of packaging. Even people who have never held a camera to their faces would recognize Kodak's little yellow film box. Sometimes, if it lasts long enough, a package becomes a pop-culture icon, à la Andy Warhol's Campbell's soup can. Marketers see the package as their last chance to influence buyers at the point of purchase.

Useful innovations in packaging help customers and therefore gain market advantages for the producers. Drip-proof spouts and easy-to-open boxes are examples. But what about those Norwegian and Portuguese anchovy bottles that cannot be opened without covering your forearms in fish oil, or the "easy-to-open" box that requires a hacksaw and protective eyewear to crack?

Incidentally, after Coca-Cola reinstituted its old contoured bottle for Coke and its dimpled bottle for Sprite in 1995, the company sold a record 3.8 billion cases, a 7 percent increase, without touching the core product. Packaging matters; it is much more than a wrapper or container.

Packaging and Conservation

Most products are overpackaged. In the United States and most of Europe, discarded packaging comprises one-third of all solid waste. There are three kinds of packaging. There's the *primary package* (for example, the bottle of Old Spice), the *secondary package* (the box that contains the bottle of Old Spice), and finally the *transport package* (the protective crate in which the whole shebang is shipped to the retailer).

Trying to decrease waste, the German government passed an ordinance stipulating that packaging must be returned by consumers to retailers, who then return the packaging to its manufacturer. In response to this "polluter-pays" legislation, German businesses established a nonprofit company to collect this waste directly from the consumer for recycling. There are some bugs yet to be worked out in this system (the main problem is the lack of a market for recycled material), but it indicates a growing trend. Customers here and abroad don't want or need, and to some extent are suspicious of, all that pointless packaging.

Price

Cash for the hard goods
Cash for the fancy goods
Cash for the soft goods
Cash for the noggins and the pickens and the frickens
Cash for the hogshead, cask, and demijohn
—*The Music Man*

Price is the value consideration—usually in money—
that the customer is willing to give up to acquire a
product. Price is contingent upon market demand, competition, and the cost of production, including research
and development, manufacturing, and marketing. In
fixing a price, the producer may set a *floor,* the lowest
price, and a *ceiling,* the highest. The former is determined by the producer, the latter by customer demand.

Unit cost is one of the first things the marketer
needs to know. How much does it cost to
produce one widget? Unit cost is determined by
dividing the total number of widgets produced by the
total cost, both fixed and variable, of producing them.

Fixed costs, or overhead, do not vary with
production or sales level. No matter how many
or how few units the company produces, it
must still pay rent on facilities, utilities, salaries, and so
forth. *Variable costs* change according to the level of
production. To produce a VCR, for example, the
company must buy materials such as electrical
components, metal housings, and packaging. These
costs vary according to how many VCRs the company
sells. Cost per unit decreases as output increases.

COST-BASED PRICING STRATEGIES

Cost-plus pricing is a strategy in which a markup, often
in the form of a fixed percentage, is added to the unit
cost. Typically, each entity in the chain, from raw-

materials supplier to retailer, adds a markup. Let's say the unit cost of a product is $20. The manufacturer adds 20 percent, charging the wholesaler $24. The wholesaler adds another 20 percent when he or she sells the product to the retailer, who in turn adds an additional 20 percent. Cost to the customer: $34.56.

Target pricing relates price to volume. The selling price provides a specific rate of return, but only if a certain volume is sold.

Target pricing, as with all cost-plus pricing, ignores customer demand and competitors' prices. If the producers fail to sell the targeted volume, then they end up with a negative return on investment (ROI). This approach is risky, but it is simple and therefore attractive to pricers in complex industries.

The American auto industry used to set prices this way. Producers determined how many cars they expected to sell, totaled the costs, added a profit, then divided the result by the expected unit sales to come up with a per-car price.

Break-even pricing might be used by a company to determine how many units of a product it must sell in order to cover production costs and how much profit the company will make as volume increases over and above the break-even point. This approach requires that the company have a firm knowledge of fixed and variable costs. "The amount by which the selling price exceeds the average variable cost is the *contribution margin* per unit of product sold. When the amount of product sold reaches the point where the total contribution margin covers all the fixed costs of a product, the firm breaks even."[1]

Experience-curve pricing is based on the fact that the total costs of production tend to decline as more units are produced. This is due to two separate cost-related factors—economies of scale and economies of experience. *Economies of scale* result when fixed costs are spread over more units of the product. *Economies of experience* result as the producers learn production shortcuts and other cost-saving steps. Higher volume and experience always lead to cost reductions, which can then be passed on to the customer, retained as profit, or a little of both.

Like other cost-based pricing, experience-curve pricing does not consider competitors' prices or consumers' price consciousness.

VALUE-BASED PRICING

Value-based pricing uses the customer's perception of value to establish prices. Pricing, along with rest of the marketing mix, is considered before the product is

manufactured. Cost-based pricing is product-driven;
value-based pricing is customer-driven. Therefore,
value-based pricing, as step 1, analyzes consumer
need, not company need.

Henry Ford put it succinctly: "We have never considered any costs as fixed. Therefore, we first reduce the
price to the point where we believe more sales will
result. Then we go ahead and try to make the prices.
We do not bother about costs. The new price forces the
cost down."[2]

COMPETITION-BASED PRICING

Competition-based pricing, also called *going-rate pricing,* is a strategy in which the producer keys prices to
those of competitors. This is especially prevalent in
heavy manufacturing industries (which are often *oligopolies*) such as steel or paper, wherein the leading
companies set the prices and the others follow suit.
Some smaller producers may set prices a bit higher or
lower, but the difference usually remains constant.
Manufacturers, both leaders and followers, assume that
the price represents the *collective wisdom* of the particular industry. Going-rate pricing also serves to circumvent price wars harmful to all producers.

SEALED-BID PRICING

Sealed-bid pricing is a specialized strategy used for
contract bidding. Prices are based on what a bidder
thinks the competition will offer. Except in unusual circumstances, bidders will not offer a below-cost bid; the
problem facing the bidder is to determine a price above
cost that will afford a practicable profit and still undercut competitors' bids.

PRICING AND THE PRODUCT LIFE CYCLE
Introductory Stage

New-product pricing is always a tricky business
because customer demand is tough to gauge. Unit costs
are known to some extent, but customer interest is
unknown, particularly with truly innovative products
such as those in high-tech fields. The marketer is left
with a choice between skimming and penetration
strategies.

Skimming price strategy refers to the employment
of a high initial price followed by price reductions. The
assumption is that people will pay a relatively high
price to be among the first to own the product at a
time when costs are greater due to the producer's
inexperience. Then, to broaden sales once the initial
market is exhausted, the producer lowers the price.

Penetration price strategy is the opposite approach, whereby the initial price is set low to generate immediate demand. With most new products, the penetration strategy is accompanied by high promotion costs in order to build product awareness as quickly as possible.

Sometimes, as distinct from both of these strategies, the marketer will offer for a fixed period a low introductory price to capture brand loyalty. After the expiration of that period, prices will climb. "If you act now"–style promotion usually accompanies this approach.

Growth Stage

During the growth stage, particularly if it is rapid, the producer is tempted to keep prices high. The trouble with succumbing to this temptation is that it invites competition; competitors recognize that the pioneering producer has found a market and that they can undercut it. If, however, the initial producer passes on to the customer the decreasing costs (due to growing experience), he or she can discourage competition and then begin to segment the market by offering generic and augmented low- and high-end models, respectively.

If growth is relatively slow, the marketer can strive to broaden the market by reducing price. The Japanese are masters at this strategy in automobiles and electronic products.

Maturity Stage

Here, stable pricing is the most common strategy. Price reductions seem to make sense at the maturity stage only when sales volume is flattening. "With some products—such as hairpins or clothespins—a price reduction is not likely to increase sales and, in fact, would probably lead to lower profits, since the quantity sold is unlikely to change. Moreover, competitors are likely to react by lowering their prices."[3]

Decline

At this stage, marketers have two options—to preserve or to drop the product. If the company opts to drop the product from its line, it makes sense to lower prices incrementally until all units are sold. However, this stage can offer a market advantage. As other producers drop the product, it becomes less widely available, and remaining producers might be able to raise prices if a segment of the market still wants or needs the product.

OTHER PRICING STRATEGIES

Product-line pricing.   Most companies produce a line of products rather than a single product. Most camera makers produce everything from disposable cameras to point-and-shoot units to sophisticated products for professional photographers. Likewise, Kodak sells an extensive line of film to accommodate all kinds of photographers. Product-line pricing sets the price steps between its various products based on the company's own costs, consumer perceptions, and competitors' prices.

Optional-product pricing. In the old days, when American auto manufacturers advertised a car at an attractive price, customers came into the showroom only to find that that price barely included seats. Everything else—power brakes and power steering, radio, air-conditioning, and so on—was extra. Customers became quite cynical about advertised prices. Following their Japanese competitors, most automakers now sell reasonably equipped cars as standard. Options, of course, increase costs to the producer, but these must be measured against the cost of alienating potential customers.

Captive-product pricing. Gillette's Sensor is the largest-selling razor in the country today. The razor itself, essentially a handle with a clever connecting mechanism, is cheap. The blades, however, are not, and other producers' blades will not fit the clever connecting mechanism. Captive-market pricing is also typical among camera makers that produce film.

By-product pricing. Some industries produce by-products. Sawdust is a by-product of lumber mills. If sawdust is priced right, it can be marketed, say, to absorb oil drips on garage floors. In some instances, by-products become a lucrative sideline, and this can allow the producer to lower the price of the main product.

Product-bundle pricing. Tour companies sell packages that include airfare, hotels, meals, tips, and transfers and price them lower than if the traveler were to book his or her own trip.

TRANSACTIONS

For a time, marketing theory focused on transactions, or *price theories.* In its distilled, almost purely theoretical form, transactions are one-time occurrences in which neither buyer nor seller has prior knowledge of the other; price is the sole criterion. In this model, each party to the transaction assumes that the other is motivated by self-interest alone—get as much as you can for as little as possible right now, never mind tomorrow.

In practice, it's difficult to find examples of pure transactions. Frederick L. Webster, in *The New Portable MBA,*[4] suggests that the sale of agricultural commodities futures might be one, but even these are based on a degree of trust and an ongoing relationship between parties to the transaction. Webster cites another example: A motorist passing through a town

Global Positioning System:
A Story of Hot Competition Amid Plunging Prices

About 20 years ago, the Department of Defense launched a series of satellites into fixed earth orbit as the hardware for a new navigation system now generally referred to as GPS. With it, a ship or an airplane could fix its position anywhere on the globe, 24 hours a day, with astonishing accuracy—within a 20-meter circle. But to do so, the navigator had to have on board a black-box receiver to gather the satellites' signals. Naturally, the system was classified.

As time passed and the Soviet threat diminished, the Defense Department released the technology—which is to say the receivers—for civilian use. At first they were very expensive, but airlines and shipping lines, for which price was no object, snapped them up. Electronics companies recognized that a huge potential market—recreational boaters—remained untapped due to prohibitive prices.

The recreational market would not pay $2,000 for GPS, particularly since an older system, called *loran* (for *lo*ng-*ra*nge *n*avigation), was already in wide use. Loran was an American land-based system; it was less accurate, subject to anomalies in certain areas, and its range was limited to about 100 miles from North America, but it was inexpensive.

With the enormous potential market as an incentive, technicians leaped at the problem of making GPS receivers cheap and easy to use. Companies such as Appelco, Garmin, Magellan, Micrologic, and Trimble, which had pioneered the technology for the military, enthusiastically entered the competitive fray. It didn't take long, a couple of years, before these companies were marketing relatively inexpensive units, and recreational boaters snapped them up. These units were mounted belowdecks and internally wired to the boat's battery. And every year, prices dropped. But navigation purists argued that these systems were only as good as the boat's electrical power source—if you lost your engine, you couldn't charge your batteries, and your GPS would falter.

Then came the Gulf War. During that conflict, ground troops by the thousands were issued handheld GPS receivers no bigger than a transistor radio, powered by common AA batteries. After the war, handheld GPS units took the recreational market by storm.

This was a remarkably useful instrument not only for soldiers and boaters, but for almost any outdoor recreationist. Not only could you learn your precise location by latitude/longitude, you could also pick your destination, called a *way point,* program its latitude and longitude

(Continued)

(Continued)

into the machine, and it would literally guide you to that point by telling you the distance and compass bearing to the way point. Since the receiver knows where it is from moment to moment, it also tells you how fast you're traveling, essential information for marine navigators.

The first handhelds cost over $1,000 in 1991. Today, smaller, improved units sell for $200 to $250. Hikers can carry them in their backpacks; mariners can use them to back up their internally wired units or in small boats use handhelds exclusively. West Marine, one of the biggest retailers of GPS receivers, calls them "one of the greatest examples of high-value consumer products." Some industry forecasters predict that GPS receivers will miniaturize, with no loss of accuracy, to the point where you will be able to wear them on your wrist—for under $100.

---

she has never visited before and is unlikely ever to return to buys a tank of unbranded gas and pays cash. "Add a familiar brand, previous transactions, the use of a credit card, a friendly exchange of greetings, the availability of a cup of coffee and a rest room, and the possibility of future transactions, and you no longer have a pure transaction."[5]

Price is obviously important, and broadly speaking, transactions are the goal of marketing strategies. However, price theory has largely been supplanted by the marketing concept.

 The new marketing thinking is based on the establishment of ongoing relationships. A relationship exists when the buyer and the seller are known to each other, and it implies a series of future transactions based on earned loyalty of the customer to the product. Absent knowledge about the customer's demographics, tastes, and interests, there can be no relationship. Likewise, the customer must know the company's products and have some means of communicating with the company. As we shall see, a new school of thought, made possible by computer information technology, holds that this communication should be individualized.

This general sort of relationship can be seen in mail-order retailers such as J. Peterman and L.L. Bean. In it, service is a huge component, because service helps build a "personal" relationship. A woman orders a dress from the J. Peterman catalog for $150 in late December. In early February, Peterman runs a sale on that dress, pricing it at $95. Unbidden, unrequested, automatically, J. Peterman sends the woman a check for $55. On a strictly bottom-line basis, Peterman loses a few bucks by doing so, but the company views this as a small price to pay for customer goodwill that will probably result in future transactions.

MR. BEAN AND THE MARKETING CONCEPT

In 1912, before anyone had ever heard of the marketing concept, L. L. Bean published the following in his first catalog (it was called a *circular* back then): "I do not consider a sale complete until goods are worn out and the customer still is satisfied. We will thank anyone to return goods that are not perfectly satisfactory. . . . Above all things we wish to avoid having a dissatisfied customer." The company has flourished because it has never lost sight of this simple objective. Today in L.L. Bean's offices, posters affirm this principle:

What is a customer? A customer is the most important person ever in this company—in person or by mail. A customer is not dependent on us, we are dependent on him. A customer is not an interruption of our work, he is the purpose of it. We are not doing a favor by serving him, he is doing us a favor by giving us the opportunity to do so. A customer is not someone to argue or match wits with—nobody ever won an argument with a customer. A customer is a person who brings us his wants—it is our job to handle them profitably to him and to ourselves.

The new marketing concentrates on creating a loyal customer, not a one-time sale. Price is not the major focus for either buyer or seller. It is the reverse of the old "penny-wise and pound-foolish" adage.

CREATING CUSTOMERS

If we want to know what a business is, we have to start with its purpose. There is only one valid definition of business purpose: *to create a customer.*

It is the customer who determines what a business is. For it is the customer alone, who, through a willingness to pay for a good or a service, converts economic resources into wealth, raw materials into goods. What the business thinks it produces is not of first importance—especially not to the future of the business and to its success. What customers think they are buying, and what they consider "value" to be, is decisive.

Because it is a company's purpose to create a customer, any business enterprise has two—and only these two—basic functions: *marketing* and *innovation.*

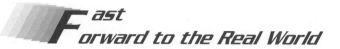

F ast **orward to the Real World**

Guarantee; Warranty; Loyalty

Jonathan Barsky, Ph.D.

A policy of standing behind a restaurant meal, a car wash, or even a haircut with a clearly stated, hassle-free guarantee may be somewhat difficult to control, but it can offer a strong competitive advantage. It can be the needed extra for some customers, especially when previous experience has made them skeptical. It can function as an early warning system, alerting you to problems within your organization. Even high-risk or high-priced services such as financial investments, real estate, or insurance can benefit from guarantees, which can contribute significantly to building customer trust and loyalty.

Many businesses hesitate to guarantee their services, out of concern that customers will take advantage of them. This is not a minor concern: Only five months after introducing it, Eastern Airlines canceled a program that offered passengers their money back for nearly any reason. Knowing the airline would accept even trivial complaints, such as the ice cream being too soft, made the offer too attractive for passengers to pass up.

But backing up products and services with a carefully crafted guarantee of refunds can be good business. There's a strong chance that by showing you take their complaints seriously, you will turn a complaining customer into a lifelong advocate. Even if you don't, whatever you spend on mollifying a disgruntled customer is invariably offset by the value of information that otherwise might not have been brought to management's attention—information that can result in overall efficiencies in operations.

Keep It Simple—and Keep Your Promise

A guarantee program can either be the centerpiece of a service company's entire operation or simply a promotional tool. Many businesses continue to make shallow promises with slogans because they are not prepared to guarantee what their customers want, or because the process for getting the company to make good on its offer is dauntingly complicated. Federal Express has returned millions of dollars to cus-

(Continued)

(Continued)

tomers as a result of its guarantee never to be even one minute late. But critics say the company doesn't take the term "guarantee" seriously enough; the policy won't be enforced unless the customers report the late shipment. Another delivery company, Guaranteed Overnight Delivery (GOD) automatically refunds money on any late delivery. Even refunds for late deliveries that would have gone unnoticed are credited to companies' accounts—a pleasant surprise for the bookkeepers when they see the correction on their monthly statement. This is an excellent example of a truly hassle-free and forceful guarantee.

For a company serious about delivering on its promises, a guarantee may even help it focus on its customers. Hampton Inns president R. E. Schultz believes that the chain's service guarantee "not only helps to differentiate us from the competition, but is just as important to our employees as it is to our customers. A maid knows that if she doesn't clean a room right, someone will go down to the front desk and ask for a refund." Franchisees recruit and train only those people who will carry out the service that the company promises. As a result, Hampton Inns reports that the number of customers invoking its guarantee is very low; so is the number of cheaters.

Bankers have also embraced service guarantees, not only for their marketing appeal, but for their impact on organizational effectiveness. About 25 banks in the United States have made operational changes to commit themselves to a permanent promise of guaranteed service. For example, the "Oops!" program of Union National Bank and Trust Co. pays $5 for "any mistake of any kind that the bank makes." This program is unconditional, easy to invoke, and quick to pay. It is also highly successful because customers want the level of service promised, not the $5 paid for a mistake. But most important, it has affected performance and reduced mistakes to one error in 7,000 transactions, a 99.9 percent accuracy rate.

Here is an example of a good 100 percent guarantee on a magazine subscription:

We stand behind everything we publish. If you're not completely satisfied with our magazine, you may cancel at any time for a full, 100 percent refund of every cent you paid. Not a prorated refund, but a complete refund of your entire subscription price. No questions, no discussion, no problems.

Here is an example of a bad money-back guarantee:

If you are not pleased with the return on investment you get from any ACE Productivity Center seminar, tell us why and we will refund up to 100 percent of the registration fee, no questions asked.

(Continued)

(Continued)

The problems with the bad guarantee are obvious. The use of the phrase "return on investment" is too ambiguous. The offer of a refund of "up to 100 percent" is also vague. How is this decided? Will they return only 5 or 10 percent? Finally, there is a glaring contradiction: "tell us why" and "no questions asked." This makes the guarantee sound evasive and difficult to invoke. The good example, however, is very explicit about the no-questions-asked return policy.

Satisfaction Guaranteed (But *How?*)

It is especially difficult to guarantee intangible products like transportation, consulting, investment banking, or health care, that can't be experienced or tested in advance. In situations like that, customers are essentially being asked to buy promises of satisfaction. Sometimes it takes real imagination to create guarantees for products and services, as the following examples indicate:

- Jaguar now offers the "love" guarantee: "If you think that love isn't a sure thing, then you haven't driven a Jaguar." The company will fully refund your money if, for any reason, you don't love your Jaguar.

- Xerox's "Total Satisfaction Guarantee" now covers all the company's equipment. Xerox promises satisfaction with each product or it will replace the product free of charge for up to three years from the purchase date. According to a Xerox spokesperson, "We're putting the customer in charge. The customer is the sole arbiter and decision maker."

- Crest involves its consumers and their dentists in a six-month promotion. If consumers aren't satisfied with the results of their examinations after using Crest for six months, they get their money back.

- McDonald's now guarantees customer satisfaction and backs it up with a free meal. A customer's next meal is free if he or she is dissatisfied with the current meal. McDonald's will also fix anything wrong with the current meal.

- Richard Chase, a professor at the University of Southern California, offers a satisfaction guarantee for his graduate course, "Management of Services." Although colleagues are scared they may be forced to do likewise, he has yet to have any student demand payment. (Students must request any rebate before their final grade is issued.)

(Continued)

(Continued)

A customer who exercises a guarantee or warranty is a complaining customer. It's important to find out why a customer is invoking a guarantee, so that patterns may be easily identified and corrected. The mail-order guru L.L. Bean gets many complaints. But it takes advantage of the potentially damaging situation. In 1988, dissatisfied customers returned $82 million worth of goods, 15 percent of all L.L. Bean's sales. The company's reaction was not to curtail its return policy but instead to identify the most frequent complaint (wrong size) and take corrective action (updating size information in catalogs and in order-taking computers).

Each time someone collects on the guarantee, have either the customer or an employee fill out a brief card explaining the reason for the complaint. (Do this *after* completing the refund process.) However, keep in mind that some customers may not provide a clue to explain their dissatisfaction, and that it may not be evident to the employee why the customer is collecting on the guarantee. Your challenge, then, is to ensure that the people who complain have ample opportunity to explain why they're dissatisfied without violating the no-questions-asked clause of your guarantee.

When a Warranty Is Warranted

Although hardly new to marketing efforts, warranties are taking on a life of their own. More than simply representing a customer service or added value, these extras are a significant source of profit for many companies. Insuring products against breakdown is among the most lucrative ideas still left in retailing.

As promotional and profit-making tools, warranties can be beneficial when they offer real value to customers and don't reduce the implicit responsibilities of the seller of products and services. Warranties were originally intended to protect the integrity of products and to be accountable for repair and replacement of defective parts. Today, many companies separate liability and the obligation of standing behind their products and services. They are selling this responsibility as an additional service, instead of being automatically accountable for what they sell.

Americans spend about $5 billion each year on extended warranties, special insurance, and service contracts. Half of this is for coverage on new-car purchases. The problem is, customers aren't getting their money's worth. Retailers are exploiting these add-ons. They are

(Continued)

(Continued)

taking advantage of the abstract concept and confusing details of warranties and of their customers' fear of the high technology in many new products.

Circuit City electronics obtains nearly half of its profits ($78 million net income in 1992) from selling extended service contracts. Macy's offers a five-year, $240 contract on electronics, covering technical assistance, maintenance, repairs, and house calls. Friedman's Microwave Ovens makes a healthy profit from selling extended service contracts for $1 per month. Some computer dealers offer extra warranties if the customer pays a 10 percent premium over the purchase price.

Many companies do offer legitimate warranties. When Compaq Computers decided to sell directly to customers to stay competitive with Dell and other mail-order computer retailers, it lowered its prices and introduced the industry's first long-term warranty. The coverage, three years (with minor exclusions), gives consumers more security and confidence in making a major purchase by mail.

Protection is now available for investment in a child's college tuition. Even weddings can be warranted against unexpected disaster, such as being called up for military duty (change of heart is not covered).

Many credit cards now offer free extended warranties and some type of protection when purchases are made with their card. Most items are covered under the extended warranty (except, for example, cars, boats, or motorized equipment) and under the purchase security protection (except, for example, lost items or jewelry, watches, or other items stolen from the customer's car). They'll also double most manufacturers' warranties, adding up to one extra year of coverage, and include gifts under this protection. Although somewhat time-consuming to cash in on (for example, before collecting any money, the customer must show original store receipts), these enhancements are valuable marketing tools. The popularity of these services underscores the importance that customers place on this protection and the market value and economic viability of these added expenses. If credit-card companies can benefit from covering your products and services, why can't you?

A product or service guarantee is an extremely effective way to improve customer satisfaction. The secret lies in the low cost and high return obtained from investments directed at retaining loyal customers. Although processing complaints is easier with advances in technology, the real gains come from the insights they provide to improve operations, and from the good chance of turning a complaining customer into a loyal fan.

Source: Marketing Tools (September 1995).

Place

The Wells Fargo wagon is a'comin down the street . . . !
—*The Music Man*

In marketing language, distribution takes place through *channels,* involving manufacturers, wholesalers, retailers, and sales reps. Marketers tend to distinguish distribution channels from *logistics,* the physical transportation of parts and raw materials from suppliers to manufacturers and the finished product from manufacturers to the wholesalers' warehouses, thence to the place where customers actually buy the product. From the producer's standpoint, distribution channels and logistics can be complex and demanding.

 But the customer doesn't care about any of that. If the customer wants or needs the product and yours is hard to get, the customer will buy someone else's, leaving moot all your efforts to produce a quality product and to give value to your customer. As Ernst & Whinny demonstrated in their 1987 survey for the Council of Logistics Management, ". . . [T]he microcomputer industry boasts a graveyard filled with companies offering competitive products backed by fatally uncompetitive distribution/service operations."

Ted Zuse, who runs Zuse Incorporated, a Connecticut-based company that sells logo clothing by mail order, puts it this way:

Most small mail-order companies like mine are killed by their own success. They haven't established the mechanisms or hired enough people to accommodate a flood of new orders. In the struggle to do so, they end up ignoring old customers, and soon they are overwhelmed by back orders, and no one is pleased. Their customers turn to their competitors. To avoid getting killed, we logged all tasks, prioritized them, and hired standby employees with various skill levels to handle these tasks. We set up what we call CPR, for consistency, predictability, and repeatability. If we can't deliver all three to the customer, we say no to the order.

Distribution is not a glamorous ingredient in the marketing mix. It tends to take place in company backwaters, the stockrooms, loading docks, mail rooms, on flatbed trucks and airline cargo terminals. Distribution managers are usually paid less well and accorded less prestige than their counterparts in, say, new-product development. Their employees are low-paid, are often part-time, and have little personal or economic incentive to please the customer. Yet you don't need to be a marketing guru to grasp that if production doesn't result in easy availability, a company's reputation will wither along with its profits.

Also, recent consumer surveys have all shown that people's enthusiasm for shopping has diminished in recent years. Fewer and fewer want to "shop till they drop." There are complicated social as well as economic reasons for this change in buyer behavior, but the message is clear. Customers want products to come to them, not vice versa. Is the obvious proliferation of mail-order catalogs in our mailboxes a cause or a symptom of this desire?

VERTICAL INTEGRATION VERSUS OUTSOURCING

Let's expand the definition of distribution, which is basically about movement, to include the movement of supplies and raw materials to the producer as well as the movement of finished products away from the producer to the customer. A fundamental change has taken place in the company's relationship between its own production capabilities and its suppliers. Hiam and Schewe contend that the old model of the vertically integrated company is obsolete.

Henry Ford, for example, built a vertically integrated company. By the time he opened his Rouge River Plant, Ford ran his own steel mill to turn raw materials into auto bodies, his own rubber mill to produce tires, and his own glassworks to turn out windshields; virtually every part on the Tin Lizzie, when it motored off the assembly line, had been produced in his plant. This made sound business sense during the 1930s when transportation and communications were, compared to

1997, ponderous, primitive, and undependable. Why should his assembly line be slowed by delinquent suppliers of essential parts?

Twenty-five years ago, the average Japanese company purchased materials approximating 70 percent of its manufacturing cost from outside suppliers. . . . If the parts purchased were defective, no matter how hard the final assembler worked, good products would not emerge. Knowing this, we began Quality Control education among subcontractors in the late 1950s. We also attempted to make these subcontractors specialists in their own fields. Today, Japan's automobiles and electronics are considered to be the best in the world. This is due in part to the excellence of their parts suppliers. In contrast, in Western countries companies try to produce all the parts they need in their own factories.

Producing everything in-house tends to . . . divert organizational focus away from the goal of giving value to the customer.[1]

KEY CONCEPT True strategic focus means that a company can concentrate more power in its chosen markets than anyone else can. Once, this meant owning the largest resource base, manufacturing plants, research labs, or distribution channels to support product lines. Now physical facilities—including a seemingly superior product—seldom provide a sustainable competitive edge. They are too easily bypassed, reverse-engineered, cloned, or slightly surpassed. Instead a maintainable advantage usually derives from outstanding depth in selected human skills, logistics capabilities, knowledge bases, or other service strengths that competitors cannot reproduce and that lead to greater demonstrable value for the customer.

INTERMEDIARIES

The company could handle its own distribution. Eliminating the go-between is an axiomatic price-cutting measure. In fact, middlemen have been economic scapegoats for centuries. Because Levantine middlemen controlled the overland trade routes to Asia, Europeans (Hudson, Cabot, Raleigh, Cartier) during the sixteenth century launched great voyages in search of a water route around North America to Cathay (China). They didn't find one, but they explored most of northeastern North America as a result of those middlemen in Asia Minor. Intermediaries exist, however, not to cadge a markup, but because they perform certain functions for a producer that the producer could not perform as well or as cheaply.

Many markets today are large and disparate. In them, intermediaries move products over long distances to their appropriate markets. A manufacturer of outerwear based, say, in North Carolina must move product to all parts of the country, but he or she is going to want a different line of winter jackets to be sold in Chicago than in Miami. In marketing language, this is called *assortment,* that is, the matching of quantity and kinds of product to the needs of different markets. Intermediaries help facilitate this match.

There are two kinds of intermediaries, *wholesalers* and *retailers,* who actually take title to the product. Many manufacturers establish regional distribution centers, run by intermediaries, from which the product is distributed to retailers. Marketers call this process *sorting,* and it consists of those two steps—first, concentration, then dispersion. Sorting is economical because for the manufacturer it reduces the number of transactions involved in actually selling the product to the customer. Because regional wholesalers are closer to the ultimate user, they are better able to gauge the quantity and kind of product local customers want. Sorting also reduces the cost to the producer of storing inventory.

 In other words, intermediaries offer economies of scale and experience, and removing the responsibility for distribution from the producers frees up their resources and personnel to focus on building quality and adding value for the customer.

DISTRIBUTION CHANNELS

The distribution channel is a set of organizations that make a product or service available to the customer by overcoming time, place, and possession gaps. Distribution channels help to complete transactions in the following ways: by providing information and research about market forces; by promoting; by finding prospective buyers; and by negotiating terms and prices whereby ownership is transferred. After the transactions are complete, other channel members actually transport the goods to market. Whether they perform some or all of these functions, distributors are specialists at what they do, and that fact makes their use economical.

The *conventional distribution channel* consists of a producer, a wholesaler, and retailers, each a separate business looking out first for its own interests, even at the expense of the larger system. Self-interest breeds conflict, either *vertical* or *horizontal.*

Horizontal conflict is that between firms at the same level. A Chevrolet dealership complains loudly that by performing shoddy service and treating customers rudely, a cross-town rival is damaging business and blackening Chevy's good name. Vertical conflict is that between different levels of the channel. A lawn mower manufacturer bypasses its usual regional distributor and sells directly to Ace Hardware franchisers in direct competition with the distributor's retailers.

Thus, a part of the producer's distribution strategy might include mechanisms to manage conflict by setting clear policy and assigning roles.

VERTICAL MARKETING SYSTEMS (VMS)

These systems seek to address the inherent potential for conflict in conventional marketing channels by unifying the channel members somehow. Under VMS, one member owns the others or is able to exert enough power, through contracts, for instance, to force cooperation at all levels. Commonly, VMS are of three types:

1. *Corporate VMS* combines production and distribution under one owner. It could be any member of the channel, but typically it is the producer. Gallo's business is to produce wine, but it also owns a fleet of trucks to haul the wine to market and to deliver raw materials to the winery, and Gallo owns its own bottling company.

2. *Contractual VMS* is a structure held together by binding agreements in which wholesalers organize to acquire retail outlets, or, conversely, retailers organize to acquire distribution capabilities. Also, franchisers, the fastest-growing form of retailing, accounting for one-third of all sales, often link stages in the production and distribution channels, among them Burger King, McDonald's, and Coca-Cola.

3. *Administered VMS* coordinates production and distribution through the size (power) of one of the participants. Such companies as Kraft, GE, and Campbell Soup exert influence over retailers as to how their products will be displayed, priced, and promoted, and from the other direction, Toys 'Я' Us and Wal-Mart can influence manufacturers' product lines.

HORIZONTAL MARKETING SYSTEMS (HMS)

Synergy is a popular word in today's business language, and that's what horizontal marketing systems are all about. Companies combine their capabilities in production, capital, and marketing to create something greater than any one company could accomplish individually. "Coca-Cola and Nestlé formed a joint venture to market ready-to-drink coffee and tea worldwide.

Coke provided experience in marketing and distributing beverages, and Nestlé contributed to established brand names—Nescafé and Nestea."[3]

CHANNEL DESIGN

According to the marketing concept, distribution, like the other ingredients in the mix, should be viewed as customer value delivery systems. (See Figure 3.1 for typical distribution channels.) The auto manufacturer with irresponsible, dishonest dealers will lose market share; dealerships that sell poorly made cars will fail. However, channel design is contingent upon certain specifics relating to the product, the company that makes it, and the intermediaries themselves.

For example, vegetables, milk, fish, and other perishables require direct, timely delivery to retail outlets; heavy products like lumber, bricks, and farm machinery call for channels that require a minimum of handling and distance. Also, the size and financial health of the company determines how much of the distribution

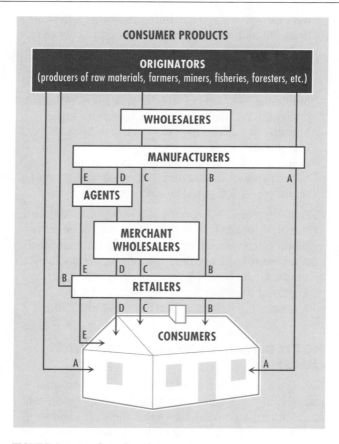

FIGURE 3.1 *Product distribution channels.*

load it can handle on its own and how much should be subcontracted. The abilities and specialties of the intermediaries themselves will affect the channel's design: Do you use intermediaries who handle a lot of different manufacturer's products and are thus cheaper, or do you hire single-line representatives because they'll sell your product harder?

Your competitors' channels are also a factor in the design of your own. Do you want to search out virgin markets, or is part of your strategy to display your product right next to your competitors'? (When you see a Burger King, you won't have to look far to see a McDonald's.)

DISTRIBUTION STRATEGY

So how does the marketer choose among the various types of distribution channels available? For mature, established products, the path is well beaten, though new wrinkles are always possible. Hiam and Schewe, for example, point to L'eggs' strategy of selling panty hose in supermarkets. If the product is entirely new or highly innovative, the way is less clear, but there are still three general criteria: market coverage, channel control, and costs.

Market coverage. The length of the distribution channel is contingent upon the size of the market. If the latter is large, say, for shampoo, then the distribution channel must be relatively longer than that for wheat combines.

Channel control. As we mentioned earlier, wholesalers and retailers take title to your product. But what do they do with it after that? Ideally, they would sell it as aggressively as you would. But will they? Or might they pass it off to another intermediary and/or retailer less appropriate for your product?

Costs. As we have mentioned, short channels do not decrease the cost of distribution; in fact, they increase costs because, ultimately, they increase the number of transactions involved in selling the product to the customer.

LEGAL FACTORS

DANGER!

Remember Standard Oil? There will never be another monopoly like it. The Clayton and Sherman Antitrust Acts and the Federal Trade Commission Act will see to that. However, a company that tries to control product distribution is heading down the road toward monopoly or restraint of trade. Yet manufacturers seek to control distribution all the time. None of the following methods of doing so are illegal as long as they don't constitute the *intent* to create a monopoly.

Developing a Distribution Strategy

In August 1984, with the contract it had reached in 1969 with Volkswagen of America about to expire, Porsche planned to alter the distribution of its sports cars in the United States. The contract between Porsche and VW specified that VW dealers would be the outlets for Porsche products. Porsche's president, Peter Shutz, wanted to bring the company closer to the customer by "doing business like no one else." A research study had found that buyers of the pricey, quality cars were not impulse buyers but, rather, saw their purchase as an investment. Shutz did not think they needed the fast-talking sales pitch of a typical dealer's salesforce. However, because he underestimated the power of the dealers, his plan failed.

The new distribution plan called for eliminating dealers completely and using agents in their place. The agents would not buy the cars, and hence would avoid inventory holding costs; instead, they would buy the cars as needed to complete a sale. They would work on an 8 percent commission compared to the 16 to 18 percent markup generally charged by VW. A total of 40 company centers would be established to stock the Porsches—but they would also sell them in direct competition with the agents.

Shutz felt that the mass retailer was the wrong outlet for his low-volume, high-price ($21,400 to $44,000) autos. He had also heard that some dealers who did not have the cars desired by consumers were buying them from other dealers at a large premium that was passed on to the customer, making the cars even more expensive. He also knew that the Japanese would soon introduce a comparable high-performance sports car, and he wanted to set up a stronger distribution system for competitive reasons. Since the VW contract called for all VW dealers to handle Porsche cars, he had no control over the selection of dealers. Hence the new plan.

Shutz's plan was such a radical departure from the distribution system in America that it met with widespread resistance. In addition, VW dealers were asked to invest in partnerships to finance the Porsche centers. The dealers felt betrayed and insulted by the offer to invest in a distribution system that attacked their traditional franchise system, one that provided them with as much as $40 million in annual sales. Shutz had reasoned that the lower inventory carrying costs would be welcomed and that investment in the centers would foster greater commitment by the dealers. He was wrong.

Three weeks after presenting the plan to what he thought would be an excited and accepting dealer audience, Shutz had to scrap the new

(Continued)

(Continued)

distribution system. The dealers were so angered that, with the help of the American International Automobile Association, they started a class action lawsuit. Dealers across the country sought damages of over $3 billion. Shutz issued a letter explaining that the company had decided against the new system. As part of his effort to rebuild the dealer network, Shutz had buttons made with the slogan, "Nobody's perfect."

Exclusive dealing. A manufacturer prohibits dealers from selling anyone else's products. This becomes questionable when the manufacturer is a monolith and the dealer is a mom-and-pop operation. In reverse, when the manufacturer is new or small, exclusive dealing can be viewed as improving competition.

Dealer selection. A manufacturer selects the dealers it will sell to—and will sell to no others. Wedgwood, a maker of top-end products, is not intending to create a monopoly when it allows only top-end dealers to sell its cut-glass items and excludes Kmart. Wedgwood is only protecting its position.

Tying agreements. The producer forces the dealer to carry other parts of its product line in order to retain the right to sell the most lucrative or popular product. This is an antitrust violation unless the manufacturer is new to the market, trying to maintain quality, or requires its dealers to carry the full product line.

Exclusive territory. Manufacturers force their dealers to sell only within a specified region.

RETAILING

Retailing is not limited to selling something from a store. In marketing terms, retailers are those at the end of the distribution channel who deal directly with the customer. By that extension, doctors, lawyers, and dentists are retailers. The Avon lady is a retailer; so is a hospital, a college, a manicurist, or a hair stylist.

In a very direct way, the face of a retailer becomes the face of the product. If you go to a store to buy a specific product and you are met with surly, rude, or ignorant sales help, you will probably go to another store, and perhaps to a different product. If at a car rental agency you are met with long lines and slow and clumsy processing, you'll rent a car from a different agency next time.

Retailing Strategies

In marketing language, retailers provide *time, place, and possession utilities* to customers. In the past, retailers were *suppliers.* They provided access to products their local customers wanted. Recently, however, retailers began to position themselves according to the market segment they served. Wal-Mart's products, personnel, and policies reflect the wants, needs—and values—of small-town America.

In contrast, other retailers narrowed their product lines while they increased assortment; among these are Toys 'Я' Us, Barnes & Noble, and Radio Shack. Because of their high volume, they can exert influence over all members of the distribution channel and undercut other retailers for whom toys, books, and electronics are a sideline with limited assortment and lower volume.

Value strategy.   This focuses on price. The value strategist tries to offer greater quality for less. This is the fuel that has propelled the growth of discount retailers such as Sam's, Price Club, and Costco.

Efficiency strategy.   Convenience has become a major concern for shoppers. In today's economic climate, it is common for both members of a household to work outside the home; some hold down two jobs. Stretched thin, consumers don't shop with the enthusiasm they used to. Superstores, convenience stores, and catalogs offer customers one-stop shopping, and they have profited and proliferated as a result.

Personal-contact strategy.   This strategy puts the onus on sales help to offer expert service tailored to individual customer needs, and some consumers are willing to pay considerably more for personal contact.

Sensory strategy.   Retailers who practice this strategy try to provide a gee-whiz experience. They stimulate in order to sell. Instead of offering lower price and convenience, these retailers try to make shopping fun again. Harrod's, the London department store, does this; so does Bloomingdale's.

 A theory of retailing holds that things happen in cycles, not unconnected to societal changes. First came general stores at a time when Americans' mobility was limited. These were supplanted by department stores in the 1950s. As department stores grew, so did their costs, and with them, prices. This gave rise to discount stores offering greater value and fewer frills. These expanded their services and displays and came to look like low-end department stores. Bare-rack warehouse stores like Sam's and Price Club arose in response. And in response to that trend a backlash has occurred as some customers have decided they want the frills and personal attention offered by specialty stores and boutiques.

PHYSICAL DISTRIBUTION

Compared to new-product development and promotion, for instance, physical distribution ranks low on the glamour/prestige scale, yet as a matter of economics, physical distribution is huge. Fully 20 percent of every dollar spent by consumers goes to pay for the physical transportation of goods. This cost varies from industry to industry; in the food industry, one of the highest, one-third of every dollar spent goes to pay for physical distribution. In total, this amounts to 15 percent of the nation's GNP!

As a process, this is much more than loading stuff onto trucks, planes, and trains. As with all aspects of the marketing mix, physical distribution must be strategized, and that strategy must mesh with the rest of your company's marketing strategy. The following aspects need to be considered in formulating your physical-distribution strategy.

Forecasting demand. Essentially, this is a matter of supplying customer needs at the lowest possible cost to the producer. If you understock at any point in the distribution channels, you will not satisfy the customer simply because your product will not be available in the quantity needed. If you overstock, you will spend more than necessary for storage and handling.

Order processing. Distribution channels have exchange points along the way. The retailer orders stock from the warehouse. The warehouse informs the producer or another channel member. The process can be long or short depending on the product and other variables, but each time an exchange is made, orders must be taken and fulfilled. The efficiency of the process—sometimes the entire marketing plan—will depend on these clerical procedures. In this, as in every step of the distribution process, computers have made things easier, but not foolproof.

Inventory management. Distributors have become the nation's inventory managers. Distribution, remember, involves not only moving finished products from the producer to the end users, but also moving parts and raw materials to the producer. The trick is to have just enough but not too much of everything where and when it's needed to balance the costs of stocking inventory against lost sales. The Japanese have pioneered *just-in-time purchasing* to accomplish this balance. It requires that the producer and its distributors enter into a partnership to control quality and scheduling.

Storage. With the aid of computerization and automation, today's marketers try to avoid storage. This goal is more or less possible depending on the fluctuation of demand for your product. In many industries, regional distribution centers, highly streamlined and automated product movers, have replaced warehouses.

Protective packaging. Obviously, breakage costs time and money. Distributors often take responsibility for protecting goods. To some extent, the product and its packaging determine the mode of transportation. For example, it is helpful to know that trains are hot and airplanes are cold, because certain products need to be protected against temperature variation.

Transportation. Railroad, truck, pipeline, waterway, airplane—these are the major modes of transport. There are four different kinds of transportation companies:

- *Common carriers* serve the general public.

- *Contract carriers* are independent firms that ship specific things to specific sites for an agreed-upon price.

- *Private carriers* are those that own the goods they ship. Grocery stores, for which timely delivery is crucial, usually own their trucks.

- *Exempt carriers* are exempt from state and federal regulation. They are usually truckers who move agricultural products.

 Physical distribution is all about service. Producers are tempted to try to cut the costs of distribution, but if doing so diminishes the producer's level of service to the customer, then competitors will step in to fill the gap in service.

*F*ast *F*orward to the Real World

Road Warriors

James Madden

Imagine walking into a sales call with every piece of information needed to introduce a product to a customer: a record of the customer's sales history, up-to-date information about the customer's industry and competitors, detailed product spec sheets, current price sheets, and all the other information needed to close the sale. One way to do this would be to bring along a team of experts, each lugging cases filled with printed information. Another way would be to make a series of calls to the support team back at the home office.

Or, you could walk into the call carrying a seven-pound notebook computer containing all of the information listed above, with the capability of making a wireless real-time connection to data stored at the home office. This is state-of-the-art sales force automation.

Sales force automation is not a new concept. What makes it of interest today is the powerful information and communication tools that are now available. These include portable computers with an enormous amount of information capacity, high-speed modems, cellular and radio data networks that allow for wireless communication, and software that allows computers to easily share information. At the same time, we are experiencing an unprecedented level of computer literacy among white-collar workers.

Then there's the high cost of keeping a sales or service representative on the road today. Ginger Trumfio, of Sales and Marketing Management in New York, reports that the average consumer sales call now costs more than $200. Many firms are turning to sales force automation in an effort to control costs, as well as to allow field representatives to work more efficiently and to gain a competitive advantage.

Naturally, when we hear the phrase "state-of-the-art," we reach for our wallets. Experience has taught us that it can mean unproven, risky, and expensive. But while there are many hidden costs to a field force automation project, there are also many hidden benefits. Perhaps the greatest benefit is the arsenal of customer, competitor, and product information that a representative can bring to a sales call. As one insurance company project manager explains her vision, "Our goal is a one-call sale, and we're getting there."

(Continued)

(Continued)

A link to the home office allows a representative to have up-to-the-minute price and inventory information. He or she can work up a quote while talking with the client and enter the order from the client's office. In addition, a remote link allows the representative to follow up on a sales call while the call is fresh in her mind. Thank you letters and collateral materials can be sent from the home office the same day a call is made.

It's hard to imagine a sales representative who would not prefer this level of efficiency to several days of follow-up work after a long stint on the road. Furthermore, having a link to interoffice networks and the ability to participate in planning and management discussions while they are away makes field force representatives immediately more productive when they return to the home office.

Who's Automating?

A 1994 International Data Corporation (IDC) survey of 402 large and medium-sized U.S. companies and government agencies revealed that 70 percent of large and medium-sized organizations are involved with field force automation. Of these, 40 percent are in their second generation and 22 percent are in their third generation of automation. The study was based on in-depth telephone interviews with 206 Information Technology (IT) managers and 196 end-user department managers, and included respondents from Ætna, Amway, Chemical Bank, Kellogg, and other large companies. To qualify, companies had to have more than 500 employees and department managers had to represent groups using five or more mobile computers. The average workgroup size was 99 employees.

Not surprisingly, the IDC study found sales departments to be the most prolific users of field force automation, followed by accounting/auditing operations, and maintenance and repair. The technology is well suited to insurance claims adjusting, project consulting, mortgage lending, and field research. Of the survey respondents, 55 percent mentioned word processing as a primary software application, 30 percent mentioned spreadsheets, 20 percent mentioned database and order entry. Fifteen percent reported custom applications to be a primary software application, 17 percent specified sales-related software, and 18 percent mentioned e-mail.

When asked about the major benefit of an automated field force, 31 percent of the IDC survey respondents mentioned better customer service, satisfaction, or turnaround; 24 percent referred to improved productivity and more efficient operations; and 14 percent focused on

(Continued)

(Continued)

better and more up-to-date information. Surprisingly, only 5 percent considered increased profitability and reduced costs to be a major benefit of a successful automation project.

The IDC study found that a typical automation project costs $6,400 per user in the first year of automation. Six percent of the firms reported spending less than $2,000 and nearly 20 percent reported spending more than $10,000 per workstation. Hardware accounted for half of the estimated cost, according to respondents. Other costs include training, application development and maintenance, network management, and communications charges.

As for development, the study found that it typically takes nearly two years to design, implement, and roll out an automation project. In cases where transaction processing is automated, allowing mobile employees to interact directly with billing, order entry, and inventory systems, implementation usually takes several months longer than it does for information-only and remote-processing systems. The average payback time on a system is 2.6 years.

Equipped for the Road

The newer generations of notebook computers are lighter, more powerful, and increasingly more cost-efficient than their predecessors of just a few years ago. Batteries last longer; CD-ROM drives and high-capacity hard drives allow field agents to carry and quickly reference enormous amounts of information; and cellular technology and radio data networks now allow for wireless communication with the home office and the information world at large.

It is possible to automate a field force with devices other than laptop computers. Andrew Seybold, author of the new book *Using Wireless Communications in Business,* explains that there are many choices for wireless communication. These include two-way radios, shared radio systems, digital pagers, messaging pagers, analog-cellular systems, and specialized data-only networks such as RAM and ARDIS.

Seybold emphasizes the importance of defining why you are interested in wireless data access. Will you save money, improve sales or service responses, or have better access to key executives? Or are you simply curious about the potential benefits of wireless data access? While each is a valid reason, it is important to know in advance who will use the system, who will control it, and what the implementation costs payback period will be. It may be more beneficial to equip some people with

(Continued)

(Continued)

cellular phones and others with pagers, wireless e-mail, or direct LAN connections. And some employees may be better off with a pocket full of quarters for pay phones.

The first hand-held personal communications devices—also known as Personal Digital Assistants (PDAs)—were the Apple Newton Message Pad and the Tandy/Casio/AST Zoomer. Users of these devices are computer users first and cellular phone users second, if at all. The strength of these devices lies in communicating with other computing devices rather than directly with people.

PDAs and other pen-based applications have not sold well to date. Seybold believes that's because "the companies bringing these products to market did not understand who would make up the first wave of buyers. They built systems that fit their vision of the future of handheld computers, but they did not concentrate on today's computer users whose primary need is to interact with their own desktops and to send and receive e-mail messages quickly and effectively."

Cellular phones have had better luck in the marketplace. The first "smart" cellular phone, Simon, was designed by IBM and marketed by BellSouth. It provides cellular telephone users with features such as an electronic daybook, address book, and to-do list. It can send and receive faxes, but it is not intended to interface with the user's desktop computer. This type of device appeals to people who interact with others by voice, fax, and other communication links.

Working Without Wires

Today's state-of-the-art laptops contain slots, which allow you to send data via a wireless modem, transmit and receive faxes, and communicate with Local- and Wide-Area Networks (LANS and WANS). Wide Area Networks are similar to the LAN in your office, but they also allow access to a much larger geographic area and a variety of dial-up, shared information sources including the Internet, electronic bulletin boards, and online services like CompuServe.

You might think that cellular modems should work with any cellular phone network. However, this is not the case in most situations. Often during a cellular conversation, you may temporarily lose contact with the other party, talk over another conversation, or have an otherwise "noisy" connection. This is not an acceptable environment for data transfer. To overcome this technical challenge to wireless data transmission, several radio-data networks have been developed.

(Continued)

(Continued)

Two of the most popular radio-data networks are ARDIS and RAM. ARDIS is jointly owned and operated by Motorola and IBM. It was first installed to provide IBM field representatives with direct access to their databases and messaging systems. ARDIS is currently the largest provider of wireless two-way data connections, with over 40,000 users nationwide.

The other leading data network, RAM Mobile Data, makes use of a radio technology referred to as "trunking." This technology uses up to 30 channels in a market area, giving the system the capacity to support a large number of users.

The third major player in this field is RadioMail. Think of RadioMail as an information clearinghouse. It allows for wireless exchange of e-mail; communication between ARDIS and RAM; and access to the Internet, MCI Mail, AT&T Mail, and other services. Over time, it will provide access to sports, weather, and many other databases. RAM was the first major data network to sign an agreement with RadioMail, thus positioning itself as the network for individuals who wanted ties not only to their own corporate e-mail systems but to public networks as well. ARDIS initially focused on connecting users with their respective corporate offices.

Today, ARDIS offers RadioMail service to its clients. RAM is working with key corporate accounts to build its subscriber base. Both systems offer comparable access to public e-mail services. They are competitively priced below $100 per month.

The now-familiar UPS package tracking system uses ARDIS and cellular networks to track parcels from the time they are picked up to the time they reach their final destination. One reason this system has been so successful is that it has been designed to place the burden of information delivery on the carrier rather than the customer.

When a tie-in to an in-house system is required, smart keys and bar codes can greatly improve the efficiency and accuracy of information transfers. These systems are built by companies such as Symbol Technologies, Husky Computer, and IBM. In the same way that a single swipe of a wand over a bar code feeds information about a product transfer into a single computer, smart keys can be programmed to transfer information to a centralized database with a single keystroke. Smart keys ensure that information is loaded into a database accurately and that it will be available for retrieval at a later date.

With the proper communications software and access to RAM or ARDIS, a card enables an entire traveling sales staff to receive a price list update simultaneously from the home office. Field representatives

(Continued)

(Continued)

would not be required to take any action to have up-to-date pricing information placed in the proper file on their systems. This could also be accomplished using more conventional methods—modem and phone lines. Programs such as LapLink Professional by Traveling Software, and SmartSync by Nomadic Systems, Inc. allow users to connect two workstations (with wires) and merge the contents of two subdirectories, retaining the most current information, and making them the same on both machines. AirCommunicator by AirSoft is the wireless equivalent of LapLink and SmartSync.

Automating Your Organization

Because of the dynamic and ongoing nature of an automation project, managers must look beyond the initial cost of hardware and software. Speaking to attendees at the Direct Marketing Association's business-to-business conference, Gary Skidmore of Harte-Hanks Direct Marketing in Austin, Texas, cautioned that there can be an intimidating learning curve, especially for the older representatives who may be your best sales people. He estimates that an automated field force requires one support person for every ten agents.

The willingness of the field force to use the system is critical to the success of a field-force-automation project. The best salespeople are highly motivated to make as many sales calls as possible. Their compensation is largely based on their revenue numbers. Sales people may perceive their new gift of a laptop as an attempt by the home office to hand off administrative chores. In this scenario, they see the proposed automation as nothing more than additional work that takes away from time spent calling on customers. When this is the case, it is unlikely that the sales force will buy into the system. On the other hand, if the sales representatives see a link to the home office as a selling tool, an efficient way to follow up on sales calls, or a way to maintain a voice at the home office, they are likely to become the driving force in implementing a system.

On a positive note, field-force-automation projects that would have failed two years ago might flourish today because of the phenomenal increase in computer literacy and the confidence today's office workers have in network computing. A sales training manager participating in the IDC survey reported, "This is our second go-around. The first time the computers were too heavy and the applications weren't geared to the field. This time we're developing it from the ground up, and the sales force is excited. They finally believe automation can do something for them."

Source: Marketing Tools (October 1995).

4

Promotion

The American Association of Advertising Agencies defines *promotion* as "interpreting to the public, or to desired segments of the public, information regarding a legally marketed product or service." Promotion is your company's public face.

Let's test that fairly simple notion against a hypothetical example. Let's say you work as a marketing manager for a conglomerate that produces, among other lines, personal-care products. That division has produced a new women's shampoo—call it Sheen. The product works, and you've augmented with a built-in conditioner. You have no question about its quality, and your consumer testing has been highly positive. Now your job is to formulate a promotion strategy. If you subscribe to the preceding definition, all you have to do is to inform the public of Sheen's existence and explain its fine cleansing and conditioning capabilities, and with your well-oiled distribution system in place, Sheen should fly right off the shelves.

Maybe it will. However, you face some stiff competition for customer attention. There are some 250 advertised brands in the hair-care category. As we said in Chapter 1, most products on the market today are mature, and at maturity the highest level of competition and market segmentation occurs. According to James C. Schroer of the consulting firm Booz Allen & Hamilton, "Most consumer goods markets are static, so to gain a share you have to outspend the competition by a huge amount."[1]

That makes things a bit more complicated. If you've got to spend a bundle to launch Sheen, you might as well do something splashy to separate yourself from the competition. You hold in-house brainstorming sessions and similar sessions with your ad agency. Everyone agrees: This launch needs to be flashy. So here's an idea. Hire Marky Mark to pose seminude and say, "I only date girls with sheen." Then you saturate the media—magazines, newspapers, billboards, even the sides of buses—with your ad, and you kick back and watch Sheen fly off the shelves. . . .

THE BATTLE FOR CUSTOMERS' MINDS

Promotion has three objectives: *informing, persuading,* and *reminding.* Promotion strives to influence demand, thus minimizing the significance of price considerations in the customer's decision making. (Hiam & Shewe put this in technical terms: "[P]romotion attempts to make the demand curve increasingly inelastic (price-insensitive) at high prices and increasingly elastic (price-sensitive) at low prices."[2])

Yes, but what about the customer? What about promotion and its handmaiden, advertising, as they relate to the marketing concept? What did your Marky Mark ad have to say about the quality of Sheen shampoo? Let's pretend that it's a good ad, winning a coveted award at the annual advertisers' banquet; again, stranger things have happened. But the ad didn't say anything about the benefits of your product to the customer. Like so many ads today, it merely proffered an image: If you want someone hip, handsome, famous, wealthy, and half naked to like you, you'll wash your hair with Sheen. Sheen itself could be a gob of goo.

 Advertising will be either effective or ineffective, but in any event, it has absolutely nothing to do with product quality, only with advertising quality.

Persuasion can thus edge over the line into manipulation and exploitation. All these efforts to create a product with the customer's best interests at heart will be for naught if the customer feels manipulated or, worse, exploited. A growing body of marketing opinion agrees with Steven Ewen, professor of media studies at Hunter College: "Advertising has filled in all the cracks of people's lives to the extent that it is seen as an encroachment."[3]

Or, as Hiam and Schewe put it in *The Portable MBA in Marketing,* "[Promotion] can be used to advance the marketing concept, or it can be allowed to conflict with it. At most companies, this key issue has yet to be addressed, let alone resolved. Promotion is still on the frontiers of the marketing concept, despite its being the most visible face of marketing from the consumer's perspective."[4]

With that in mind, let's turn to the nuts and bolts of promotion.

PROMOTION MIX

Promotion mix is a company's total communications program. It consists of *advertising, personal selling, sales promotion,* and *public relations.*

Advertising is generally defined as any impersonal form of communication about ideas, goods, or services paid for by an identified sponsor. Most advertising uses such mass media as newspapers, magazines, television, radio, direct mail, and billboards. The remainder—about one-third—uses everything from matchbooks to circulars, calendars to catalogs. Since it is impersonal, advertising addresses *basic* human appeals such as sex, prestige, hunger, and social approval.

Personal selling entails presentation by a firm's sales force. This could be a business-to-business approach or it could take the form of the person who sprays perfume on you as you enter Bloomingdale's.

Sales promotion involves short-term incentives such as discounts or throw-ins—buy a pair of Air Jordans and for a limited time only get a Chicago Bulls gimme hat—that encourage purchasers and build customer relations.

Public relations is a way of gaining favorable publicity and heading off unfavorable publicity to build a positive corporate image.

ADVERTISING: THE TEXTBOOK NUTS AND BOLTS

Advertising has become more than just commercials, more than an effort by companies to inform and persuade; it has become a major part of our pop culture. Advertising as an industry is a monolith, accounting for about $140 billion in 1993. As a subject for study, advertising is also immense, and space does not allow an in-depth discussion in this book. However, here are some basics.

Advertisements need *objectives* to be effective. Objectives should be articulable and specific. Here are three:

1. *Sales objectives.*   All advertising has this objective, in general, but your sales objectives should be specific, including numerical increases in bottom-line areas such as revenue, unit volume, or market share.

Advertising, particularly of the mass-market sort, is hard to measure for effectiveness, no matter what its boosters claim. This question of measurability in promotion generally is one of the most interesting and controversial issues in marketing today. It is also one of the main attractions of direct marketing.

2. *Prepurchase objectives.* These are basically exposure goals. For example, a client might tell an ad agency that he or she wants to reach 90 percent of the targeted audience ten times in one week.

3. *Image-building objectives.* As a strategy, these ads are as self-explanatory as they are ubiquitous.

Advertising objectives are mated to a specific message, or *advertising platform,* to be conveyed to the audience. The next step, how the message is conveyed, is a matter of advertising technique and not our province here.

The Advertising Agency

Madison Avenue: Everyone's heard of it, even if they couldn't find it on a map of Manhattan. Back in the 1950s, advertising was portrayed as an exciting, glamorous, if slightly hocus-pocus, profession in Doris Day–Rock Hudson romantic comedies. *The Man in the Gray Flannel Suit* took some of the blush off that rose. During the heyday of mass-media advertising, powerful giants such as Ogilvy and Mather and J. Walter Thompson ruled the canyons of midtown Manhattan, which was to say, the world.

Today the world is much changed. A decade ago, the average U.S. company spent over 40 percent of its promotion budget on advertising; that percentage has dropped to 30 as businesses shift their budgets to other ingredients in the promotion mix. The keynote speech at the 1991 American Association of Advertising Agencies was called "The Year Best Forgotten."

No one seriously predicts that the ad agency will vanish from the economy of business, but nothing in the industry will ever be as certain, at least in the foreseeable future, as it was when everybody wore the same suit.

Like distributors, ad agencies perform a specialized service better and more efficiently than, say, a large soap manufacturer could perform them. That manufacturer might have its own advertising and promotion department, but it would still hire an agency for anything out of the ordinary, such as new-product promotion. Also, agencies know the media, mass and otherwise, and they are in the business of selling their experience as well as their expertise.

In the halcyon days—in other words, until very recently—most agencies worked on a commission basis, paid not by the client but by the media the agency hired to run their ads. If an agency bought (with the client's money) $100,000 of media coverage, the media paid 15 percent, or $15,000, in commission to the agency. The agency's fee from the client was relatively small, thus encouraging the use of ad agencies— similar to the relationship between a travel agency and its client.

Nobody much likes this system anymore. Big companies don't like it because they see themselves paying more for the same services smaller advertisers get for less, and because the commission system places more emphasis on the high-cost media. Agencies don't like it because they don't get paid any more if they do special work for the client. Today a little over a third of the advertisers pay agencies straight commission. The others pay either a flat fee or a combination of fee and commission.

In the face of bedrock change, many agencies, large and small, are offering more diversified services in response to advertisers' growing interest in diversified media. One writer referred to the new agency–advertiser relationship as "marketing partners." Additionally, the conglomeration of ad agencies, part of the 1980s merger-and-acquisition fever, has made smaller, perhaps freer, agencies more attractive to some advertisers who don't want partners, only specific services.

PERSONAL SELLING

Personal selling is the most individualized component in the promotion mix, and so consumer targeting can be very precise indeed. However, the number of personal contacts are limited by time and expense. Therefore, personal selling is most appropriate in the following circumstances: when the price of the product markup is high enough to warrant the increased costs; when the product is complex enough to need explanation and demonstration; and when product benefits need to be tailored to fit the individual customer. Though companies such as Avon and Mary Kay use personal selling directly to the consumer, most personal selling takes place between businesses. Industrial equipment is almost always sold face-to-face.

Hiam and Schewe point to *Sales & Marketing Management* magazine's six categories used to identify the best sales forces in America:

1. Recruiting top sales forces
2. Retention of top salespeople
3. Quality of training
4. Opening new accounts

5. Product and technical knowledge

6. Reputation with customers

Procter & Gamble, winner of *Sales & Marketing Management*'s award in the health- and beauty-aids category, has reorganized its sales force to allow a single salesperson to handle an entire category for retailers, who are its direct customers. Retailers appreciate this new structure because they need to see only one salesperson per category, not a long line of them representing each product, and the salesperson becomes a specialist in cooperative problem solving with the retailer.

Hiam and Schewe also cite Nabisco Biscuit Company, winner in the food-products category, for its spirit of the marketing concept in its work with retailers. Nabisco strives to make their lives easier. "First of all," says Harry Lees, senior vice president of sales, "we deliver product to the back door so they don't have to go through a warehouse. Then we literally set up the biscuit department. We help our customers pick the best location for the products. Our salesperson can sit down with a customer and . . . share our information on the retailer's market position, who its customers are, what its average purchase is, and how to create the most effective merchandise mix for that environment."

RJR Nabisco and Procter & Gamble, among others, are not merely making sales to their retail customers, they are building a long-term relationship based on trust and cooperation. Advertising and direct-mail sales cannot do that.[5]

SALES PROMOTION

According to the American Marketing Association, sales promotions are "those marketing activities, other than personal selling, advertising, and publicity, that stimulate customer purchasing and dealer effectiveness, such as displays, shows and expositions, demonstrations, and various nonrecurrent selling efforts not in the ordinary routine."[6] Though expensive, sales promotion is becoming more important to most companies because it has enormous power to create customer awareness and positive attitude. Companies often spend more on sales promotion than on advertising.

PUBLIC RELATIONS

Public relations tries to put the company's best foot forward. In this usage, *public* certainly includes customers, but also members of the distribution channels, stockholders, government regulatory agencies, neighbors, the media, and the company's employees.

Publicity is part of the public relations function. *Publicity* in this case refers to any message about the company that appears in the media but is not paid for by the company. The headline ACME, INC. BUILDS PLAYGROUND FOR LOCAL KIDS is an example of good publicity; ACME, INC. ACCUSED BY FEDS OF ASBESTOS DUMPING IN LOCAL PLAYGROUND is not.

The Pinto was a public-relations disaster for Ford in the 1970s, since it tended to burst into flames when struck from behind. Though Ford was exonerated in the courts, it had to withdraw the car from the market. The company that produced flammable pajamas for kids underwent a similar PR nightmare. The tobacco companies are presently living their own nightmare. They've given up as a lost cause good publicity. Their only hope is to win the court fight over whether tobacco should be regulated as a drug.

David Merrick, the Broadway producer, was a master manipulator of PR. Among his box-office ploys, he once boosted flagging ticket sales by finding in the phone book people with the same names as the New York theater critics. He took these people to his show as his guests, and in the next day's newspapers ran ads saying: "Brilliant! Don't Miss It," (Frank Rich); and "A Delight from Start to Finish," (Walter Kerr). Merrick's clever tactic wasn't meant to deceive. He wanted you to know how he got his quotes. That was the whole point.

But if you're not David Merrick, you'd better not try to kid the media. They tend not to find it funny, and they particularly dislike being manipulated. Companies designate people in their PR departments to handle press relations. It's in the best interests of the company to maintain an honest, open, working association with the press and other news media.

TYPES OF MESSAGES

Promotional messages are usually directed to a target audience. They may consist of nonusers, potential users, or present users. The target audience will determine, or at least shape, the type of message sent:

Rational appeals relate to the buyer's self-interest on the basis of quality, economy, value, or performance.

Emotional appeals attempt to activate feelings that will motivate purchase. Michelin seats an infant in the center of one of their tires and says you should buy them because there is so much riding on your tires. If you don't brush your teeth with such and such, they'll fall out in your lap.

Moral appeals speak to the audience's sense of right and wrong, to moral obligations. Charities such as the Christian Children's Fund and the March of Dimes use moral appeals.

COST AND THE PROMOTIONAL MIX

Some companies, like Coca-Cola and PepsiCo, seem to have unlimited promotion budgets, but most companies have to make certain decisions about how to spend their money. Promotion expenses vary wildly according to the product being sold. A cosmetics company may spend 30 percent of sales on promotion, whereas a manufacturer of high-pressure valves for medical applications might spend less than 5 percent. (Ralph Lauren has said, "In the laboratory we mix chemicals, in the marketplace we sell dreams." Dreams cost relatively more to promote.)

Though it's hard to generalize, there are four common methods of promotion budgeting:

1. *Affordable method.* In this method, the budget is set at the level of spending the company can afford. Most basic, this method works well for small businesses that sell their products or services to a local market. In fixing the actual dollar amount, the operator will start with total revenue, deduct costs, and allocate a portion of the remainder for promotion. This places promotion last among priorities and makes long-range market planning imprecise; that's usually no problem for, say, the small sporting-goods retailer in western Pennsylvania, but not for a chain such as Herman's.

2. *Percentage-of-sales method.* A percentage of current or forecasted sales is allocated to promotion. The knock on this method is that it considers sales as the cause of promotion rather than the result. Thus it tends to neglect promotion opportunity. The history of marketing is peppered with examples of how increased promotion spending turned around flagging sales of good products.

3. *Competitive-parity method.* Here, a company's promotion spending is keyed to that of its competitors on the assumption that, taken together, competitors' spending represents the collective wisdom of the industry. Also, this method forestalls promotion wars. It is often used in heavy industry. Strict application of this method is, however, somewhat like the captain of a vessel who enters a strange harbor by following another vessel that *seems* to know what it's doing.

4. *Objective-and-task method.* This method sets a promotion budget based on what the company means to accomplish with its promotion. First, of course, the company must set and articulate those goals; second, it must determine the tasks necessary to achieve the goal; and third, it must estimate the costs involved. This method is the most logical, but these three steps are hard to make because advertising effectiveness is hard to gauge.

 **FACTORS USED TO SET THE PROMOTION MIX**

Type of product and market. As we've said, consumer-products producers spend more on advertising than do industrial-products consumers. These two types of producers approach the mix from different directions. Con-

ADVERTISING-TO-SALES RATIOS

Industry	Ad Dollars as Percent[a] of Sales[a]	Ad Dollars as Percent of Margin[b]
Air cond, heating, refrig equip	1.5	5.8
Air transport, scheduled	1.8	16.0
Apparel & other finished prods	2.9	8.0
Beverages	9.5	17.0
Bolt nut screw rivets washers	0.9	2.9
Btld & canned soft drinks, water	2.9	6.2
Can/frozen presrv, fruit, veg	6.9	17.1
Carpets & rugs	0.7	2.8
Catalog, mail-order houses	5.7	15.8
Computer & office equipment	1.2	2.7
Cutlery hand tools, gen hrdwr	10.9	21.6
Educational services	5.0	9.4
Electronic computers	5.1	10.3
Games, toys, child veh ex dolls	14.2	29.3
Groceries & related pds-whsl	1.5	10.7
Grocery stores	1.3	5.5
Guided missiles & space veh	5.3	170.1
Hospitals	5.0	29.7
Industrial inorganic chemicals	16.5	34.4
Investment advice	8.6	19.8
Iron & steel foundries	1.2	4.2
Lawn, garden tractors, equip	4.0	11.3
Lumber & other bldg matl-retl	1.8	6.9
Membership sport & rec clubs	11.0	13.5
Motion pic, videotape distrib	13.0	15.1
Perfume, cosmetic, toilet prep	10.4	16.1
Phono records, audio tape disc	8.3	23.2
Prepackaged software	4.8	9.2
Radio, tv consumer elec stores	5.3	23.8
Retail stores, all	5.8	12.7
Security brokers & dealers	3.1	7.3
Special clean, polish preps	14.5	24.8
Sugar & confectionary prods	10.6	28.9
Women's clothing stores	2.7	7.5

[a]Ad dollars as percent of sales = Ad expenditures/net sales.
[b]Ad dollars as percent of margin = Ad expenditures/(net sales – cost of goods sold). Based on 1989 industry data.
Source: Schonfeld & Associates, 1 Sherwood Drive, Lincolnshire, Ill. 60069, 1990.

sumer-products producers place their emphasis on advertising, followed in declining order by sales promotion, personal selling, and public relations, whereas industrial producers invest first in personal selling, then sales promotion, advertising, and public relations.

Push strategy.   The company uses its sales force to "push" the product through distribution channels. Producers promote the product to wholesalers, wholesalers to retailers, and retailers to consumers.

Pull strategy.   The producer orchestrates its own marketing activities directed primarily at final customers, thus building demand for the product to which the channel members will respond. Public demand "pulls" the product through channels.

Most large companies employ a combination of both methods.

MASS MEDIA: THE NOT-SO-NEW FRONTIER

The decades since the close of World War II gave birth to and saw the maturation of mass marketing. Mass marketing would not have been possible without mass media—more specifically, television, also born after the war. But if TV made mass marketing possible, another technological development, the computer, has called into question among most modern marketers all the old assumptions about mass marketing.

Mass markets are no longer comprised of masses. They have fragmented. (Remember the product life cycle? Most products today are in their mature phase, a time characterized by deep market segmentation and heavy competition.) But far and away the most influential change is that caused by information technology, which offers marketers access to great quantities of knowledge about customer needs. So significant is the shift away from the efficacy of mass marketing that a group of marketers envision a "one-to-one future," in which companies can literally market their products to individual consumers.

In the halcyon days of mass marketing, during the early 1960s, an advertiser buying time on the network TV stations could be reasonably certain that the message would reach 90 percent of the population in one week. Today that accessibility has declined to a little over 50 percent as networks lose market share to ever growing numbers of cable TV stations. The ballyhooed 500-channel TV is, according to most critics, just around the corner. Some critics also point to the remote control as a cause of mass-media decline. Many viewers don't even watch commercials anymore; they mute them or channel-surf during them.

Likewise, print media has fragmented. You can hardly think of a subject or a field of interest to which a special-interest magazine is not devoted, and special-interest magazines themselves have fragmented. In the 1960s, choices of magazines for boaters basically amounted to *Boating* or *Yachting*. Today, readers—and those marketing products to them—can choose among *Sailing World, Cruising World, Motorboating, Sea Kayaking, Canoeing, Multihulls,* and *Megayacht,* to name only a few.

The result of this fragmented market and media represents a loss to advertisers generally. Companies that once spent well over 50 percent of their promotion budgets on mass-media advertising, including but not limited to TV, now spend around 25 percent. Most marketers contend that that percentage will slip even further, perhaps all but replaced by one-to-one interactive media such as on-line services or interactive television or some new form we can't predict.

In the next chapter we will look more closely at the "one-to-one future," but for now let's examine direct marketing, one of the most obvious and fastest-growing trends in marketing communications.

DIRECT MARKETING

Bob Stone, in his book *Successful Direct Marketing Methods,* defines *direct marketing* as "an interactive system of marketing which uses one or more advertising media to effect a measurable response and/or transaction at any location."

 *Measurable* is the important word here. Mass marketing can be likened to throwing rice at the problem. Some grains hit, but most don't. One traditional way to measure the effectiveness of mass-media advertising was to track sales figures. But this didn't tell you *whom* your customers were, what segment was actually buying.

Direct marketing, as distinguished from mass-market advertising, offers the following advantages:

1. A firm, definite offer is made on the spot.
2. All decision-making information is provided in a self-contained form.
3. A response mechanism is supplied, usually in the form of a toll-free telephone number or mail-in coupon. If direct marketing fulfills its predictions, the response mechanism will be even more direct—with the press of a key on your computer or television.

In his book *Direct Marketing,* Edward Nash claims that one of the main reasons for the surging development of direct marketing is a thing called *statistical projectability.* This makes direct marketing much more scientific than other forms of advertising because

COMPARISON OF DIRECT MARKETING AND GENERAL ADVERTISING

Direct Marketing vs.	General Advertising
• Selling to individuals. Customers are indentifiable by name, address, and purchase behavior.	• Mass selling. Buyers identified as broad groups sharing common demographic and psychographic characteristics.
• Products have added value or service. Distribution is important product benefit.	• Product benefits do not always include convenient distribution channels.
• The medium is the marketplace.	• Retail outlet is marketplace.
• Marketer controls product until delivery.	• Marketer may lose control as product enters distribution channel.
• Advertising used to motivate an immediate order or inquiry.	• Advertising used for cumulative effect over time to build image, awareness, loyalty, benefit recall. Purchase action deferred.
• Repetition used within ad.	• Repetition used over time.
• Consumers feel high perceived risk—product bought unseen. Recourse is distant.	• Consumers feel less risk—have direct contact with the product and direct recourse.

Source: *Bob Stone, Successful Direct Marketing Methods, 3rd ed. (Chicago: Crain Books, 1985), p. 2.*

results can be quantified. Ideas can be tested with little financial risk. "If a test mailing to a valid sample produces a 5 percent response, there is a reasonable probability that the rest of the list or similar lists will, within a predictable margin of error, produce the same results. It is therefore possible, by spending relatively small amounts, to accurately determine the best copy, offer, or lists for a given proposition, or even to test one product against another."[7] In 1978, direct marketing accounted for $60 billion in annual sales. By 1985, that total had soared to $200 billion.

Types of Direct Marketing

Direct mail and catalog marketing are becoming increasingly popular. Are you a surfer, in-line skater, small-business owner, architect, artist, computer person, musician, and on and on? Almost without exception, no matter what you do (as long as it's legal), no matter what you are interested in, a direct-mail company knows about you. Mailing lists, the buying and selling of them, are the lingua franca of the industry.

Direct mail is attractive to marketers because of the high degree of selectivity it offers. Cost per customer is higher than in mass-media marketing, but you trade higher costs for better prospects.

Catalog marketing should be distinguished from direct-mail marketing on the grounds that the established companies sell entire lines of products, as opposed to the single product direct-mail marketers often sell. In essence, however, they have the same goals—to get their offerings into the hands of the people most likely to buy them and to make purchasing easy. (The decline of retail selling skills brought about by retailers' attempts to chop overhead has done much to propel the growth of direct marketing generally.)

The average household receives over 50 catalogs a year, totaling over 15 billion copies of about 8,500 different catalogs. Business-to-business catalog marketers mail over 1 billion catalogs each year, realizing $50 million in sales.

Telemarketing, at this writing, is the most widely used form of direct communication. The average household receives 19 sales calls per year, and makes 16 calls to place orders. In 1990, AT&T logged upward of seven billion 800-number calls.

Business-to-business marketing takes place almost entirely over the phone, to the tune of about $15 billion in annual sales of industrial products. Telemarketing is a boon to businesses large and small, because it reduces travel and other costs needed to support personal selling campaigns.

Telemarketing sometimes earns a bad reputation over "nuisance calls," the telephonic equivalent of junk mail. The whole point of direct marketing is to aim your message at those most likely to respond. If you annoy people with unwanted calls, you've missed your target. When industries don't self-regulate, legislators will. Most marketers don't want to alienate potential customers or others who don't want to be targeted, and these marketers support such developments as national "Don't Call Me" lists and legislation banning sales calls during, for instance, the dinner hour.

Television marketing, like sitcoms and TV dramas, can be divided into the short and the long form. Called *direct-response* advertising, the short form describes a product or service in a commercial-length spot, supplying—as always with direct marketing—a means of easy, immediate customer response, usually a toll-free phone number. Though today all manner of products are sold this way, two of its pioneers, the Popeil's Pocket Fisherman and Ginsu knives (which sold $40 million worth of cutlery) have become part of American popular culture.

Infomercials, running a half hour or more, represent a relatively new wrinkle in television marketing. This form was pioneered by some fast-talking, get-rich-quick salespeople whose success has caused marketers at mainstream companies such as GTE, MCA, Johnson & Johnson, and Revlon to take notice. Infomercials accounted for a billion dollars in sales in 1994.

Home shopping channels, a new twist in TV marketing, devotes entire channels (most visibly the Quality Value Channel and the Home Shopping Network) and 24 hours a day to nonstop selling at closeout prices. The format is breezy and upbeat, and the number of channels is climbing as such firms as Value Club, Spiegel, Sears, Kmart, and JCPenney get in on the act. Marketers have big hopes for this outlet, and if predictions hold true, interactive TV will become a leader in direct marketing. In 1993, about $2 billion worth of merchandise was sold this way.[8]

On-line shopping uses interactive on-line computers to connect sellers and buyers. This form almost completely replaces the retail function—if not now, soon—by offering electronic catalogs of myriad products and services. You can do everything on-line, from buying a television set to booking a trip with Club Med, and you can comparison shop and pay for your purchases by credit card. On-line shopping has suffered some growing pains, and some systems have dropped by the wayside through lack of interest, but as more and more people go on-line, marketers predict big things for the future. Presently, CompuServe, Prodigy, and America Online are the major players, and with these and other providers, consumers can do their banking, handle investment portfolios, and schedule travel arrangements, including airlines, hotels, and car rentals; they can even call up back issues of *Consumer Reports* to comparison shop.

DATABASES

Fundamental to direct marketing, databases are collections of information about individual customers from a demographic, geographic, behavioral, or almost any other perspective, all with the intention of more accurately targeting consumers.

The "20-80 rule" of mass marketing holds that 20 percent of the market accounts for 80 percent of sales. Thus, if your database can be winnowed to the one in five individuals who account for that 80 percent, you can garner four times the response of the usual 5 percent generally expected from group mailings. There are those who quarrel with these numbers, but if they are even close to

A Brief Guide to Infomercial Literature

The ThighMaster belongs right beside the Pocket Fisherman and the Ginsu knife in terms of multitudinous audience awareness, awareness being one of the major objectives of the genre. Peter Bieler, author of *This Business Has Legs,* subtitled "How I Used Infomercial Marketing to Create the $100,000,000 ThighMaster Craze,"[9] is one of the form's historic boosters. "The infomercial industry," says Bieler in his introduction, "offers excellent opportunities for start-ups. The initial investment is relatively low. The industry has dependable vendors to handle every aspect of the campaign and help newcomers steer clear of big mistakes. It's a cash business. You get your money before you ship your product. And best of all, when you have a success, the cash flow is quick and massive. This book shows you how to get there."

And it does. *This Business Has Legs* is a real lesson in marketing strategy and also an energetic romp through Hollywood (Suzanne Somers starred in the ThighMaster show) and life at the entrepreneurial edge.

Frank Cannella published *Infomercial Insights* himself. It's full of clear-eyed information and frontline experience compiled from writings by the industry's major players.

Tim Hawthorne's *The Complete Guide to Infomercial Marketing* (NTC Business Books) is just that. If you have a product to sell, you won't need anything more than the gleam in your eye to make your own infomercial.

And Ron Popeil of Pocket Fisherman fame has written his own book on infomercials, mostly rah-rah salesmanship, called *Salesman of the Century* (Dell).

actual, then it is clear that direct marketing is much more cost-effective than mass marketing. Databases are not cheap to build or maintain, but they can pay big returns.

Consider the usefulness of a database to the large home-appliance manufacturer. In addition to the usual demographic and psychographic information on each customer, the company would keep records of the customer's purchasing history. The company would also know how long you've owned your stereo receiver and when you might replace it. The company might at that point send you announcements of sales, gift certificates, and other promotional material at precisely the time when you're considering buying the product.

*F*ast *orward to the Real World*

Plus c'est le Même Chose

Gene Koprowski

The Nielsen Families, those demographically correct Middle Americans whose tastes have determined the fate of TV shows and marketing campaigns since 1950, have some New Media neighbors.

They're called the Videoway Families. For the last few years, these new kids on the block have helped rate and shape the world's first fully operational, commercial interactive TV system, Videoway, offered by LeGroup Videotron. Little known outside its hometown of Montreal, Canada, LeGroup Videotron's Videoway system has about 300,000 subscribers in Quebec, Alberta, and London. Videoway subscribers receive a range of 110 interactive offerings, from video games to game shows, to data services such as weather forecasts and lottery results, to interactive advertising.

Researchers at the University of Montreal and LeGroup Videotron have been collaborating for the last six years, as the system went from conception to creation, determining the likes and dislikes of the interactive TV consumers.

Since 1989, the University of Montreal has surveyed more than 2,400 Videoway families and 9,000 French-language individuals. Company officials, cable industry observers, and advertising industry executives agree that the results of these studies provide the first real assessment of the possibilities of interactive TV. Judging from the results, Time Warner in Orlando, Florida, and Viacom and AT&T in Castro Valley, California—which plan to offer movies on demand and related interactive services starting later this year—may be in for a rude awakening when they learn exactly what viewers want.

"We in the U.S. media industry have been sleeping south of their market," says David Maran, senior vice president of media research at J. Walter Thompson, New York. "While some very exciting exercises are in the preparatory stages here in the U.S., what LeGroup Videotron is doing right now is serving the needs of the customer."

Andre Caron, director of the New Technology Research Laboratory at the University of Montreal, has pioneered the research that has chronicled interactive TV viewing habits of the Videoway Families. LeGroup

(Continued)

(Continued)

Videotron approached the university as it broached the idea of launching an interactive TV service in the late 1980s. Executives such as CEO Andre Chagnon wanted to know what obstacles there were to interactive-TV success. "We had been involved in studying the adoption of PC's in Canada, and there were two aspects that we found in common with interactive TV," said Caron. First, "there was very little interest on the part of manufacturers in what people wanted or were interested in." Second, what people wanted were products driven by their wants and needs, as opposed to the engineering department's abilities and imagination.

To succeed, LeGroup Videotron would have to design a system that followed those rules. Research began in the fall of 1989, when the university randomly selected more than 400 families to receive free Videoway services. The surveyors avoided including "innovators," those individuals prone to trying the latest gadgets and then tossing them aside. This was done to avoid skewing the results. They selected families that already had cable TV, as well as those who did not.

University personnel performed in-depth family interviews, laboratory trials, telephone surveys, group interviews, and written questionnaires. Participation rates in the studies were from 70 to 95 percent of families receiving the subscription during the studies.

By the fall of 1991, when Videoway reached 100,000 subscribers, another 800 households were randomly selected for study. A year later, when subscriptions had reached 150,000, more than 1,270 new Videoway Families were studied. Last fall, another 1,000 families were surveyed. Individual data are kept confidential, though participants are allowed to use the research for academic articles.

The combined results of the surveys may startle some in the U.S. who are expecting interactive TV to render the broadcast media obsolete.

"We estimate that people spend 20 to 30 percent of their TV watching time using Videoway," says Caron. "That's a pretty large chunk of time. But TV remains the entertainment medium."

Janet Callaghan, vice president and national media director at J. Walter Thompson, Toronto, agrees: "Life isn't going to change that much. Why count out the broadcasters already?"

The studies show that, overall, Videoway users spend about 13 hours per week on the system. About 5.5 hours of that time are spent playing 40 different video games—everything from chess, checkers, and puzzles, to video versions of card games and mazes. Video games were used by every member of the household, says Caron, including many adults aged 34 to 59.

(Continued)

(Continued)

Videoway Families spent 7.5 hours a week using data services—scanning an electronic version of *Le Monde* newspaper, for instance, or reading their horoscopes or biorhythms, examining the latest Lottery scores, or gaining more educational information on nutrition or classical music. Viewers can even take a test for their driver's license over Videoway.

"What they are doing is everyday things they would already be doing, but switching them over to another media," Caron observes.

Basic cable rates are $25 per month for the Videoway system; interactive TV costs an additional $7.95 per month. Subscribers rejected the idea of usage fees. "They are not willing to pay for something every time they use the system," says Caron. "So the way it is structured is very user-friendly. They can play with it 100 times a week if they want to. There's an illusion among some in the media that people will pay for things, even though they don't want them."

The service had 26 percent market penetration after four years and helped retain subscribers for basic TV service and pay TV, Caron says. It attracted new subscribers to cable as well and served as a marketing tool for outside service providers.

During this year's Winter Olympics, while much of the world was focused on the Nancy Kerrigan and Tonya Harding controversy, Ford Canada ran interactive advertising over the Videoway System. Using their remote controls, Videoway subscribers were able to choose one of four Ford TV commercials produced by Young and Rubicam, Montreal, according to Yves Plouffe, vice president of interactive TV for Videoway. "If you choose your commercial, it becomes less of a pain to watch it. It's your commercial," Plouffe explains. "The commercials were tied to a contest, which was offered over the videotex system. Viewers were asked if they remembered how many airbags there were in the new car. They had to watch closely and understand everything in the commercial to win."

Other companies are conducting similar experiments. Coca-Cola and McCann-Erickson used the system three years ago to ask Videoway users trivia questions, says Plouffe. Callaghan notes that J. Walter Thompson, Toronto, will use the Videoway video games as the staging area for a promotion it plans for one of its cola clients, perhaps as early as next fall.

Revenues in 1993 from Videoway topped $50.5 million (Canadian), according to the company's annual report. That's up from $44.2 million in 1992. Overall, LeGroup Videotron is a $583 million enterprise, with holdings in broadcasting, cable, and related services. "Videoway is about

(Continued)

(Continued)

to reach the critical mass needed to finance all annual research and development costs out of its own income before depreciation and amortization, at which time development will be financed by the cash flow from its operations and will no longer require additional investment," the annual report says.

LeGroup Videotron has taken these results and incorporated them along the way, Plouffe says. It is currently moving on to the second stage of its interactive-TV system. Along with partners such as Hearst Corp., New York, Canada Post Corp., Hydro-Quebec, and the National Bank of Canada, LeGroup Videotron has announced a $750 million program called UBI, for Universal Bidirectional Interactive. This two-way interactive goes beyond what Videoway is currently offering. When it is running next year, it will offer consumers interactive banking, online utility payments, and that holy grail of interactive advocates, electronic yellow pages.

The transactional and interactive multimedia service—designed to deploy 1.4 million TV-set-top boxes in the province of Quebec—is expected to provide even more insight into what the future holds for the new media. It will build on both the infrastructure, customer base, and experience of LeGroup Videotron.

"The approach being taken is to build the equipment and put it into the home and lease cyberspace much the same way a shopping mall leases space," says Al Sikes, president of Hearst's new media and technology division (and President Bush's chairman of the Federal Communications Commission). "At Hearst, we want to provide an electronic gateway into the teleshopping mall, and offer couponing and reservations. We'll be able to do that because they'll have the delivery system in place."

Adds Thompson's Callaghan: "We have a lot of clients interested in UBI." The reason for that interest is the fact that more market research will be conducted into the Videoway Family's acceptance of the new system—in one market.

Some in the advertising community view the research on Videoway Families as too "early stage," and reckon that the UBI data will provide a more accurate picture of what the new media age will look like for marketers. "The problem with Videoway is there's no meter hooked up to the TV to monitor people's TV-watching behavior. They're just asking them to recall. You couldn't go to someone 20 years ago and ask them how much they would like to watch MTV or CNN," observes J. Walter Thompson's David Maran. "Unfortunately, it is all we have. We shouldn't bet the house on these preliminary results."

(Continued)

(Continued)

But Caron of the University of Montreal defends his research by saying that the America media's vision of an all-encompassing information superhighway is "a false image." With the Internet or an online service, Caron points out, the customer provides the content. With television, the content is provided by someone else. He describes this as the difference between a "telematic culture" and a "television culture."

"Most people will still use TV as an entertainment medium," he argues. "They may become more active couch potatoes . . . but they do not always want to talk back to the TV. They want others to talk to them."

LeGroup Videotron is expanding into the U.S., in markets such as Dayton, Ohio and Tampa, Florida. U.S. advertisers will soon be able to see for themselves just what all the fuss is about up north. What might that mean for U.S. cable operators?

"The important thing is that they've sold this in the U.K., as well as in Montreal," says Mike Schwartz, vice president of Cable Labs, the Lewisville, Colorado R&D consortium for 75 cable companies. "So, it is obviously an exportable item."

Source: Marketing Tools (September/October 1994).

Fast Forward to the Real World

Ads That Win vs. Ads That Work

Philip W. Sawyer

It's that time of year again, when various advertising and publishing organizations announce the "best" ads of the past year. The winners are usually selected by panels of notable people, who painstakingly review scores if not hundreds of different entrants and then rate the ads according to each judge's criteria for excellence.

The process is interesting and exciting, and it's probably good for the industry. But we should all recognize that in many cases, the winning ads are not necessarily the most effective ads. Confusing the two standards is an expensive—and, unfortunately, all-too-common—mistake.

For my purposes here, effectiveness refers to an ad's ability to reach the audience for which it is intended. Thus, an ad that makes a great impression on a panel of experts may have very little effect on the readers of the magazine in which it appears. Likewise, an ad that falls flat with the panel may prove to be a very powerful attention-getter for its target audience. (And which of these two constituencies does the advertiser most care about?)

In short, the panels of experts undoubtedly pick winners fairly often, but they are also likely to pick losers, which is reminiscent of John Wanamaker's old saw: "Half the money I spend on advertising is wasted, and the trouble is, I don't know which half."

Panels of experts will not help advertisers figure out which half of their advertising budget is wasted. Research will. And for more than 70 years research has yielded some principles of advertising that have consistently asserted themselves, starting in 1923 with Daniel Starch, carried on by David Ogilvy, and continuing to the present day, when we have the advantage of splendid technology, magnificent databases, and hundreds of thousands of ads available for analysis.

What follows are ten guidelines that we believe advertisers should keep in mind whenever they sit down to create an ad. As we offer these, we are well aware that any number of ads ignore these guidelines yet are very successful. That's fine. Mark Twain broke almost every rule of

(Continued)

(Continued)

grammar when he wrote *The Adventures of Huckleberry Finn*. But he had to know the rules before he could break them effectively.

1 Keep It Simple, Stupid.

The KISS principle has no better application than in advertising, yet it is probably the most abused principle of all. Here is the best argument for simplicity: a great many magazine readers do not read magazines to look at the ads. Therefore, advertising needs to catch the eye quickly, deliver its message quickly, and allow the reader to leave as quickly as possible. Ads that clutter the page with multiple illustrations and varied sizes and styles of type offer no central focus for the eye, no resting place. Because of these visual disincentives for staying with "busy" ads, readers naturally move on, having spent little or no time with them.

2 You're Not Selling the Product; You're Selling the *Benefits* of the Product.

An old *New Yorker* cartoon depicts a pompous-looking young man at a party, talking to a young woman. "Well, that's enough about me," he says. "Now, what do *you* think about me?" Most advertisements suffer from the same kind of egotism. They assume that the reader is as interested in the product as the advertiser. In reality, most readers do not enter the advertiser's realm readily. They do so only when convinced that the product will do something for them. If an advertiser does not answer the reader's implicit question—"What's in it for me?"—he is unlikely to attract any real interest.

Most ads are simply descriptive; they explain what the product or service *is*. The worst ads give you a long history about the company, its values, commitments, and size—as if anyone really cares. But the best ads directly address the problems that the product or service solves and suggest how that solution makes life better for the potential consumer.

3 When Appropriate, Spice It Up with Sex.

Psychologist Dr. Joyce Brothers once predicted that "the days of sexy advertising are numbered. The reason is that within five years, the number of marriageable women will be greater than the number of marriageable men. This will be the beginning of the 'she' generation, which will be a generation unimpressed with sex as a selling point."

(Continued)

(Continued)

Dr. Brothers makes the common (and, it could be argued, sexist) mistake of assuming that men are interested in sex and women are not. In truth, the publications that carry the sexiest advertising today are women's publications. And that kind of advertising attracts considerable notice and readership and will continue to do so until human beings reproduce exclusively by parthenogenesis.

At the same time, it should be emphasized that sexy ads tend to be simple ads—perfectly reasonable since clutter and salaciousness are not really compatible. The best ads of this type may feature nudity, but are not explicitly erotic.

To the politically correct, we say: Sex sells. Get used to it.

4 Use Celebrities.

Opinion surveys indicate that Americans do not believe an ad simply because it features a well-known person hawking the product. However, according to our data, ads with celebrities earn "Noted" scores that are 13 percent higher than average. They are particularly effective with women readers, scoring 15 percent higher than average, compared with 10 percent higher for men. Ads with testimonials from celebrities score 11 percent above the average, whereas testimonials from noncelebrities actually earn below-average scores. Celebrities may not be believable, but they are very effective at attracting reader attention, the first job of any advertisement.

5 Exploit the Potential of Color.

Print advertising has a potent rival to contend with: television. The moving image is a profoundly effective means of communication, and anyone who has ever tried to amuse a baby knows that the eye has an inherent attraction to motion. At the same time, the eye is also attracted to bold, bright, and beautiful color. Our data indicate that one-page color ads earn "Noted" scores that are 45 percent higher on average than comparable black and white ads; two-page color ads earn scores that are 53 percent higher than similar black and white ads. And generally, the more colorful the better (as long as the advertiser keeps in mind the other nine principles in this article).

Television has a lock on the moving image, but print's ability to generate astonishing, eye-catching colors is substantial, and publications should do everything possible to stay current with new advances in color technology.

(Continued)

(Continued)

6 Go with the Flow.

Every ad has flow to it, and the flow is determined by the positioning of the various creative elements. Ads with good flow send the reader's eye around the page to take in all the important elements: the illustration, headline, body copy, and brand name. Ads with bad flow may attract a fair amount of attention at first, but send the reader off the page. For example, a number of advertisers make the mistake of placing a flashy illustration toward the bottom of the page and the copy and headline at the top. In such cases, the most powerful element of an ad can turn out to be the most detrimental, because that alluring illustration steals attention away from the copy.

For another example, consider the automobile industry and the way some advertisers position the automobile on the page. The eye, our data indicate, tends to follow the car from back to front. Thus, if the car is facing right to left on the page and stands above body copy, the eye, moving back to front, ends up over the beginning of the copy, exactly the right place if you want to have your copy read. But consider how many advertisers position their cars facing left to right, thus "leading" the reader to the right side of the page, the point at which the reader is most likely to continue on to the next page without studying the rest of the ad.

7 Avoid Ambiguity.

Although it appears that Europeans accept, if not welcome, ambiguous themes and symbols, we have found that Americans have little tolerance for advertising that does not offer a clear and distinct message. Several years ago, Benson & Hedges attracted a great deal of attention with an ad featuring a man clad only in pajama bottoms and a bewildered expression, and standing in a dining room in the middle of what appears to be a brunch party. The trade press evidently was far more attracted to the ad than were readers, who, our data indicated, (a) were as non-plussed by the ad as its star was by his predicament, and (b) reacted with considerable hostility to the advertiser who dared to confuse them.

Americans like it straight. They choose not to spend a great deal of time thinking about the messages in their advertising. If the point of the ad is not clear, the typical American reader will move on to the next page.

8 Heighten the Contrast.

We live in a visual culture, and one thing that delights the eye is contrast. So advertisers would do well to employ what might be called

(Continued)

(Continued)

"visual irony" in their advertising. One suggestion: contrast the *content* of the ads.

American Express produced one of the best ads of 1988 by featuring the diminutive Willie Shoemaker standing back to back with the altitudinous Wilt Chamberlain. The contrast was humorous and eye-catching. Another way to fulfill this principle is to contrast the elements constituting the *form* of the ad—color, for example. Our data indicate that using black as a background makes elements in the foreground pop off the page. Stolichnaya earned average scores with a horizontal shot of the product against a white background. When the same layout was produced with a change only in the background, from white to black, the scores increased by 50 percent, on average.

9 Use Children and Animals.

Almost any advertising can succeed with an appeal to the emotions, and children and animals appeal to all but the most hard-hearted. It's logical, of course, to use a close-up of a child when selling toys. (Yet flip through an issue of a magazine for parents and notice how many products for children's clothing, for example, do *not* use children—a missed opportunity if there ever was one.) And pets, of course, are naturals for pet food.

The trick is to find an excuse to use a child or furry little beast when your product is not even remotely connected to those models. Hewlett-Packard pulled this off beautifully by featuring a Dalmatian and the headline, "Now the HP LaserJet IIP is even more irresistible." The ad won the highest scores in the Computer & Data Equipment product category for 1990. Hitachi has used the double lure of celebrity Jamie Lee Curtis and various animals—cats and parrots primarily—to hawk the company's televisions in a campaign that has consistently garnered the highest "Noted" scores for the category.

10 When an Ad Has a Good Deal of Copy, Make It as Inviting as Possible.

A source of never-ending astonishment to us are the advertisers who insist on shrinking and squeezing copy into a tight corner of an ad in order to maximize "white space"—a triumph of style over common sense. Others present copy over a mottled background, making it almost impossible to read easily. Two other common problems are reverse print over a light background, offering too little contrast, and centered copy

(Continued)

(Continued)

(i.e., unjustified right and left margins), which forces the reader to work too hard to find the beginning of each line.

An advertiser who includes a fair amount of copy obviously hopes that it will be read. Relatively few readers choose to spend the time to read most of the copy of any advertisement—if you get 20 percent of magazine readers to delve into your copy, you are doing very well. So the challenge is to make the whole process as easy for the reader as possible. Good content alone will not attract readers. The best-written, wittiest, and most powerful copy will be overlooked unless it is well-spaced and sufficiently large and clear to invite the reader in.

Although the vast majority of awards programs employ a less-than-ideal methodology for testing advertising effectiveness, some still yield the "right" answers. For example, several years ago, we cross-checked the Magazine Publishers of America's Kelly Award nominees with our own data to determine the extent to which the MPA's judges chose ads that resonated with the magazine-reading public. Our findings indicated that the Kelly nominees, without exception, earned higher-than-average scores for at least one readership measurement. Our conclusion is that the MPA's judges had their fingers on the magazine-reading public's pulse.

Nevertheless, we believe that the MPA is the exception. Those who really want to ascertain which advertisements and which advertising approaches are the most effective are better served by embarking on a continuous plan of research that tracks performance through time, allows for comparisons with competitors' ads, and encourages creative experimentation and feedback.

Lastly, the principles offered on this page are not intended to be regarded with the same reverence as the Ten Commandments. Rather, they are more useful if seen as akin to the instruments on the dashboard of a car. They are meant to impart important information that should help advertisers reach their destinations as smoothly, safely, and efficiently as possible. In short, the purpose of advertising research is to help advertisers become more informed, and, therefore, better drivers.

Source: Marketing Tools (March/April 1995).

*F*ast *F*orward to the Real World

Brave New World

Katy M. Bachman

The very first book to roll off Gutenberg's printing press in 1454 is one of the earliest books to embrace the new media. Yes, the Bible, the best-selling book of all time, will be published on CD-ROM.

If the word of God is moving from stone tablets to digital disks, you might conclude there's a mad rush to the exciting, glamorous world of online services (CompuServe, Prodigy, America Online, et al.), CD-ROM, and interactive TV. And, in fact, *Fortune* magazine reports there are 700 businesses—most of them high-tech, business-to-business companies—on the World Wide Web, the trendy commercial neighborhood on the sprawling Internet.

In the consumer arena, marketers from Detroit's Big Three to Lillian Vernon and McDonald's have invested time in establishing a beachhead on the new media. There are about 80 merchants in CompuServe's Electronic Mall. Prodigy says it has more than 100 advertisers or marketers. Shopping 2000, the Internet shopping mall from Contentware, is touting JC Penney, Spiegel, and a dozen other high-profile direct marketers. In the CD-ROM world, there are 39 catalogers on Magellan's The Merchant and 28 on Redgate's 2Market. The much ballyhooed and often-delayed interactive TV trials boast much the same roster of blue-chip marketers willing to take the plunge in these promising, yet largely uncharted, waters.

What do catalogers, financial-service providers, florists, and auto companies know about the new media that you don't? Ask them why they're getting into the media and more often than not, the response will be that it is well worth testing, that the current efforts are "experiments," with an eye to the future. What is the future they are seeing? And should your company be a part of the fabled information super-highway?

Rabbit Ears and Rotten Reception

In many ways, what's happening today with the new media is greatly reminiscent of the earliest days of television. The technology is crude

(Continued)

(Continued)

and the pictures are fuzzy. Only a relative handful of consumers are willing to buy the needed equipment—the computers, the modems, the CD-ROM drives, and the interactive TV converters. And only a handful of marketers are willing to put their ads into the 1990s equivalent of a plywood box with a flickering 9-inch screen.

However, like the TV pioneers of the 1950s, intrepid new media marketers are betting that online services, CD-ROMS, and interactive TV will be as dominant a force in marketing as television. What gives the new media its promise is not the "gee whiz" technology, but the new roles played by both the consumer and the marketer.

The old media are one-way streets: program producers speak, and the audience listens (or not, as the case may be). The new media take a hefty portion of control away from the programmer and hand it to the receiver. Consumers will be in a position to interact with as little or as much material as they like, asking for information or advertising only when they want or need it, making choices about the content as opposed to passively accepting (or ignoring) what's offered them.

The consumer isn't the only one with something to gain from this new arrangement. Marketers will now have the ability to establish dialogs with individual customers, getting instant feedback on their efforts, unfiltered by the noise of the marketplace. "The potential of the new media is in the interactivity," says Jack Smith, senior vice president, new media, ASI Market Research. "The major benefit they offer is people connecting with other people."

Every marketer who has tried the new media has found them to be a great way to establish a relationship with customers. Modem Media, an interactive ad agency in Norwalk, Connecticut, created Zima.com, a "broadcast tributary" named after Zima, the clear malt beverage from Coors. Net surfers visit Zima.com to meet other Coors aficionados and take away games and digital geegaws.

Establishing relationships sounds wonderful, but it requires a significant commitment on the part of the market. Toyota learned that lesson the hard way when it established Toyota Interactive on Prodigy, the largest of the consumer online services. "It represented a breakthrough in the use of new media by marketers," says Laurie Peterson, editor of *The Cowles Report on Database Marketing*. "It wasn't about showing off content, but about creating a place for its customers to go." Before long, Toyota's Prodigy site was like a hot nightclub with long lines out front. Sadly, Toyota didn't invest enough resources to handle all that traffic,

(Continued)

(Continued)

and recently pulled the plug on its bulletin board. You have to be careful what you wish for.

Who Are the New Media Marketers?

Is your company ready for the new media? "Certain types of advertisers are more appropriate," says Craig Gugel, senior vice president and executive director of Interactive Media and Research at Bates USA. Among those who could benefit immediately: "high-ticket or information-driven products such as leisure travel, airlines—the types of advertisers where people will want to find out more information before they make a decision."

This is why so many of the earliest pioneers on the new media are information-rich categories. Fidelity Investments is one of the biggest users of online services, CD-ROMs and interactive disks, and has forums on Prodigy and CompuServe. Other insurance companies, mutual funds, and financial services companies have also created interactive communications that allow a consumer to input specific information about income, financial goals, and levels of risk tolerated, enabling the company to help the buyer select and create the specific product that best meets his or her needs.

"You can nest a lot of information about a product, based on individual needs," says J. G. Sandom, president, Einstein and Sandom, the interactive marketing unit of DMB&B. "You don't have to go through a linear process."

Just about every automobile advertiser has embraced the new media for its ability to deliver a wealth of information to the consumer. Many of them began with interactive computer disks several years ago, such as Ford with its "Simulator" series. Cadillac found that a large percentage of its car owners also possess computers, CD-ROMs, and online service memberships; hence, the company operates its own areas on CompuServe and Prodigy, as well as distributing an interactive disk called "Impressions."

"In those disks, we allow the user to access information about our current products, features, and benefits, and make direct comparisons with competitive vehicles," says Peter R. Levin, director of advertising for Cadillac Motor Car. "They can select the vehicles they want, call up the information they want, and get a printout. The user is in control and making the decisions."

For any business that sells directly to the consumer, there's little question about who should play: "Anyone whose product appeals to

(Continued)

(Continued)

enthusiasts is not limited by geography," says Barry Edison, media planner, DMB&B, Bloomfield, Michigan.

The Electronic Gift Shoppe

There are even a few marketers who have created a deliberate strategy of being on the new media. Bill Tobin, founder of PC Flowers, has said that he became interested in interactive and then chose the business best suited to the new media.

A similar gift company, 1-800-FLOWERS, has enthusiastically embraced just about every interactive service. At the end of 1994, the direct-to-consumer florist offered its floral gifts on four major online services and on Bloomberg Financial Network, a business-to-business network; all the major CD-ROM shopping ventures; and even a couple of the nascent interactive TV services. Plans for 1995 include AT&T PersonaLink, and Interaxx television. By mid-1995, 1-800-FLOWERS will be available through a dozen interactive services.

"Our vision is to make our services available anywhere and everywhere our customers want to reach us," says Elaine Rubin, manager of interactive services, 1-800-FLOWERS. "With the increasing acceptance of PCs and their multimedia capabilities, and in the longer term, the availability of interactive TV in the home, our customers will be shopping this way."

One company most pundits never expected to see so soon in the new media arena is Lillian Vernon. The company, which was literally founded on a kitchen table, has put its relatively prosaic consumer catalog on Magellan's "The Merchant," one of the major CD-ROM shopping ventures featuring major consumer catalogers. "The way the consumer shops is constantly evolving," explains David Hochberg, vice president for public affairs. "CD-ROM may not be as strong a shopping experience today as it will be in the future. It's a long-term commitment. CD-ROMs are the same thing as microwaves and telephone answering machines. It was a gradual process for people to accept them."

More than just a hedge for tomorrow, Lillian Vernon expects its CD-ROM venture to reach a consumer segment they have not been known for targeting: men, the biggest users of computers and CD-ROMs. "We saw this as an opportunity to broaden our customer base," says Hochberg. While he won't quantify results from the catalog's March mailing, Hochberg did characterize them as "decent" and as having "met our limited expectations." Results were satisfactory enough to encourage Lillian Vernon to venture onto one of the online services in 1995.

(Continued)

(Continued)

If information-rich selling or direct-to-consumer marketing is best suited to the new media, then the question becomes: are packaged goods ill-suited to interactivity? After all, how much do consumers really want to know about their frozen veggies or bathroom cleaner? "There's not as much need for information with grocery-store products," says Craig Gugel, of Bates USA.

Yet DMB&B's J. G. Sandom believes that even grocery categories can use the new media to enhance brand image. could create nutritional centers or forums, sponsored by brands," he says. "Packaged-goods companies are thinking about these ideas now. Take toothpaste, for example. There is no reason why you can't put together an interactive disk teaching dental hygiene. There are ways of using interactive new media, even with the most mundane of products."

Unmasking the New Media Market

While no one really knows exactly when the new media will reach critical mass, there is a growing population segment that is most likely to accept the new media in their lives. Bates USA has dubbed this group of 44 million consumers as "techthusiasts" and has commissioned a study in order to quantify and qualify this growing population segment.

Compared with the typical American consumer, techthusiasts are more comfortable getting their information and entertainment from magazines and newspapers than they are from television—television viewing among techthusiasts is about 20 percent lower than that reported for total adults in the U.S. On the other hand, techthusiasts are more receptive (42 percent) to interactive advertising and advertising on demand than the population at large (32 percent).

"You almost have to look at PCs, online services and the Internet as a new medium. People are no longer spending all their time in front of the television," says Gugel. "You're going to see a change in the marketing mix. What we consider ancillary media today will come to the foreground as we approach the next decade. Anything over telephone wire to computer will have to be considered."

Today's new media marketers have their eye on this potential change in America's media usage. "As marketers, we have to be where the consumer wants to be," says Gerry O'Connell, a founding partner of Modem Media. "As more consumers converted to telephones, as more consumers watched TV, that was the place to go. There's no difference between that and going online. There are more people using the Internet than there were three years ago."

(Continued)

(Continued)

As "the place to go," today's available new media have a long way to go before they close in on radio or television's 98 percent penetration. "The Internet needs considerable development before seriously threatening the television networks, newspapers, yellow pages, radio and billboard companies that today comprise the best ways to reach large numbers of consumers," says Thomas E. Miller, vice president for Find/SVP's Emerging Technologies Research Group. Find/SVP's 1994 American Information User Survey of 2,000 U.S. households estimates there are only 3.1 million households on the Internet and on the online services, a far smaller number than the 20 to 30 million bandied about in the press.

Still, research conducted by CompuServe and Find/SVP indicates that the profile of those on the Internet or using online services is a very desirable advertiser target: male, upscale, affluent, and well-educated.

What if your customer profile is less upscale? Can you ignore the new media with impunity? The experts think not. If you accept the eventuality that more consumers will sign on and the inevitability of the changing marketing mix, they say, the time to jump in is now.

"It is important for marketers to learn the new media," says Jack Smith of ASI Market Research. "Those testing will have an advantage as long as they don't spend a fortune."

Look Before You Leap—Then Leap

Such explorations need not be expensive. Take the CD-ROM catalogs, for example. The 20 or so catalogers on one disk can share distribution costs and still get a sense of whether or not the new media will be profitable in the future. Sandom says marketers can do an interactive disk for $50,000 and a CD-ROM for $100,000. "The investment is not that great," he observes. "You can learn and experiment and pass the benefits along to your corporate culture."

"No one is spending a ton of money," O'Connell concurs. "So why not test and get your research first hand?"

There is a caveat: most practitioners agree that you can't take what you might know about advertising and cataloging and simply push it into the new media. "New media have a different thinking paradigm and skill sets," says Sandom.

Take the McDonald's experiment on the NBC area of America Online. The fast-food marketer digitized an existing 30-second spot, overlooking the fact that it takes a computer hundreds of times longer

(Continued)

(Continued)

to "read" the information than it does to transmit a signal through the air or cable. "I would have been furious if I had tied up my computer for 45 minutes, only to run a commercial on my computer that I had already seen on TV," says Barry Edison, media planner, Darcy, Detroit. "They did not provide me with any information of value for me to spend my time with them."

Interactive sales pioneer Bill Tobin, president of PC Flowers, provides a second cautionary note. "Regardless of if you have the best product, the best prices, and the most innovative marketing and promotional programs, you must have a flawless order processing, credit-card processing, customer support, and delivery system," Tobin told attendees at the Fall 1994 Direct Marketing Association conference. "Interactive consumers are far more demanding than those who shop through retail outlets, 800 numbers, and catalogs."

Furthermore, the same new media that pave the way for interaction between marketers and consumers also give the disgruntled consumer the power to vent displeasure to an audience of millions. Says Tobin: "If interactive consumers are unhappy with your service, they have the ability to log onto a bulletin board and inform millions of other members how unhappy they are with your service and what a terrible job you have done."

A Measure of Success

The new media will put a bigger burden on the message provider. "One-to-one relationship building is the marketing goal to be achieved online," says Edison. "Marketers have to position sponsorships within relevant content and provide users with information value. Determine what it's worth to turn interested consumers into experts on your product. Set a value on the relationships you're able to build. Evaluate these alternatives on a cost per inquiry or cost per transaction basis."

Unlike television, radio, and print, there is as yet no set standard, no rigorous definition for marketing success in the new media. Says Sandom: "The accountability is cost per transaction; you are not counting number of eyeballs. It's much more the paradigm of direct mail. The measurements are built in."

Don't count on the built-in measures that come with the new media to fill all your marketing information needs. "I get hit rates (the number of times a given area is accessed) for my areas on the online services," says Edison. "But I don't have numbers on various content sections that I might want to sponsor. Nor do I have any idea about how much time

(Continued)

(Continued)

people are spending online. I think some of this information would prove helpful in getting budgets for interactive experimentation."

Experienced new media marketers agree that it is important to set up a measurement instrument so that you can constantly monitor your progress. Cadillac, for example, checks its progress two ways. For its disks and CD-ROMs, the company counts the responses to the ads that feature its new media offering. Online services provide the car manufacturer with information on the number of times its area was accessed.

Colonizing Cyberspace

None of the markets see the new media as a replacement for the tried and true. For example, "If you're doing image and awareness advertising, then the new media aren't it," says Sandom.

"Image advertising is difficult," says ASI's Jack Smith. "You don't have the penetration you need in the new media, but you will have information about how to move from selling by saying, 'This is what I have, it's terrific', to 'This is my information, do you want it?' "

"Don't expect these new tools to replace previous marketing communication tools," advises Edison. "Before users will interact with you, they will first have to be aware of who you are, and have an interest in what you have to say. This part of the communication funnel will continue to be better served through traditional methods."

"We don't see [new media] as a replacement," says Cadillac's Levin, "but as a complement to our brochures. It's a brochure with more flexibility. It's another way for us to provide access to our customers."

Despite its limitations as a brand advertising vehicle, presence on the new media does carry a certain cachet, sending a powerful message about the brand's image. "Some of this advertising you see on the Internet is interesting just because it's there," observes Gerry O'Connel of Modem Media. "There's a major halo effect, associating their brand with what is new and on the edge."

What's more, you'll be establishing a foothold that can only help you in the future. Sandom's recommendation: "Companies should invest a certain percentage of media dollars now and spend 5 to 10 percent of that budget on new media by the year 2000.

"It's okay if you jump in just because your boss read an article in *Newsweek*," he adds. "We'd rather you have a strategic approach, but it's better to do something than nothing."

Source: *Marketing Tools* (March/April 1995).

Fast **orward to the Real World**

Turbo-Charging Your Lists

Michael Edmondson

You're in charge of putting together your company's next direct-mail campaign. It's crucial that you reach the best prospects at the lowest possible cost. You've studied results from previous mailings, reviewed your list broker's test recommendations, and tracked down a few really great special-interest lists. You're feeling pretty confident that you have found the people most likely to respond to your offer. But still you have a nagging doubt. Could you do more to make sure this promotion gets to the right people?

Yes, you can. In fact, there's quite a bit you can do, before and after selecting lists, to help you execute better-targeted, more profitable mailings. The key is using additional sources of information about households and consumers. Learn where to find these data and how to use them, and you'll obtain optimum results. The most important aspect of campaign planning is list selection. At this stage, knowing more about your customers really pays off. Before even starting list research, review everything you know about the people who buy from you—and the people who don't. Update your customer profile and refine it to add detail about your prospects. For example, if survey data indicate a high level of computer use in your customer base, you should explore lists of computer magazines or computer-related product buyers.

Of course, you should already know the basics—your customers' median age, income, and household type. This information can help you locate areas with the highest concentrations of individuals most likely to purchase from you. Here's how to do it.

The **Census Bureau** has population data for the entire U.S. by age, income, household type, and much more. While it doesn't rent individual names, the bureau's data can help you identify the neighborhood blocks and zip codes with high concentrations of people matching your profile. The census is taken every ten years. Private data companies use estimates to produce yearly updates.

The Census Bureau also produces periodic long-range projections of the population by age, sex, and race. These are published in **Current**

(Continued)

(Continued)

Population Reports, Series P-25 and P-26. A subscription costs $20, available from the Government Printing Office. This information is useful for strategic planning. It tells you where growth will occur by state and which demographic groups will increase in size at the fastest rate.

Another helpful tool available from the federal government is the **Consumer Expenditure Survey (CE),** which is used by the Bureau of Labor Statistics to calculate the Consumer Price Index. This survey provides marketers with a staggering amount of data on the full range of household expenditures by age cohort, income, and household type.

The **Bureau of Labor Statistics (BLS)** can also provide business mailers with occupational information. Every other year, the BLS projects the size and characteristics of the labor force as well as growth projections for various industries and occupations. Summaries of these projections are published in *Monthly Labor Review.* A subscription costs $20 and is available from the Government Printing Office. This information can be used by business mailers to gauge their universe and measure current penetration.

House files are probably the best source of information about your customers. Studying purchase and promotion history on your customer file can help you categorize your prospects and forecast future results.

For some mailers, it may pay to use a service bureau to attach customer-specific demographic or other data to your internal files. This can enhance the value of your list and provide opportunities for effectively parsing your in-house mailing lists.

List enhancement usually makes the most sense for mailers who have large databases, limited information, and adequate computing capabilities. Companies with smaller databases may find that the cost of adding and maintaining outside data is outweighed by the promotion efficiencies it provides.

In general, using demographic data for **customer segmentation** is most valuable for separating marginal from optimal customers. According to a 1990 Direct Marketing Association survey, 64 percent of all companies append demographic data to their files to improve response to customer mailings.

Companies like Infobase and Metromail offer extensive consumer databases that contain detailed demographic and economic information about U.S. individuals and households. These can be matched to your customer files to add detail to your records. Typical data items include income, size of household, ages of members, type of home, length of residence, car ownership, telephone number, and mail responsiveness.

(Continued)

(Continued)

Individuals on your file that don't show up on an outside database can still be profiled by adding neighborhood-level information. The Census Bureau reports data for block groups, census tracts, or zip codes. These data are updated annually by the estimates of private companies like Strategic Mapping, Urban Decision Systems, and Equifax National Decision Systems, which resell them to businesses for use with sophisticated cluster analysis software packages.

Neighborhood data offer an extensive array of information. Marketers can work with more than 350 census variables at this level, including standard demographics like sex, age, race, education, and marital status, as well as more exotic topics such as commuting time, language spoken at home, and age of house.

Business mailers should not feel left out. Companies like Dun and Bradstreet and American Business Information offer list enhancement through appending **business demographics.** Data such as Standard Industry Classification (SIC) code, annual sales volume, and number of employees are readily available. Depending on the composition of your file, you can expect a 60 to 70 percent match rate to these business databases.

The more you know about your customers, the better your chances for success. You can find out a great deal about them by using readily available public and private data. Once you understand what information is available and start using it, you can begin to plan and execute better targeted, more profitable promotions.

Source: Marketing Tools (May 1995).

Fast **F**orward to the Real World

On With the Show!

William Dunn

Just a few miles from Disney World and a few hours' flight from most anywhere in the United States, the sprawling Orange County Convention Center is getting even bigger. Having attracted 5.2 million conventioneers since it opened in 1983, the center is in the process of close to tripling its present size. At 1.1 million square feet when the expansion is completed in 1998, the facility will extend a half-mile in length. It won't go empty; conventions are booked straight through to the year 2022, including the PGA Merchandise Show and the National Automobile Dealers Association.

Meanwhile, in Waco—smack in the heart of Texas—the city-run convention center has been landing such trade shows as the National Funeral Directors and the National Woodcarvers, as well as an increasing number of regional and state shows.

"Now why would anybody want to come to Waco?" asks Jeff Tanner, a marketing professor at Baylor University in Waco and the research director at the Center for Professional Selling. Because, he answers, "There are trade associations of all sizes, and they tend to go to cities that fit their size. And so a lot of cities are cashing in on the business, including small cities like Waco. There are also a lot of state and regional meetings held, where a place like Waco—in the center of Texas—is highly attractive."

Expansions like that in Orange County and the appeal of unlikely destinations like Waco are driven by a number of factors. These include the ongoing restructuring of and heightened competitiveness in corporate America, the emergence of the global marketplace, the testing and fine-tuning of selling and marketing, competition among localities to bring in visitors to stimulate local economies, and the efforts of associations and trade shows to respond to a changing marketplace fraught with opportunity and risk—not to mention the ongoing popularity of the shows themselves.

"Despite what some people say in terms of the cost of shows, it still is the least expensive way of reaching the marketplace in a given period of time and seeing buyers en masse that you normally wouldn't see over a period of six to eight months," contends Steve Sind, president of the Trade Show Bureau. The bureau, based in Denver, conducts research on and promotes the trade show industry.

(Continued)

(Continued)

TradeShow Week Data Book, a leading industry journal published by Reed Publishing, counted 4,316 trade shows in 1994 in the United States and Canada, 90 percent of which took place in the U.S. The *TradeShow* survey covered events over 10,000 square feet in size. While not all the eligible shows responded, the report is believed to have captured about 90 percent of the shows in this category. The Trade Show Bureau estimates there were another 1,200 to 3,000 so-called private shows, which tend to be smaller occasions staged by corporations for their own distributors.

Of the 1994 shows tracked by *TradeShow Week Data Book,* 49 percent were strictly business-to-business affairs, 11 percent were designed for consumers, and 40 percent were combination business-to-business/consumer events. According to the *TradeShow Week Data Book,* the shows hosted a total of 1.3 million exhibitors and attracted 85 million attendees.

The number of shows in this survey has risen each year since 1989, when there were 3,289 shows. Attendance has also grown, from 60 million in 1989 (with decreases in 1991 and 1993). The number of companies exhibiting at shows is up from 1 million five years ago, although the number was stalled at 1.2 million in 1991–93.

The average business-to-business show boasted 381 exhibit companies and 9,977 attendees, although in actual practice 49 percent have 1,000 or fewer attendees, and only 13 percent have attendance over 10,000. Shows designed primarily for consumers average more than 54,000 attendees, but fewer than 300 exhibitors.

Of the 4,316 shows tracked in 1994, the most heavily attended categories, in descending order, are: gifts and merchandise, manufacturing and engineering, computer and electronics, jewelry and apparel, sports and recreation, hospitality and services, food and beverage, medical and related fields, home and office, and broadcast and communications.

Baylor's Tanner attributes the continuing popularity of trade shows to the buyers, who "want more efficient ways of buying.

"Buyers don't have time to listen to as many sales people as they used to, because there are fewer of them. They have been downsized like everybody else," Tanner explains. "The trade show is a very efficient way for them to find out about a lot of different vendors."

Choosing Shows Where the Buyer Goes

The shows themselves are changing. There are two countervailing trends: some shows are getting bigger and broader, while many others

(Continued)

(Continued)

are narrowing their focus, becoming more specialized. Show organizers are staging more efficient, more high-tech events, and are offering exhibitors more services and intelligence on attendees, a response to the exhibitors' demands for all of the above and more in return for their sizable investments. On average, exhibitor companies spend 18 percent of their annual marketing budget at trade shows, a figure topped only by the 23 percent they spend on business magazine advertising, according to a 1991 Cahners Advertising Research Report. The big cost is not the space rental at the exhibit hall but the transportation of equipment and the hotel costs for company representatives.

Trade Show Bureau projections indicate that after two decades of robust growth, the pace will slow in the 1990s; there will be increases in the number of trade shows and attendance, but the growth will moderate as the industry matures. A 1991 survey of 1,200 trade and consumer show managers, conducted by *TradeShow Week,* found that some 573 new shows would be launched between then and the year 2001. Show managers in that same survey cited three major impediments to growth: rising costs for exhibitors (cited by 82 percent of respondents), too many shows (67 percent), and rising costs for attendees (62 percent).

The Innovative Foods Expo will be one of the new shows launched in 1996. Slated for Boston, it's being organized by Diversified Expositions of Portland, Maine. Diversified produces half a dozen shows each year, including the International Boston Seafood Show each March—the biggest annual trade show in that city, with some 20,000 attendees.

Diversified's Nancy Hasselback says trade shows allow people to "interact face to face. You can meet with your current suppliers, meet with new vendors, and develop the relationships that are so important."

They also provide exhibitors with a stage on which to demonstrate their product in a controlled environment. In the case of food shows, notes Hasselback, "Attendees can try the product there. And the exhibitor has the control. You prepare the food; you're not shipping it to a client and saying, 'Try this.' You control the preparation and the serving."

Ocean Garden Products, a major seafood importer based in San Diego, attends the International Boston Seafood Show each March, as well as Seafare in Long Beach, California, each September. "We have a very large, self-contained exhibit that has a complete cooking unit in it that we take to the seafood shows," reports marketing manager Dixie Blake.

(Continued)

(Continued)

"The seafood industry is quite vertically integrated, from the harvester through processors through brokers and distributors to end users: restaurants or retailers," she adds. "There's quite a bit of opportunity at these shows for all of these spectrums of the industry."

Besides the shows in Boston and Long Beach, Ocean Garden exhibits at eight to ten events a year, including shows targeted at chefs, club managers, cruise lines, and food retailers. In addition, its seven regional offices exhibit at smaller distributor shows.

"The shows we attend, we attend because they are more narrowly focused," Blake explains. "When we go to shows for chefs, for example, we are talking directly to the people who are using our product. They are the ones who have to be familiar with the different brands and attributes, so they can ask for our products by name."

Even as the Trade Show Bureau predicts the launching of more shows in the future, some companies are finding that less can be more. Vibra Screw Incorporated, a New Jersey-based manufacturer of dry solids processing equipment, now finds it can effectively exhibit at fewer shows than it did 20 years ago. The company used to exhibit and demonstrate its bin activators at separate shows catering to the chemical, food processing, mining, paper manufacturing, and plastics industries. In recent years, however, trade shows have emerged that cater to more than one industry at a time. Vibra Screw now concentrates its exhibition efforts on the Powder & Bulk Solids Conference/Exhibition, which is held each spring in Chicago. The only other trade show the company will do this year is in Asia this fall—a first excursion outside the U.S. that came about because of Vibra Screw's growing export business to the Pacific Rim.

The Chicago show "drew people who had a need for our type of equipment from all the industries that we used to go into specific trade shows for," explains Richard Wahl, Vibra Screw vice president. "So instead of having to be in several shows, we did away with all that and put a bigger booth in the Powder & Bulk Solids Show." The show still offers exhibitors the option of being in areas grouped by specialty, or in a general exhibit area, which is where Vibra Screw has chosen to go.

What's more, the Powder & Bulk Solids Conference/Exhibition is located at Chicago's Rosemont Convention Center, only six miles from O'Hare Airport. Wahl likes the central location, quickly accessible from the airport by courtesy bus—and the fact that it's not too close to any downtown distractions. "It's not that easy a trip to downtown Chicago. So it tends to keep people out there, right by the expo hall. And there isn't much to do out there, except eat, go to the show, and sleep at night."

(Continued)

(Continued)

Not that there is a great deal of the legendary carousing with which conferences—however accurately—have been associated in the past, no matter where the event is held. "Air-bowling"—a pastime devised by exhibitors to amuse themselves after the attendees had hurriedly fulfilled their obligations and left to tour the hosting city—is definitely on the wane, as buyer and seller expectations for a solid business return on their investment rise. Cocktail receptions and dinners have dwindled in popularity, because of their expense and unproved benefits. Wahl and many other exhibitors and trade attendees confirm that shows have gotten much more serious in recent years—less partying, more work. "The pretty girls standing out in the aisles—they still have that, but less and less," reports Wahl. "There's more serious interaction with the customer, less hype, more down-to-earth stuff."

Even in Las Vegas, conventioneers are getting down to business. The COMDEX/Fall computer show attracts a crowd of 78,000 to Las Vegas each autumn. It can take three or four days to see all the 2,000 companies exhibiting at COMDEX/Fall—and the attendees have developed a reputation for actually trying to do just that, rather than hitting a reasonable percentage and spending the rest of the convention in the casinos.

Taking Care of Business

The result of this more business-like approach: more business! A 1992 survey by Simmons Market Research Bureau found that 26 percent of decision-makers signed a purchase order at the last trade show they attended. Fifty-one percent requested a sales representative be sent to their company, 76 percent asked for a price quotation, 77 percent found at least one new supplier, 94 percent compared similar products, and 95 percent asked for literature to be sent. The Simmons study, which was commissioned by the Trade Show Bureau, was based on telephone interviews with 1,009 decision makers.

"Numbers I have seen have shown that there may be fewer attendees at some shows, but it will be the most highly qualified decision-makers who are still attending," reports Paula Marlow, senior editor of *Exhibitor* magazine. "On both sides of the coin, you have people who are serious about getting business done at trade shows."

Those attending business-to-business trade shows go to an average of four a year. The number of shows that companies exhibit at varies widely, and is often related to company size and the number of markets a company is trying to reach. IBM will exhibit at a few hundred shows a year; most companies exhibit at only one or two.

(Continued)

(Continued)

It's a labor-intensive and expensive way to reach customers, yet those who exhibit on a regular basis do so because they consider trade shows a potentially effective way to meet and pitch to motivated, potential buyers.

Ocean Garden has enough faith in the medium to devote about 15 percent of its advertising and promotion budget to trade shows. "It's always difficult to assess the total impact of the shows," concedes Blake. "But I think the fact that they continue to grow in exhibitors and attendees indicates that they get benefits from going."

Those benefits include a lot of intangibles, such as an opportunity for good old-fashioned face-to-face communication, she says. "There are a lot of people who have seen our ads, or are aware of the company, who just want to come to the booth to make a personal assessment of who we are or what we do that they wouldn't get from a mailing or telephone call."

Then there's the question of showing the flag. "One of the age-old marketing questions is what happens if you're not there," observes Blake. "People tend to forget about you."

"If we are not at a trade show, people are wondering, 'what's wrong with these guys?' " agrees Vibra Screw's Wahl. "Even though you can't prove it, we all tend to be impressed that we're in this very big show and that we've got this very attractive booth. Our reps come out and see what we do, and that impresses the reps, and maybe encourages them to sell more for us, because of the big investment that they've seen we've made in the sales effort. So you impress yourself, you impress the customer. And there's a lot of cost effectiveness to that that you really can't weigh."

While people do disagree on how to best gauge the cost-effectiveness of various selling methods, the Trade Show Bureau cites studies that calculate it costs $292 to contact a sales prospect in the field versus $185 to reach a visitor at a trade show. Again according to the Trade Show Bureau, it costs $1,080 to close a sale in the field, compared with $419 to close a sale with a qualified trade show prospect. (In each of the two examples cited, the in-the-field statistics come from Cahners Advertising Research Report; the trade-show cost comes from Exhibit Surveys, Inc.)

Vibra Screw might develop 350 good leads at the Powder & Bulk Solids Conference/Exhibition. The company spends half of its advertising budget on the show, the biggest cost being the shipment of equipment there and the hotel expenses of the sales force. "Compare that to running a postcard, which is mailed out once a month to a particular list of

(Continued)

(Continued)

people. That might cost me $1,500. And that alone may produce 100 leads. So the cost per lead by direct advertising is much more cost effective than a trade show," maintains Vibra Screw's Wahl.

But, he quickly adds, the contacts and leads developed at a trade show tend to be much better prospects than those developed by cold calling or getting a response to ads or direct mail. "If somebody comes to the show, especially if he sits down and talks to you, you have learned more about his problem—and can maybe convince him that you have the solution—than you can if he just responds to an ad and sends in a request for a brochure. You haven't talked to that person at all. You only know that he'll turn into a good lead once the salesperson goes into the field or makes a telephone call to find out. So, yes, when you get the lead back from the trade show, it is much more qualified than a lead from an ad response would be."

Looking to the Future

Besides, "It's where everybody tends to go. They can touch the pieces of equipment, they can talk to engineers there," Wahl explains. His firm's exhibit at the Powder & Bulk Solids Conference/Exhibition includes working models of their bin activators, plus computer-generated schematic presentations of just how the equipment works.

Baylor's Tanner contends that "if you compare the cost of a sales force with the cost of choosing your shows well and following up selectively, your cost savings are just tremendous at a show."

Can trade shows replace a sales force? "In the right industry, yes," Tanner responds. "When I say replace, yes, in the sense that the selling is done at the show and then what the salesperson does isn't really sell; the salesperson takes care of the customer. It's more of a customer service role."

The trade show and exposition industry grew by 72 percent during the 1980s. During the 1990s the industry is projected to grow by 35 percent. "Regional off-shoots of established events will generate nearly half of the new expositions," asserts *A Guide to the U.S. Exposition Industry,* a 1994 study by the Trade Show Bureau.

Nearly one-fourth of the new shows will be created by taking specialized vertical segments from broad-based expositions. Roughly 11 percent of the new shows in the 1990s will be horizontal broad-based shows, like the Powder & Bulk Solids Conference/Exhibition. "Emerging technologies such as environmental technology, biotechnology, and even

(Continued)

(Continued)

some not yet developed will spark 21 percent of new shows in the next ten years," predicts the *Guide*.

Even as shows evolve and gain an increasingly secure foothold as a marketing tactic, industry observers are gauging the potential of new technology to put a new spin on the game. For example, "One of the real fears that some people in the industry have is that things like virtual reality will take the place of trade shows—that I'll be able to do via technology the same things I can do at a show except talk to you face to face," Tanner explains. "It's something that is going to be important to keep an eye on."

Source: Marketing Tools (July/August 1995).

Fast **F**orward to the Real World

Smart Companies Use Public Relations Tactics to Get Good Ink

Gene Koprowski

Jerry Della Femina was at the point of penury when public relations saved his struggling ad agency. It was 1967. Della Femina Travisano, Inc. had come close to winning several accounts, but still hadn't received its first big break. Desperate, Della Femina called the editor-in-chief of the leading advertising trade magazine of the day, *ANNY*, and related the tale of how his company was *not* going to win the Panasonic account. The magazine printed his story, and soon everyone was talking about the hot young agency that had come so close to nabbing a big client.

Della Femina turned a disaster—his company's inability to win an account—into a success; his company was now viewed as an aggressive newcomer, rather than a pathetic also-ran. Della Femina went on to become one of the most famous names in the agency business—and he did it by aggressively shaping the public perception of his company.

What Public Relations Is—and Isn't

Public relations techniques are essential to the success of your firm. Your company's image is a primary asset. Conveying that image through the media is an effective way to win a place for your business in the public consciousness; and, ultimately, to boost your bottom line.

"The growth of public relations and its acceptance as a valuable, sometimes essential marketing practice, is practically universal," observes Thomas L. Harris, a former agency executive and author of *The Marketer's Guide to Public Relations*. "Companies assign public relations staff specialists to their product marketing teams and engage public relations firms to help them get the maximum mileage from product introductions, to keep brands prominent throughout the product life cycle, and to defend products at risk."

Leonard Saffir, author of *Power Public Relations: How to Get PR to Work for You*, believes the craft of public relations has grown during the

(Continued)

(Continued)

last century, in much the same way that advertising has. "Good publicity can help sell products," says Saffir. "Public relations is a necessary part of the marketing mix."

This is as true for the two-person SOHO (small office/home office) operation as it is for the multi-national corporation. Lack of a big budget for PR is no excuse: Public relations has been called the last free thing in America, and that's very nearly true. It's possible to run a whole PR campaign with a pen, a fax machine, and a little brainpower.

Jay Conrad Levinson, author of *Guerrilla Marketing* and the forthcoming *Guerrilla Marketing On-Line,* is a former creative director at a major agency. Levinson thinks that many smaller companies can generate great PR campaigns with in-house staff and a limited budget.

"A lot of PR has to do with timing," he observes. "The real name of the game in public relations is contacts"—the editors, reporters, and other media people you need to get your story out.

Crafting a public relations strategy requires a lot of research. You need to decide which audience you wish to reach, and to perform a media analysis, just as you would if you were constructing an ad campaign. Are your company's immediate needs best served by in-depth stories in the print media, or more cursory coverage on the local television news? Could your company's long-term image be better served by a profile of its president in a regional magazine, or by booking him (or her) as a guest on a national radio talk show?

Making Headlines: How to Feed an Editor

Let's say you are interested in placing a story about your company in the national print media, where (you hope) businesses that might need your product will see it. There are thousands of newspapers and magazines published in the U.S., and many of them have very specialized readerships. Getting a press release published in a magazine for florists—no matter how favorable—won't help you if you're targeting engineers. "Media planning can make as big a difference to the PR client as it does in advertising," says Saffir.

Bear in mind, however, that public relations is *not* advertising. You are working with the news media to get your message across to a targeted audience, but you aren't paying for the placement. A third party—the news organization's editor—decides whether and when and where to position the article. These people earn their living by providing their audience with interesting stories. They're not going to give

(Continued)

(Continued)

you coverage just to make you happy. You have to meet the needs of the journalist, supply her with truly newsworthy items, before she can help you.

This is not an impossible job. "The news needs you. They are hungrier than any denizen of Jurassic Park," says Levinson. "They want to hear from you." Still, you'll make your story a lot more appetizing to finicky journalists if you do some background work before you approach them with a story idea.

First and foremost, read the publications you're targeting to determine how you can provide them with the content they need. Request writers guidelines; if possible, talk to the editors. What kinds of stories are of interest to them? Do they like new product announcements, or would they prefer an analysis of a new trend in the marketplace? Although any PR person worthy of the name is shooting for the big cover story, it pays to be flexible; almost any kind of coverage can give your organization a public relations lift. A news story that details positive earnings at a company can help show existing and potential customers that others have faith in the firm as well. A new product announcement may be a potent influence for those who are in a position to buy.

"Sometimes, if there's nothing happening at your place, you can stage an event," says Levinson. "You can bring in a celebrity. You can have a fair or seminar or contest around your business. You can tie in with other companies, which I call fusion marketing, and reduce your costs. If you do that, you can attract the media: 'Look, a group of companies is getting together to do this.' That's creating news, and you can do that all in-house."

Levinson also recommends relaying interesting information about your industry to the media. Data about new trends can be gathered from clipping services or trade journals and repackaged with your company's name on it. The media will cite you as the source of the data. "Nobody ever really is the single source of information, but if you collect it, you can be quoted on TV as the expert," says Levinson.

Making controversial predictions based on your knowledge of the industry can also net you publicity. If the predictions are accurate, you will soon gain a reputation as an industry visionary. Giving speeches to local organizations can also lead to favorable media coverage. "These are things you don't need a pro to do, and they're real news," says Levinson. "If you're the expert, the media will want to talk to you."

(Continued)

(Continued)

The Right Man (or Woman) for the Job

If your organization has decided to handle its public relations program in-house, it pays to take care in assigning the job—don't just hand it over to an existing employee who doesn't seem to have enough to do, or who didn't duck fast enough when you asked for volunteers. Generally speaking, a company's PR person should have a good sense of the kinds of information that will play favorably with the media. A degree in journalism or communications is a big help. Good writing skills are an absolute necessity: Sending an editor a press release with a poorly constructed sentence will not help your cause, so examine each applicant's writing samples carefully.

The person you hire must also have the networking skills needed to cultivate journalists—a PR person cannot be a wallflower. And every public relations professional should be thoroughly knowledgeable about the industry he or she has been hired to promote.

This writer has dealt with publicists—both in-house and agency—for over 10 years. The best flacks, as we call them, are those who provide essential information for a story—and then get out of the way. They let the writer determine the angle, and don't try to force their point of view on him. They provide access to senior corporate officials to answer questions. And they never lie, because they understand how important it is to maintain credibility in the eyes of the media; they know that once credibility is lost, the whole company's reputation can go down the tubes.

Whether you handle your public relations program in-house or hire an agency, you'll want to monitor it periodically to make sure it is doing the job for which it was designed. A survey by Thomas L. Harris & Company of Highland Park, Illinois, an agency search consultancy, provides a framework for evaluation. The 1994 study examined the attitudes of 877 executives at companies which employed PR agencies. The average PR budget at these companies was close to $1 million.

The most important attribute for a successful agency—listed by 84 percent of respondents—was that it "keeps promises." Next on the list was delivery of good "client services," an attribute most sought after by 81 percent of clients. Honest and accurate billing also rated high. Good writing skills were valued. Creativity was considered essential to a successful agency, and, of course, quality and quantity of media coverage was essential as well. Creating a list of these attributes, and then rating your in-house PR person or agency on a scale from 1 to 10, can serve as an effective measuring tool.

(Continued)

(Continued)

Increased sales leads are another indicator. If you have a telemarketing operation, instruct the operators to ask those who call to request product information where they heard of the item. List the magazines where you have had story placements, and keep a tally of which magazines provide real leads and which ones don't. This can be quite valuable in evaluating performance.

The real test of a public relations program, of course, is the bottom line. If you have targeted a market for public relations activity, and sales increase there, you will know the publicity did its job.

Source: Marketing Tools (October 1995).

*F*ast *F*orward to the Real World

The Age of Accountability

Thomas Robinson

It's a simple phrase, but it's guaranteed to strike fear in the hearts of marketing's most battle-hardened veterans: "We need to conduct some research to prove that our advertising campaign is working."

Welcome to the age of accountability, where the bottom line is top of mind and marketers are under increased pressure to implement advertising programs that can be quantitatively measured in a language that management understands: results. Not computer-generated assumptions showcasing the percentage of the target population who have the opportunity to see an ad; not carefully crafted recall scores produced in a sterile test environment; and not whether a few people sitting behind a mirror feel warm and fuzzy after seeing an ad; but an accurate measurement of how an advertisement changed people's attitudes and motivated them to take the desired action.

The obstacles to quantifying advertising effectiveness are numerous and well-known. Advertising is just one of a host of variables—pricing, production, distribution, sales support, and market demand, to mention but a few—affecting the success of any product or brand. The challenge is to try to isolate this lone variable and gauge its impact. To further complicate the task, results can take many forms, from increased sales at the register to an enhanced awareness of a company's reputation.

The primary obstacle to measuring advertising effectiveness, however, is usually created by the advertisers themselves, who fail to define the specific objectives of the campaign up front. Like a long-distance runner who forgets to bring along a stopwatch, many campaigns run on and on, with no predetermined criteria for gauging the advertising's ultimate success or failure.

Determining the Criteria

The most crucial step in measuring the effectiveness of any advertising effort is to identify the specific benchmarks against which the campaign will be measured. This may sound simplistic, but how many times have

(Continued)

(Continued)

you heard people express their advertising objective as simply "to increase sales"? If the primary objective of a campaign is to move product, a set of specific criteria should be defined. For example, is the primary goal of the advertising to increase sales regardless of profit potential in an attempt to capture market share? To stimulate impulse sales to balance inventory? To announce special promotions designed to entice competitive product users? Or is it intended to encourage increased frequency of use?

Similarly, if the broadly stated objective of the advertising is to increase awareness of a company, what specific criteria should be measured? Is the goal to enhance an existing franchise position? To offset aggressive competitive offenses? To cultivate new geographic or demographic markets? To support the ongoing efforts of the sales force? And is overall familiarity of the company the best indicator, or should we be quizzing respondents about more specific attributes, such as the quality of the company's management or its investment potential?

Once these questions have been answered and the campaign's specific objectives have been prioritized, the advertiser should assess its current situation and establish a series of benchmarks. In many instances, existing sales and market share data may not be sufficient. For example, companies attempting to increase corporate or brand awareness may determine the need for a pre-campaign survey among a representative sample of the target market. By measuring aided vs. unaided recall, current product-usage habits, and the degree to which respondents are favorably disposed to try the company's products, the advertiser is collecting quantitative data that can serve as a benchmark for future measurement.

Finally, it should be agreed upon by both marketing and top management that these predetermined objectives are realistic. Has enough money been allocated to the advertising budget to accomplish the task? Is advertising really the best way to achieve these objectives? Does management have the patience to cultivate long-term results, as well as realistic expectations of the short-term returns? Only after addressing these specific concerns is the advertiser in a position to launch the campaign.

Models and Methods

To determine the appropriate method for measuring the campaign, it is useful to examine existing advertising response models to decide at what phase of the process tracking should occur. The most widely recognized model for evaluating media was adopted by the Advertising

(Continued)

(Continued)

Research Foundation (ARF) in the early 1960s. This traditional model is frequently referred to as the standard by which advertising effectiveness should be gauged.

The ARF model is linear, following an advertisement through six distinct stages, from a media vehicle's initial distribution to the ultimate sales response. For most advertisers, intermedia comparisons and advertising measurement occur in the initial phases of the model—for example, relying on total audience estimates to project vehicle exposure, advertising recall techniques to estimate advertising exposure, or qualitative focus groups to gauge advertising perception. Although these traditional methods provide useful indicators, they do not necessarily equate to sales or consumer action.

Clearly, the need to generate quantitative data that justifies the advertising investment—combined with today's proliferation of media—would suggest that the traditional model has its limitations. Today's consumer is continually bombarded with a deluge of advertising messages from both traditional and new forms of media. As the fine line between advertising and information continues to blur, a new model can be introduced that better represents the natural media environment, one that is based on the consumer's perspective and takes into account the fact that advertising is just one element in a complicated media mix.

Unlike the traditional model, the Media Proliferation Model acknowledges the volume and diversity of advertising messages constantly confronting consumers. Some of these messages are complementary, some conflicting. Some are obvious; others are more subtle. The Media Proliferation Model suggests that the first step the consumer goes through when evaluating this influx of advertising messages is media filtering. By subconsciously assigning a credibility rating to each media vehicle, the consumer is, in effect, evaluating the messenger.

Unlike the methods associated with the vehicle exposure phase of the traditional model, this alternate approach discounts concepts like pass-along readership or out-of-room viewing. It favors those core media that consumers have willingly chosen to interact with, such as a magazine read by paid subscribers, or television programs that are viewed in their entirety and not in ten-minute increments. Once the media are filtered, consumers can then analyze and evaluate the claimed benefits of the advertising message from a personal perspective to determine if these benefits address their individual needs. If so, a positive attitude is adopted about the product or brand that may ultimately affect their behavior.

(Continued)

(Continued)

With the Media Proliferation Model as a guide, the quantitative methods and measurement tools for successfully gauging advertising effectiveness should now focus on the final phase of the process: consumer action.

Measurement Tools for a New Age

To identify what specific actions consumers have taken as a result of advertising, many leading marketers are relying on one of the most effective advertising measurement tools available: new computer-based technologies that enable them to identify customers in a database, track individual sales at the point of purchase, zero in on the best markets, and more. Often underutilized, emerging technological solutions have had a tremendous impact on successful ad measurement, and are helping to transform the ways in which researchers justify advertising expenditures. Unlike most traditional methods that deal with forced exposure to an ad in an unnatural environment, this technology helps track advertising results in a natural state.

Surprisingly, many companies currently employ this kind of technology effectively in areas of their operations such as production or distribution—yet their advertising programs do not benefit from the same competitive advantage. If advertising is to be held as accountable as other functions within the organization, however, researchers must utilize all the technological tools at their disposal.

By capturing as much customer information as possible, companies can build extensive databases that have direct applications to their advertising programs. Product registration information, service records, or similar data gathered at the point of purchase or after the sales transaction can help to define a company's best customers and prospects. Custom databases can also be merged with a variety of outside resources to create an even clearer picture. By profiling customers' demographic and psychographic traits, purchase habits, and buying preferences, advertisers can effectively define their advertising objectives in advance and establish benchmarks for future measurement.

Effective database management can also aid in the execution and follow-up of the advertising. By overlaying a customer database with media subscriber lists, advertisers can gauge whether or not the media should carry a particular advertising message. In addition, technology enables companies to track their advertising success against specific products, and to identify new areas of opportunity. For example, the use

(Continued)

(Continued)

of Universal Product Scanners has greatly enhanced the ability of retailers to track sales at the point of purchase and to quickly and effectively evaluate the impact of an advertising campaign. Or by simply categorizing a customer database by zip code, a company can determine which zips represent their best customers based on past spending levels or other customer loyalty measures, and then target those specific zip codes using regionalized editions of the media.

Technology is also having a positive impact on the effectiveness of traditional measurement techniques. Computer-aided personal interviews (CAPI) are helping to eliminate some of the interviewer bias usually associated with the method, and computer-aided self-administered interviews (CASI) are currently being tested by some media research companies in an attempt to enhance the traditional methods of advertising measurement.

The Future of Ad Measurement

Because advertising represents a substantial investment for most companies, management increasingly expects a return on that investment. As a result, marketers are responsible for making calculated business decisions and accurately predicting results. In this environment of media proliferation, however, the task isn't getting any easier. There are obvious inefficiencies inherent in traditional methods of advertising measurement, but there are also a host of technological innovations on the horizon that will enhance ad tracking in both passive and active media environments.

Today, researchers must focus on establishing the specific benchmarks by which a campaign will be measured, employ the most innovative methods to track those benchmarks, and incorporate technology into the advertising process so that the company's advertising strategy can be constantly reevaluated. Then, the next time management walks into your office and announces the need to show solid, quantifiable data, you can say, "No problem boss, I have those results right here."

Source: Marketing Tools (June 1996).

5

Customers

I Let's say you accept the marketing concept, its principles and implications. You subscribe to the view that top-to-bottom business decisions must be customer-directed, not product- or company-directed. You *want* to give the customers what they want because you recognize that profit is your reward for doing so. But what do they want? For that matter, who are they? Why do they buy what they buy?

In this chapter we'll examine the means and sources of market research, the purpose of which is to help you understand your market, to learn about your customers. As we shall see, part of the goal of modern market research is to understand customers' conscious *and* unconscious motivations for buying a thing or a service, and here market research extends beyond customer profiles and statistical analysis into the realm of psychology. For its sources, market research runs the gamut from the U.S. census reports to inkblot tests.

Except for the most specialized products, today's markets are large, complex, and varied. Consider batteries, for example. Since electronic products proliferate almost daily (everything from the Walkman to those handheld GPS units), the battery market is enormous. Consumers ask two questions about batteries: Do they work? How long do the work? Batteries that don't work or that leak acid have, we can safely assume, been driven from the market. The question for the marketer then becomes, how and why do customers choose between one brand and another?

Do Energizer batteries really last longer than the other brands, or do they just have a clever bunny who claims so? Do people of color buy different batteries than do white people? Does one brand sell better in the Northeast than in the Southwest? Do teenagers, heavy battery users, prefer one brand over another? If so, do they think one brand is better than another, or are they responding to something in the packaging or to the bunny? Each year, millions of dollars are spent to learn the answers to just such questions about hundreds of different products.

CUSTOMER BEHAVIOR

Customer behavior, in the aggregate, is observable on the bottom line. This aggregate is "the market." But, individually, who are those buyers? If you knew for certain (say, as a result of extensive questionnaires filled out at the cash register by purchasers of all products), then you would know, among other things, if your product was properly positioned or marketed. You might even glean market directions and be able to determine what would be selling well years hence.

Factors Affecting Behavior
Cultural Factors

Culture is a learned set of behaviors, values, and responses. The "American dream," for example, is a learned notion. Irish-Americans might subscribe to the American dream, but Irish men and women probably do not, or if they subscribe to those sets of values they call them something else. In movies produced in the 1940s, everyone smokes; in 1990s' movies, only the villains smoke. In the interim, there has been a shift toward health consciousness. As a result, a huge industry has arisen for products such as vitamins and nutritional supplements, exercise gear, and gym wear. In urban areas, expensive health clubs flourish, and health-food stores are now commonplace. People who once thought that bacon and eggs constituted a nutritious breakfast now eat only low-fat and low-cholesterol foods. Marketers who caught the wave of this cultural shift got rich.

Consider the huge market for recreational products, everything from Rollerblades to fly-fishing rods, in terms of cultural shift. First-generation immigrants paid much more attention to work than to play in the belief that through their labor their children would lead better lives. Jewish pushcart merchants probably wouldn't have bought a lot of mountain bikes had they been available. But today the pursuit of leisure is approached with all the seriousness once reserved for work, and that change in culture has given rise to a multibillion-dollar industry.

While these examples are clear, cultural generalizations are often risky. Therefore, marketers divide cultural behavior into subcultural behaviors.

Subcultural factors

These are made up of nationalities, religious and racial groups, and regional residents. There are others, of course; a recent New York City mayoral candidate spoke of the city's cultural mosaic, but just how finely do you separate one tile from another? Are homosexuals part of a subculture? What about mixed-race spouses? Here are three broad examples of consumer subcultures.

African-American consumers. Thirty-one million Americans are black; they spend about $218 billion every year. They tend to spend more than whites on clothes, personal-care products, and shoes. Blacks tend to be more brand-loyal than whites, and they prefer to buy from local merchants. The publishing industry used to contend that blacks didn't read much; therefore, it didn't publish books specifically directed to black audiences. Along came Terry Macmillan, and now editors actively pursue black writers. Marketers in many fields have begun to appeal strategically to black purchasing power by including blacks in advertising and promotion.

Latino consumers. Population projections hold that early in the next century, Latinos will outnumber all other subcultural groups in the United States. The 26 million living in the United States today buy $206 billion in goods and services annually. Goya food products are found in supermarkets nationwide. Spanish-speaking media have become major advertising outlets. Also brand-loyal, Latinos buy quality products instead of generic ones. They tend to patronize Latino businesses or those that cater to and actively welcome their patronage.

Only recently has the Latino market itself begun to segment. Peruvians probably never liked being lumped with Hondurans, or Argentineans with Mexicans, and now marketers are recognizing that each nationality buys things differently.

Mature consumers. There is a lot of speculation about the effect that maturing baby boomers will have on everything from social security to medical costs. (As of this writing, the first of them have turned 50.) Even now, there are 32 million people over the age of 65 in this country. Senior citizens spend over $200 billion annually. They have redefined the real estate markets in Florida and the Southwest. They tend to buy in blocks, and their purchases consist of more than just trusses and wheelchairs. They are interested in recreational and personal-care products because they are in

FAMILY LIFESTYLE CYCLE STAGES

Age Group	Age	Behavioral Characteristics	Products of Interest
Early childhood	Birth–5	Total dependency on parents; development of bones and muscles and use of locomotion; accident- and illness-prone; ego-centered; naps; accompanies guardian shopping; may attend nursery school.	Baby foods; cribs; clothes; toys; pediatric services; room vaporizers; breakfast cereals; candy; books; nursery schools.
Late childhood	6–12	Declining dependency on parents; slower and more uniform growth; vast development of thinking ability; peer competition; conscious of being evaluated by others; attends school.	Food; toys; clothes; lessons; medical and dental care; movies; candy uniforms; comic books.
Early adolescence	13–15	Onset of puberty; shifting of reference group from family to peers; concern with personal appearance; desire lot more independence; and transition to adulthood begin.	Junk food; comic books and magazines; movies; records; clothing; hobbies; grooming aids.
Late adolescence	16–18	Transition to adulthood continues; obtains working papers; obtains driver's license; concern with personal appearance increases; dating; active in organized sports; less reading for fun.	Gasoline; auto parts; typewriters; cameras; jewelry and trinkets; cigarettes; books and magazines; sporting goods.
Young singles	19–24	Entrance into labor market on a fulltime basis; entrance to college; interest in personal appearance remains high; increased dating; varying degrees of independence; activity in organized sports decreases.	Auto; clothing; dances; travel; toiletries; quick and easy-to-prepare foods.

Age Group	Age	Behavioral Characteristics	Products of Interest
Young marrieds	25–34	First marriage; transition to pair-centered behavior; financially optimistic; interest in personal appearance still high; learning to be homemakers, working wives, and husbands.	Home renting; furniture; major appliances; second auto; food; entertainment; small household items.
Young divorced, without children	28–34	Lifestyle may revert back to young single; both males and females financially worse off than when married; most men and women will remarry.	Discos; therapists; clothing; auto; household goods; apartments.
Young parents	25–34	Transition to family-centered behavior; decline in social activities; companionship with spouse drops; leisure activities centered more at home.	Houses; home repair goods; health and nutrition foods; family games; healthcare services; early childhood products (see above).
Young divorced, with children	28–34	Wife usually retains custody of children; husband provides child support; woman must look for employment; low discretionary income.	Child-care centers; household goods; condominiums.
Middle-aged, married with children	35–44	Family size at its peak; children in school; security-conscious; career advancements; picnics; pleasure drives.	Replacement of durables; insurance; books; sporting equipment; yard furniture; gifts.
Middle-aged, married without children	35–44	Small segment, but increasing in size; lifestyle less hectic than when younger; emphasis on freedom and being "care-free."	Vacations; leisure-time services; athletic products; personal health-care services; party-related products.

FAMILY LIFESTYLE CYCLE STAGES (Continued)

Age Group	Age	Behavioral Characteristics	Products of Interest
Middle-aged, divorced without children	35–44	Small segment; major lifestyle adjustment for both spouses; financial condition dependent on occupation and socioeconomic status; very unlikely ever to have children.	Self-help books; therapy; cruises; vacations; condominiums; household goods.
Middle-aged divorced with children	35–44	Lifestyle changes are significant; some children may have resumed some responsibility for family's livelihood; divorced father has financial constraints; mother seeks employment if not already employed.	Condominiums; sports equipment; financial planning services.
Later adulthood	45–54	Children have left home; physical appearance changes; increased interest in appearance; community service; decline in strenuous activity; pair-centered.	Clothing; vacations; leisure-time services; food; gifts; personal health-care services.
Soon-to-be-retired	55–64	Physical appearance continues to decline; interests and activities generally continue to decline; pair-centered.	Gifts; slenderizing treatments; manicures and massages; luxuries; smaller homes.
Already retired	65 and older	Physical appearance continues its decline; mental abilities and health may decline; homebody and ego-centered behavior.	Drugs; dietetic canned foods; retirement communities; nursing home care; vacations; home care services.

Source: Adapted from Fred D. Reynolds and William D. Wells, Consumer Behavior (McGraw-Hill, New York, 1977); Patrick E. Murphy and William A. Staples, "A Modernized Family Life Cycle," Journal of Consumer Research, vol. 6 (June 1979). pp. 12–22. Reprinted by permission of the Journal of Consumer Research.

better health than their counterparts a generation ago. Marketers and merchants of all stripes are interested enough in their patronage to offer deep discounts for products and services such as movie tickets and early-bird dinner specials.

Social Factors

Social scientists and economists argue whether *class* distinctions are permanent or plastic or a little of each, but class structure does exist and obviously affects spending. Class is determined by income, education, and/or profession. Here, as in all these factors, the lines blur. A Brazilian-American orthodontist with a healthy stock portfolio buys a Rolex. What is the determining factor: class or subculture?

Groups. Liberals or conservatives, fishing enthusiasts or sailors, union or nonunion workers, motorcyclists or country-club members, soccer fans or baseball fans—to what extent are their buying decisions influenced by membership in these or a hundred other groups? For marketers, the *opinion leaders* come into play. These people, due to talent, knowledge, or force of personality, exert influence over members of their group. Playground basketball players might be influenced if Michael Jordan said he thought your company's sneaker was the best buy.

Family. Most marketers believe that families are the most influential purchasing structure in existence because they are one of the most potent societal structures. At one time, the stay-at-home wife made most of the family's buying decisions, but today well over half the nation's women hold jobs outside the home. Markets have reflected this shift. Men now buy about half the total household products, and women buy about half the cars sold in the United States. And a lot of marketing is directed at children, even though they have no money. When children see an ad for an action figure, is it the mother or the father who first hears the request for that toy? Marketing strategies will turn on the answer.

Personal Factors

Personal influences include *age, occupation,* and *lifestyle.*

That tastes change with age is obvious, but more useful for marketers is the attendant notion of *life cycles.* A college kid would probably buy a different couch than would young marrieds or new parents. Marketers have noticed that these neatly bordered cycles have blurred due to changes in mores since the late 1960s. "Nontraditional family" is the latest buzzword that applies to unmarried couples, same-sex couples, single parents, and others. Does "nontraditional spending" apply as well? Studies abound.

Occupation is certainly related to social class, depending on how you define these terms. From a marketing standpoint, a person can make certain decisions about the hand-tool market for part-time odd-jobbers by studying the kinds of tools professional carpenters buy.

Lifestyle is a subdivision of a subdivision and somewhat difficult to classify. Marketers sometimes use terms such as "AIO dimensions" (for *activities, interests, opinions*) when defining a customer's psychographics.

MARKET RESEARCH

Generally speaking, marketers can turn to *formal* or *informal* sources of information. Informal sources, including customer-complaint lines, word of mouth,

CONSUMER TRENDS
Middle-Aged Affluence

Age of householder	Households (in millions) 1995	Median Income 1994	% change Income (1984–1994 constant $)
15–24	5.4	$19,300	−3.6%
25–34	19.5	33,200	−2.3
35–44	22.9	41,700	−2.2
45–54	17.6	47,300	+4.9
55–64	12.2	35,200	+2.3
65 and older	21.4	18,100	−1.1
all households	99.0	32,300	+0.7

Source: Census Bureau

Nontraditional Family Gains
(Numbers in Thousands)

	1985	1995	% change 1985–1995
All households	86,789	98,990	14.1%
Families	62,707	69,311	10.5
Married couple, without related children under age 18	25,312	27,498	8.6
Married couple, with related children under age 18	25,038	26,367	5.3
Other family	12,357	15,446	25.0
Nonfamily	24,082	29,686	23.3
Male-headed	10,114	13,190	30.4
Female-headed	13,968	16,496	18.1

Source: Census Bureau

anecdotal evidence, and employee observations, while sometimes useful by themselves, usually augment more formal sources of hard market information. Formal sources are of two types:

1. *Primary,* involving the customers themselves
2. *Secondary,* involving existing information about customers

THE RESEARCH PROJECT

Now let's walk step by step through a typical market-research project.

Today most marketing experts believe that knowledge about customers accumulates over time; that is, it is an ongoing process, not merely a response to an abrupt drop in sales of an established product or a pioneering effort around the introduction of a new product, though it can be useful in both these situations. In general, marketing research can help in three areas: *marketing planning, problem solving,* and *monitoring.*

Planning, problem solving, and monitoring pretty well cover the gamut of marketing problems and questions. Let's use a specific, if imaginary, scenario. Pretend that your company markets a line of recreational equipment including skis, in-line skates, and small boats such as canoes and kayaks. Your ski division is losing market share. Though your skis are of high quality and you have a range of prices, the entire line is not as profitable as it was three years ago. What should you do?

You have several alternatives. You can (1) drop skis altogether, (2) redesign them on the assumption that they don't suit customers' needs as well as your competitors' products, (3) lower your prices, or (4) spend more money to promote your skis. You are unsure of the cause of the loss of profitability, so you aren't sure which alternative is best. A market study seems called for. Do you hire the study from a custom company or do you handle it yourself?

Before proceeding any further, you might want to educate yourself as thoroughly as possible. Again, syndicated sources might be preliminarily useful. They will tell you something about your competitors' skis. They might tell you, for example, what kinds of skis are favored by Western powder skiers as opposed to Northeastern skiers who encounter icy conditions. You might learn what portion of the nation's skiers have given up downhill skiing in favor of cross-country skiing, or what portion—and profile—of the market has eschewed skis for snowboards. Even if syndicated sources are too broad to be directly relevant to your problem, you

Often-Missed Sources

Are you overlooking good sources of information? The following is a list of sources most commonly overlooked by managers:

- *Government patent fillings.* Watching such data discloses potential technological advancement within a firm's industry.

- *Competitors' annual reports.* In an attempt to enhance stockholders' image of the firm, the annual report may disclose new technology in research and development or other useful information.

- *Competitors' employment ads.* Such ads may suggest a competitor's technical and marketing directions.

- *Professional associations and meetings.* The competitors' products, research and development, and management philosophy are often disclosed in displays, brochures, scientific papers, and speeches.

- *Various governmental agencies.* Under the 1966 Freedom of Information Act, many federal agencies must provide requested documents, files, or other records of a federal agency, such as the Federal Drug Administration's inspection reports of competitors' plants, competitors' cost data in a competitive bid, and reports filed with the Federal Trade Commission to support advertising claims.

- *Newspaper and magazine reports.* Tracking events at competitors' sites and in the industry and environment as a whole. It is often worthwhile to assign someone the task of clipping articles and compiling a weekly circular of the important ones.

Syndicated Marketing Research Services

- *A.C. Nielsen Company, Northbrook, Illinois.* The specialty of Nielsen, the world's largest marketing/advertising research company, is monitoring TV program viewing. Its "audimeter" device is attached to 1,700 household TV sets throughout the nation. The company also provides syndicated and custom audits of retail product sales.

- *Arbitron Ratings Company, New York.* The focus of this company is measurement of radio and TV audiences in local markets. The company also offers a computerized program that provides audience data merged with information on viewer lifestyle.

- *Burke Marketing Services, Cincinnati.* Burke provides both syndicated research services and various customized services through its multiple divisions. It offers pre-and post-TV advertising copy testing and custom survey research, educational seminars, special market modeling, television campaign testing in controlled laboratory settings, and psychological measurement of reactions to advertising.

(Continued)

(Continued)

- *The Gallup Organization, Princeton.* Gallup specializes in quantitative attitude and public-opinion research and provides syndicated surveys in the areas of packaged goods, video, and financial services.

- *IMS International, New York.* IMS's research activities consist mainly of syndicated audits in the pharmaceutical, medical and health care industries throughout the world. The company tracks the movement of products through panels of doctors, drugstores, hospitals, medical laboratories, nursing homes, and the like.

- *Information Resources, Chicago.* This company's main business is its BehaviorScan system, which collects product sales data via in-store scanner equipment; monitors buying behavior through a panel of households that use an identification card tied to the optical scanner; controls TV advertising to selected homes via cable to test the relationship of advertising to purchase behavior; and measures in-store promotions.

- *NFO Research, Toledo.* The main business of NFO is to track purchases of beverages, home furnishings, women's tailored apparel, and home computers and video games, using a fixed panel of 240,000 households.

- *Simmons Market Research Bureau, New York.* Simmons conducts an annual survey of 19,000 adults regarding their media usage, purchase behavior, and demographic characteristics. These data are combined with the Dun & Bradstreet databank to produce measures of advertising effectiveness by geographic area.

- *Yankelovich, Skelly & White, New York.* This marketing and social research company offers two widely used services: Monitor, a survey of opinions and trends in special segments of society, and *Laboratory Test Market,* a market simulation that evaluates new products in the planning stage.

- *Custom research firms.* As the name implies, custom research firms tailor their studies to the specific needs of their clients. Naturally, they are more expensive. Their usefulness will depend to a large extent on how clearly the marketer understands what he or she wants to know. These firms often have access to secondary sources unknown to the company that hires them.

- *Specialty-line suppliers.* These resources are more specific still. They specialize in a single aspect of the total research process. Most typically, they conduct field interviews with people who match customer profiles.

will learn something about your market at a low cost to your company.

Stage 1: Define the Problem

Marketing questions are intellectual in nature, and, like all such, to be addressed effectively they need to be *defined* with all possible specificity. The question, simplified, is: Why are your skis losing profitability? And by extension, what are your company's alternatives? The effectiveness and cost of the marketing study will be directly related to a clear definition of the problem and the possible actions that can be taken in response to the study, no matter what its findings are.

Fix the specific objectives of the study before you hire the researcher, and make sure that all persons involved, both in your company and outside it, have a common understanding of those objectives.

Stage 2: Establish a Plan

In-house discussion combined with applicable information from syndicated sources will help you formulate a plan. What kind of information will be necessary—and how much? Part of intellectual problem solving involves determining what information is necessary, but equally important is determining what is *not* necessary. People want to be helpful, and if asked for a response they will offer it, but many a research project has been deflected dangerously off course by a welter of irrelevant, secondary objectives. Therefore, a plan should result in a widely distributed *written* proposal.

Stage 3: Select a Technique

To circumvent this problem, researchers have taken to random-number dialing.

There are many new computer applications to help researchers handle telephone survey response more efficiently, but most seekers of audience response should hire a professional research firm to design telephone surveys.

Finally, there is the *mail survey,* and it, too, has advantages and disadvantages. That it is standardized removes interviewer bias, and that it is often anonymous makes the interviewee freer with personal revelations. One of the disadvantages is that mail surveys often go straight from the mailbox into the trash. Response rate averages about 25 percent. What are the nonresponders thinking? Marketers may try to increase the response rate by notifying people in advance that they will be receiving the questions, and sometimes by paying respondents a small fee for their time. The latter seems to work best.

A growing number of researchers combine telephone and mail surveys.

Stage 4: Sample Design

If you are seeking an explanation as to why your skis are selling poorly, you don't want to waste time and money approaching respondents who have never been on a pair of skis. You need to direct your questions to an appropriate sample. How do you pick the sample?

Though they tend to use different names, researchers employ three types of *probability sampling.* (In *nonprobability sampling,* respondents are selected according to the researcher's judgment.) The three types are *simple* random sampling, *stratified* random sampling, and *area* sampling.

Simple random sampling takes the names of "all" skiers in the country—obviously, you can't talk to them all—and randomly chooses those to be contacted. Researchers might acquire their sample by buying customer lists from ski magazines, retail stores, and/or ski resorts.

Stratified random sampling divides the sample into groups of like kinds—young skiers, mature skiers, wealthy skiers, middle-class skiers, skiers for whom the sport is a way of life ("ski bums"), and occasional skiers. Having divided the sample into strata, the researcher then chooses respondents randomly from each.

Area sampling comes into play when it is not possible to find the total population. Instead, the researcher picks a geographic area and extrapolates from there. Let's suppose, as we said earlier, that sales for your skis are climbing in New England but flattening or falling in the West. In that case, area sampling might help you determine why.

There are three types of nonprobability sampling: *convenience, judgment,* and *quota* sampling.

Convenience sampling picks respondents because they are available, such as those at the mall or on the street who are willing to stop for questioning.

Judgment sampling bases its choices on criteria set by the researcher as most representative of the broad population under study.

Quota sampling picks a sample that matches the overall population in some specified way, for example, weekend skiers who take vacations in another region.

Stage 5: Process and Analyze Data

Raw data must be turned into useful information. This is a counting and tabulation function to come up with three different numbers: *Mode* is the most frequently appearing number; *median* is the middle number; and *mean* is the average. Sometimes the study requires professional statisticians to turn raw data into useful information. Part of the statistician's function is to find a mathematical mechanism for distinguishing chance and error.

Once the data has been analyzed and perhaps depicted in some visual form such as a graph or chart, it must be interpreted. Most research firms do this interpreting and, based on the results, offer recommendations.

 Research and marketing used to be separate functions. Many companies now strive to unify the two. Research is inextricably linked with and vitally important to management decisions because it is one of the most useful ways to know your customers.

FORECASTING

If a genie came out of a bottle of Evian water in the CEO's office and offered to grant three wishes, the ability to *accurately* forecast sales over the long term would be high on the wish list. Imagine what a boon that would be. You wouldn't make mistakes; you'd know which products would sell and which wouldn't, so you'd know how to allocate costs. You'd know precisely how to manage all aspects of your operation.

And it almost takes a genie. Even the best demographic information is old when it comes out. Even the keenest statisticians, those who can glean all the implications and ramifications from mind-numbing columns of numbers, can't predict the future. It would be simpler if sales happened in a vacuum, unrelated to society, domestic and international politics, and the overall economy—but they don't. They remain vulnerable to all manner of change.

Forecasting Techniques

These techniques are generally of two types: *quantitative,* involving the collection and explication of objective fact, or *qualitative,* involving someone's judgment or opinion in the collection and explication of the facts. There are many techniques. Here are the most common.

Trend analysis implies the belief that the future will behave like the past, but trends by definition don't last very long. Since the baby boom (which no one foresaw, incidentally), U.S. population growth has been slowing. Families have grown smaller. Let's say you market a consumer product such as laundry soap. If the trend toward slower population growth continues, how will this affect your marketing plans? What if the trend doesn't continue? Should your giant "family size" contain less soap? If you find from data that more people are living alone or without children, should you market soap in one-wash packets?

Market-share analysis works best in stable markets, because it assumes that the company's market will remain constant. Thus, this technique focuses its sales projections on the market as a whole. If the market's sales advance, then so will your sales, though your percentage of the market will not change.

Test marketing is broadly employed, and it is essential when no other information exists. In consultation with your test-marketing firm, you might decide to test your new product before you risk a bundle on a nationwide launch in a chosen regional market. Your findings from that test will become the benchmark on which to gauge and project national sales. Trying to extrapolate the whole from a part makes intellectual sense, but the practice has some drawbacks.

Test marketing assumes that one area is typical of another. And sometimes it is, but not all the time. Moreover, your competitors won't be sitting on their hands while you run your test. They might boost their own promotion efforts in your test area to disrupt your results, or they might use your new product to improve their own. And, as we've mentioned, your competitor might even buy up all of your product in the test region before it gets into the consumer's hands. Rude, perhaps, but it happens all the time.

Market buildup uses sales in one segment of a product's market to project future sales for the whole company. Like the test-market technique, buildup is a logical effort to see the whole from an aggregation of its parts. Your ski company expanded to produce snowboards. In order to project companywide sales, you project sales for skis and for snowboards, then combine the two. This particular example slices the whole into only two parts. In reality, most bigger companies have multiproduct lines, and some of these products are used in different ways by different segments, further complicating the question.

Market breakdown works in reverse. By some means, marketers project sales for the entire industry or some large chunk of it, and then that figure is sliced into its component parts to forecast sales for each product.

Surveys and discussions seek to elicit customer response to your product or customer needs vis-à-vis your new product ideas. The forecaster extrapolates consumer response over the larger market based on that sample. Most marketers find it necessary to hire a firm with specialized experience in picking an appropriate sampling, because the accuracy of this technique is dependent on it.

Statistical techniques collect data in order to quantify as many variables affecting sales as possible. Having assigned numerical values to the variables, statisticians build a mathematical model. This is akin to the work actuaries perform for insurance companies. For our ski manufacturer, the variables are relatively simpler than those that giants such as Procter & Gamble or General Mills must grapple with, but they are generally the same kind: relating demographic changes, changes in the political, social, and economic landscape, and of course cost fluctuation.

 Computers allow for extremely sophisticated statistical analysis and broad flexibility to manipulate numerical variables, to play a serious what-if game with the company's future. The arcana of statistical analysis is often best left to professionals, but desktop technology has made it possible for small companies to project sales by building a mathematical model of tomorrow. Much software—Lotus 1-2-3, to name one—is available to assist, but that mathematical proclivity you discovered in high school algebra will come in handy.

Scenario analysis is another kind of what-if approach, only more subjective. Often, researchers approach the future from three perspectives: optimistic, pessimistic, and most likely. Scenario analysis works best for long forecasts. It helps establish contingency plans by isolating cause and effect. What will happen in the huge and variegated transportation industry if someone perfects the electrical motor for automobiles? What will happen in that industry if the Feds pass stringent clean-air legislation? The company that makes carbon-fiber blades for power-generating windmills will be concerned with longer-term projections than will designer Bill Blass.

The delphi technique employs a panel of experts to consider and by some means categorize and rank variables that might influence the future. Think tanks were founded on this approach, but strict application of the delphi technique requires that panel members remain anonymous and that their musings be submitted in writing. Then panel members review each other's work. Out of this process, which requires time, some consensus arises. The theory is that if enough experts agree that a thing will happen, chances are it will.

Executive opinion is a fairly simple—and ancient—technique. Executives take on the role of forecasters and, based on their experience, estimate future sales for their provinces and then try to hammer out a consensus.

Historians agree that one cause of the decline of the auto industry was that the CEOs of Ford, GM, and

Chrysler were totally out of touch with the real world inhabited by their customers. Chauffeured everywhere, these men didn't even drive automobiles. While executive opinion can result in quick action, it is only as good as the executives themselves.

Salespeople's estimates takes an opposite approach by polling those on the front lines rather than those in the executive suites. If the salespeople work in territories, for example, they will be asked to estimate sales on that basis; then someone will combine the figures to come up with an aggregate projection. "You gotta know the territory," the notions salesman exhorts in *The Music Man,* and salespeople are in a fine position to know their own customers—a better position than the boss. While that doesn't make them any more prescient, their opinions should never be ignored, especially since to get their opinions you don't have to hire a research firm or formulate a market research study—all you have to do is ask.

 Just because a thing happened yesterday doesn't mean it will happen tomorrow, and even if it does it might not happen in the same way. To one extent or another, all these techniques use the past as a compass because there is no other basis for comparison. Try to use as many different techniques as possible to forecast sales. If they all produce the same result, you can have relatively more confidence in their accuracy—but only relatively more.

MARKETING AND PEOPLE

"The market" as a phrase suggests something static and stable that can be probed and analyzed and quantified—certainly thousands of practitioners, academics, consultants, and gurus are in the business of doing so—but just when you think you have it in focus, the market has a tendency to slither out from under your lens and career wildly off in some unpredictable direction. Markets shift constantly, sometimes in response to cultural, economic, demographic, or political change, and sometimes for seemingly inexplicable reasons. The market is like history in that it never stops happening and it makes the most sense in retrospect.

This isn't particularly surprising when you look at the market's makeup—customers. All customers are people, even when the customers are other businesses, and people's behavior, comprising so many different aspects and influences, is intrinsically difficult to understand, let alone to predict. Artists from the first Neolithic cave painters to Samuel Beckett have sought to portray and explain human behavior. Sociology, anthropology, ethnography, ethnology, and psychology arose to do the same thing.

It's little wonder that marketers have trouble trying to pin down human behavior, but they must continue to try. Predicting future sales, for instance, is essentially a matter of predicting the future behavior of customers, since in our complex society buying (or not buying) things is a significant aspect of human behavior. The marketer cannot succeed entirely in this, but he or she can try, saying, "Okay, I can't know everything, but I can know something. What variables, aspects, influences, and components can I know, and what can these parts tell me about the whole?" For the marketer specifically, the question is, "Why do my customers behave as they do today, and will they behave similarly tomorrow?" Perhaps for now we should think of marketing as customer science.

In this section, let's distinguish between external influences on buyer behavior and internal, psychological influences, even while we recognize that human nature is not established by either genetics or environment alone.

Self-Image

Neither psychologists nor marketers understand entirely the origins of an individual's self-image, but they recognize its existence and that it influences behavior.

Many companies purvey an image of their product on the assumption that if it matches the self-image of enough customers it will sell. The "Marlboro man" is an image that has transcended cigarette sales to become a pop-culture icon. (In "I Can't Get No (Satisfaction)" Mick Jagger wrote, "He can't be a man 'cause he doesn't smoke the same cigarette as me.")

Certain sport utility vehicles depict in their advertising a ruggedly handsome man plowing through streambeds and forest trails to get to his favorite trout stream where, presumably, he will contemplate nature and solitude, while a voice-over reads the first paragraph of *A River Runs Through It,* in which Norman McLean compares trout fishing to religion. Never mind that there are very few places where the man wouldn't get arrested by a park ranger for driving through streambeds. Never mind also that, though SUVs come equipped with four-wheel drive, only a tiny percentage of their owners ever use it.

Some people buy products because they want to, others because they think they should. Young Hollywood agents drive BMWs—not the big BMW but the smaller, sporty one; the big one would seem showy, as though they were acting above their station. To paraphrase an early sociologist, we behave not according to how we think we should, or how others think we should, but according to how we think others think we should.

But the line blurs in today's popular culture. Most promotion and advertising people will tell you that in formulating a product's image, they consider the degree to which people might subscribe to that image. However, advertising's image making is so deeply pervasive in our lives that it shapes our self-images. The media—including advertising—celebrates sports figures for being aggressive, stoic, and hard-nosed, and at the same time talking heads wonder aloud what happened to all the role models in professional sports.

AIOs and VALs

How does an individual's psychology get objectified in the real world? By modes of behavior, according to the short answer. So how do we categorize behavior as a means to learn something about buyer behavior?

Lifestyle is that pattern of living expressed by a person's *activities, interests, opinions* (AIO). Psychographics is the attempt to measure lifestyle by establishing categories and classifications according to AIOs. We touched on lifestyle and AIOs earlier in this chapter, but now let's go a little deeper.

Values and *lifestyle,* or VAL, classifies people according to how they spend their time and money. Some traditional marketers like to distinguish between *principle-oriented* customers, those who buy things according to their view of the world; *status-oriented* customers, who base their buying decisions on outside opinion; and *action-oriented* buyers, who make decisions on the basis of variety, uniqueness, and chance taking.

Though the names may vary, marketers have categorized VALs into eight different types:

- *Actualizers.* These are people with the highest incomes, who can indulge their taste for quality. They do not necessarily follow the crowd, but they buy images as a reflection of their taste and character.

- *Fulfilleds.* These tend to be professional, mature, and family-oriented. They spend liberally but are practical and value-conscious.

- *Believers.* Practical and conservative, this group buys established and American brands. Their incomes place them solidly in the middle class, and their lives are connected to American institutions such as church, family, and country.

- *Achievers.* Successful, hardworking, and conservative, these people favor established, quality products that reflect their success or respect for success.

- *Strivers.* Their values are similar to those of achievers, but their resources are fewer. They tend to pick products that imitate the styles of wealthier consumers; they are status-oriented.

- *Experiencers.* These are youthful consumers who spend money on clothes, entertainment, and recreation. They tend to be action-oriented. Novelty appeals to them.
- *Makers.* Practicality, simplicity, and usefulness are their criteria for consumption. They are concerned with the environment and the state of society. They spend money on recreation, but it tends to be non-motorized. They don't buy style.
- *Strugglers.* Since these are people with few resources, they tend to be excluded from the picture. However, marketers recognize their brand loyalty.[1]

INDIVIDUAL INFLUENCES ON BUYING BEHAVIOR

These influences are also referred to as *personal* or *psychological* influences.

Motivation

Motivation is a drive or impulse that leads to action. Motivation is broadly divided into two categories: *biogenic,* or those related to bodily wants and needs, and *psychogenic,* or psychological needs for prestige, love, recognition, and so forth.

Motivation According to Freud . . .

One among the seminal figures who changed the world (Newton, Darwin, and Einstein being others), Freud held that behavior is largely the result of unconscious forces. Buyer-motivation researchers who subscribe to this view design tests for small groups that try to glean the deeper motives behind buyers' behavior. These researchers use word associations, inkblots or other picture interpretations, and role playing. Cold-eyed marketers sometimes look askance at these so-called projective techniques as being too touchy-feely, but psychology is far too determinant of behavior to be flatly rejected.

. . . And According to Maslow

Abraham Maslow's 1970 study proposed a hierarchy of human needs to explain why people behave in certain ways at particular times. Here's his hierarchy of needs in descending level of importance:

A. Physiological
B. Safety
C. Social
D. Esteem
E. Self-actualization

According to Maslow's model, people satisfy the most important needs first. You've got to eat, drink, and sleep. After these primal needs are satisfied, a person looks to the next, relatively less potent, need, and so on.

Perception

"It is not reality that drives our behavior, but our perception of reality."[2] (Remember the story of the blind men and the elephant?) Perception is sort of the grammar of experience, its ordering principle, but if reality itself is partly a matter of subjective experience, then so is your product. Not only must it have all the features we discussed in Chapter 1, but it must also be *perceived* as having them.

Marketers, therefore, are faced with the task of shaping our perceptions. But first they must grab our attention. As we walk down a city street, for example, we experience (on some level at least) all kinds of sensory perceptions, most of which we tune out, a tendency marketers call *selective attention*. Its cousin, *selective distortion,* refers to our tendency to filter out information that doesn't support that which we already believe. Media studies estimate that the average American is exposed to between 1,500 and 2,000 commercial messages a day. How many of these get noticed, let alone considered? Not many, the same studies agree. Most become part of the white noise of our unconscious.

So, what are marketers to do? They can work harder to figure out how to capture our attention, how to elevate their own message from out of the nebulous mass. Or they might to some extent give up on the mass market as the best vehicle for communication, turning instead to the other outlets we've mentioned, such as direct marketing in one or more of its forms.

Learning. As used here, *learning* is different from knowledge acquired through education. Rather, it refers to changes in behavior as a result of experience. Psychologists and learning theorists hold that most behavior is learned. Incidentally, animal behaviorists tend to put less weight on instinct and more on learning as a determinant of behavior in nonhumans.

Borrowing from learning theorists, marketers think of learning as a shifting interplay between drives, stimuli, cues, responses, and reinforcement. To enhance demand for their products, marketers try to associate them with powerful drives (à la the Maslow hierarchy, for example), employing cues to motivate and positive reinforcement to sustain customer loyalty. Benjamin Franklin's old adage "once burned, twice shy" certainly applies to customers and their learned choices.

Beliefs and attitudes. Distinctions between the two can blur, but generally a *belief* is a descriptive thought about a thing, whereas an *attitude* is a more stable and consistent set of feelings about a thing, exerting a positive pull or negative push. The attitude that Japanese products are well made and American ones are shoddily made was pervasive during the 1970s and 1980s. Regardless of its truth, this attitude formed a countercurrent that took American automakers years to stem. Once a belief is hardened into an attitude, either positive or negative, there will be a commensurate reflection in sales. That's why managers so tenaciously protect their brands.

How Buyers Decide What to Buy

Traditional marketers talk about the five steps of purchasing behavior that consumers go through:

1. Need recognition
2. Information search
3. Evaluation of alternatives
4. Purchase decision
5. Postpurchase behavior

These steps need little explication, except to say that marketers have focused their most strenuous efforts on the fourth step, the purchase decision. There is today that large body of marketers who focus their attention on the entire purchasing process.

Let's pause on step 2, the information search, because it is a step in which the marketers participate. The customer receives information about a product from four sources: (1) personal, (2) commercial, (3) public, and (4) experimental. Far and away the greatest bulk of information comes from commercial sources, those controlled by the marketer. But the most compelling source is personal, by word of mouth. In marketing language, commercial sources inform, while personal ones legitimize by confirming or denying commercial sources. This fact supplies further evidence of the need for customer communications. What information are customers acting upon? How did they learn about the product? How did they evaluate alternative brands? And, having purchased the product, are they pleased enough with it to buy another?

THE ONE-TO-ONE FUTURE

As previously noted, there has been by marketing pundits and practitioners a shift away from reliance on mass media and mass marketing. Marketers in growing numbers predict that the shift will be of historic proportions, affecting not only mass media and mass marketing but mass production as well, such that the rules of competition and growth will never again be as

What about Subliminal Advertising?

We often think of the period we routinely refer to as the fifties as a time of serenity and simplicity in which we shared a common set of values about what constituted the good life. But this view ignores the atomic bomb and the Cold War. This was the generation that came up with and practiced "duck and cover" as a means of civil defense.

During this time, rumors of a pernicious new kind of perception arose. It was subliminal, and we were powerless to resist. During movies, it was widely believed, sneaky advertisers flashed their messages in $1/300$ of a second across the screen (e.g., "Drink Coca-Cola") too fast to be consciously perceived by our eyes. But our minds got the message. We grew thirsty and bought a Coke. Just imagine if the Russians got their hands on a manipulative tool that powerful and brainwashed the lot of us.

Subliminal-message advertising has been tested thoroughly by psychologists—and advertisers—and none has showed that it works. But media critics contend that advertisers still use techniques that approach the subliminal. To capture our attention and thereby shape our perceptions, advertisers try to knock us off balance, to confuse us with blurry images, quick cuts, and compelling sounds such as babies' cries and ambulance sirens, using any means to drag their message out of our selective attention into conscious scrutiny. Some advertisers take the opposite tack to the same end, reasoning that amid all the quick-cut clamor the slow, subtle, even black-and-white message will, by its exception, land with impact on our perception.

Though the jury of passing time is still deliberating the effectiveness of this approach to advertising, some marketers believe that it is beside the point—which is to deliver value to, not to manipulate, customers—and that it's old-fashioned. We are not the same audience we were in 1957, when mass media was new and exciting, and its power to captivate was somewhat threatening.

important as they are today. Some people go further still, saying that the future has already arrived.

Among the most vocal of this group are Don Peppers and Martha Rogers, authors of *The One-to-One Future.*[3]

They claim that "products will be increasingly tailored to individual tastes, electronic media will be inexpensively addressed to individual consumers, and many products ordered over the phone will be delivered to the home in eight days or less."[4]

Similarly, Garth Hallberg in *All Consumers Are Not Created Equal* says, "New data shows that for most categories (of mass-produced brand-name goods), one-third of the buyers account for at least two-thirds of the volume. This 'high-profit' segment generally delivers six to ten times as much profit as the low-profit segment. . . . The profits of most mass-market brands clearly, then, do not come from the mass market. The small segment of profit-producing consumers must have a high priority in the marketing plan."[5]

Because of its consumer-oriented underpinnings, this new field of thought is a logical extension of the marketing concept. Whether we borrow Peppers and Rogers' term *one-to-one marketing* or call it, as Hallberg does, *differential marketing,* the underlying principle holds that the marketer should no longer think in terms of his or her share of the market as a whole. Think, rather, about single customers.

Information-gathering technology—in other words, computers—makes it possible for marketers to know their *individual* customers in much the same way as the old small-town general-store owners knew their customers. Modern technology, then, ushers in a return to a pre-mass-production way of marketing. In fact, "return to the future" is a favorite phrase of these new thinkers about the subject.

Most marketers agree that it is five times more expensive to acquire one new customer than it is to retain one current customer. "Moreover, most businesses lose about 25 percent of their customers annually. If you could cut just 5 percent off of that customer loss, you could add as much as 100 percent to your bottom line. Yet companies allocate six times as much to the expensive process of trying to generate new customers as they do to the less expensive process of trying to retain their current ones."[6]

By its nature, mass marketing is directed toward obtaining new customers, even though studies show, as Hallberg says, that the masses don't respond en masse. What you want is the lifelong customer, and that is what your marketing strategy should be geared to. But how do you gain that customer loyalty? Airlines and car-rental companies offer discounts or frequent-flier miles to gain repeat customers. Yet price breaks or other rewards by themselves are not enough. In fact, some customers might see them as a mild form of coercion. You *must* fly your family on American Airlines for their Club Med vacation because you've earned all those air miles from your job-related travel, whether or not American's schedules are as convenient as another carrier's.

What Peppers and Rogers suggest is that you *collaborate* with your customers. "What the typical customer wants—particularly a high-volume purchaser—is a company that recognizes who he is, understands his importance to that company, and helps him solve his own individual problems or meet his own needs."[7] Obviously, this could not be accomplished without computer technology; as Garth Hallberg puts it, "the first harbinger of the transforming power of information technology is the consumer database."[8]

 Will the future indeed be one-to-one? Will micromarketing rule the day? Maybe, maybe not. The future, like the customer, is hard to pin down precisely. As we shall discuss in the next section, segmentation is not without costs, and not all products need to be segmented to a one-to-one extent. But one fact remains: You can know more about your customers today than ever before, and tomorrow you will know still more. This fact will change marketing— it already has—and no one in the business can ignore the power of the database.

A NOTE ON PRIVACY

"How much do they know about me? How much can they know? And at what point does their bulging database become an invasion of my privacy?" These are valid questions, and the general issue of privacy is inherent to the new information-gathering potential. Every time you order something by mail, buy a magazine subscription, return a warranty card, or make a contribution to or join an organization, your name goes on somebody's database.

Most of the time customers benefit from this, and to benefit customers is the marketing purpose behind getting to know them. But there are a few direct marketers whose only aim is to take advantage of customers. That could be said about all industries, however. There is a larger issue at work here than nuisance calls or even crooked marketers. In a democratic society, should businesses have access to personal information about such things as your net worth, where your children go to school, your credit history, whether you're overweight?

The future of marketing in the information age will depend to a large extent on how marketers handle that information; or, put more directly, it will depend on marketers themselves. If they overstep, or are perceived to overstep, the boundaries of privacy, there will be a consumer backlash. And that will result in restrictive legislation. If the industry doesn't regulate itself, some other body, perhaps customers themselves, will.

However, most direct marketers want what their customers want—intelligently designed strategies that speak to, and only to, those customers who want to listen.

Fast
orward to the Real World

Focus: Hocus Pocus?

William Weylock

You hear a lot about focus groups these days—at cocktail parties, in business meetings, and even on television sitcoms. You also read a lot about focus groups—in national magazines, in business journals, and even in college-level textbooks.

On the positive side, you hear that focus groups have helped political campaigns, increased sales of faltering products, raised customer satisfaction levels, and helped build award-winning advertising campaigns. Some accounts make it sound as if focus groups are an almost magical technique, working marketing miracles with little help from human beings.

On the negative side, you hear that groups are unscientific voodoo—a crutch for lazy and irresponsible marketers. Pointing out correctly that groups are easily misused, detractors go on to damn the entire approach as pseudo-research.

I make a lot of my living from focus groups, so you won't be surprised that I come down on the positive side. It's my contention that if focus groups are used when appropriate, and if they are properly designed, conducted, and analyzed, they are extremely valuable.

On the other hand, I agree that if they are used for inappropriate tasks, if they are designed carelessly or run by unskilled moderators, and if they are not analyzed carefully by a professional, they can be dangerously misleading.

Many people have the idea that focus groups are an alternative to surveys and other quantitative research. This notion is simply not true, and it causes a lot of trouble for both marketers and marketing researchers. In fact, focus groups and surveys are ideal partners.

Groups can generate questions to be asked in surveys. They generate hypotheses that can be tested quantitatively. They can also help phrase survey questions properly, in language that really speaks to respondents.

The Yin and Yang of Campaign Research

Jerry is a political campaign manager in a Senate race. He needs to market his client to the broadest possible audience and avoid offending

(Continued)

(Continued)

as many people as possible. He needs research into the public's opinion on issues facing the state.

He can conduct a survey asking how many people approve of this or disapprove of that, but he wants something more useful. He wants to know what kinds of things his candidate should be saying in response to these problems.

He needs to know what different points of view there are on the key issues, how many people hold each opinion, how firm their positions are, what might change them, and what kinds of programs seem appealing in response.

His first problem is that he doesn't really know how to ask questions about some of the issues. They are complicated, and he doesn't want to use language that the public will not understand. He also wants to be careful not to bias the responses by inadvertently using inappropriate language to describe them.

Focus Groups to the Rescue

Jerry convenes several focus groups of frequent voters and opinion leaders (important, because who wants to hear from people who won't play a role in the election?). The groups discuss the issues in general and provide many insights into how voters talk about things among themselves, how the various issues interrelate, what differences of opinion there are, and how concerns might be met.

Jerry then does a survey to find out how many people in the state feel each issue is important and how they feel it should be addressed. His candidate emerges with live ammunition to use in the campaign.

Groups can also be used to probe issues that emerge in quantitative studies. Let's suppose Jerry's candidate is being hammered in the polls. His credibility goes way down, and surveys reveal that voters "don't relate well" to him.

Focus groups can pull together people who say they "don't relate" to the candidate. Under careful moderation, they can discuss what it is about Jerry's candidate that rubs them the wrong way. They can watch commercials and television appearances and point to key moments:

"There! When he shifts his eyes like that. You can tell he doesn't believe what he's saying."

"It always seems as if he's angry at the reporters. They're just doing their job."

"I don't like the way he crosses his legs."

(Continued)

(Continued)

All of those things are changeable. Since the numbers show that the problem is real and not just the cranky opinion of a few picky people, it is probably worth Jerry's while to coach the candidate on public behavior.

For another example, an advertising agency sends three test television commercials out for audience response analysis. The agency's favorite commercial scores low on persuasiveness. Of course, the client has no interest in producing a commercial that has tested poorly. The agency believes in the approach, but does not understand what to do in order to make a more persuasive commercial.

Focus group respondents can look at the three commercials and discuss them among themselves, going deeply into the reactions they have to various elements and sharing their views. The moderator can suggest ways in which the commercial might be altered to make it more persuasive, and the panel can give feedback on which changes might be effective.

A Question of Balance

It is fairly easy to see why the match of focus groups and surveys works well. It may not be quite so easy to see why using only one method has risks.

If Jerry does a survey on the issues without doing the focus groups, he may not ask the right questions. Or he may not ask the questions in the right way—and if questions are not very carefully phrased, they can bias answers. If some people misunderstand the question, even slightly, they may be providing incorrect answers. Later, when Jerry and his team look to the survey results for guidance, they may be misled.

If Jerry merely accepted the results of the other survey and didn't do focus groups to follow it up, he might conclude that the candidate should smile more, kiss more babies, or trot out his family. None of those things would work, because the key problems would not have been identified.

If Jerry does the focus groups without the survey, he runs an even greater risk. The campaign may respond perfectly to a concern that is shared by only a few people who happened to come to the focus groups. They may waste precious media dollars that could be spent on issues that concern a much broader segment of the public.

If the candidate responds to one or two focus groups without any polls to indicate that he's in any kind of trouble, he might stop crossing

(Continued)

(Continued)

his legs, start chatting with reporters, and stare directly into the camera at all times. In fact, these may not have been problems at all, and the wider public might lose their identification with him as his "personality" changes in public appearances. ("Why has he started sucking up to the press?")

For some reason, when surveys are proved wrong, people question the skill of the pollsters. When focus groups are misused or presented as completed research without supporting quantitative data, groups get blamed for being "unscientific" or "misleading." Focus groups are quite "scientific." They are simply not a substitute for statistical sampling techniques.

Surveys, by the way, are not all "science." There is considerable art to constructing appropriate questions and putting them in the appropriate order. There is also a great deal of intuition required for constructing the questionnaire and performing the analysis.

These general rules should be helpful, but knowing what kind of research to perform for what kind of marketing issue is an art in and of itself. It's one of the main things a research consultant, familiar with various techniques and options, can provide. At least, you should be better prepared to approach a researcher, and should have a better sense of why you need to.

Source: *Marketing Tools* (July/August 1994).

F ast orward to the Real World

Don't Know Much about Geography?

Ann S. Badillo and Elizabeth A. Kunze

As a marketing professional, how many times have you asked yourself: "Are my company's sales and service coverage adequate for this region? How can we improve our direct marketing? Where are our customers located relative to our store locations?"

Understanding the physical relationships among people, places, and resources is critical to your business's success. Yet because the nature of these relationships is not always immediately apparent, you may tend to overlook location-sensitive factors. Desktop mapping and its parent technology, geographic information systems (GIS), are changing the way marketing professionals look at both location-sensitive factors and the many gigabytes of data stashed in corporate databases.

Desktop mapping and GIS are software tools that identify relationships between database information and geographic data, and display the results in map form. Desktop mapping is a scaled-down spinoff of GIS, the mature mapping technology developed in the late 1960s. GIS is used extensively by utility and telecommunications companies to map and manage delivery networks—power and telephone lines—that connect customers to services. Federal, state, and local government agencies also use GIS to map and manage land use for resource planning.

Desktop mapping products, adapted from traditional GIS tools for easy use with smaller data sets, are ideal for the less complex location-sensitive problems common in marketing. Desktop mapping is well suited to users who are not trained geographers and who do not need the horsepower of a graphics workstation.

If you still doubt that your business really *needs* maps to improve its marketing, remember that a picture is worth a thousand words. A single map can discover thousands of dollars of potential revenue by revealing new customers. Desktop mapping and GIS identify and highlight the hidden implications of location-sensitive relationships among people, places, and resources. Whether you realize it or not, your business depends on these relationships.

(Continued)

(Continued)

Desktop mapping can also work as a database mining tool to unlock the wealth of information stored in corporate databases. *WIRED* magazine calls data or database mining nothing more than "extracting value (money) from the seemingly useless bedrock of numbers, statistics, and information." In its simplest form, database mining is what desktop mapping and GIS do best: providing you with an easy way to use and visualize data to determine the impact of location-sensitive factors on your business.

Increasing Sales at CIGNA

Consider the simple question: "Where are our customers relative to our facilities?" In the managed-healthcare field, this is one of the most important concerns of clients, prospects, and consultants. The issue is no longer simply how many providers a managed-care organization offers in its network, but how varied and how close those providers are to a prospective client company's employees. GIS, with its ability to link information with location, is uniquely able to make sense of location-sensitive factors and provide quick, useful solutions.

Connecticut General Life Insurance Company (CIGNA), a leader in the field of health-care coverage, offers group health-care products through a vast array of service providers. CIGNA salespeople must demonstrate to prospective clients what the company's provider network will look like, how the managed-care network is structured, and how accessible CIGNA facilities will be to the prospective client's employees.

In March 1992, CIGNA began using a customized GIS designed specifically for health-care companies engaged in building, maintaining, and marketing managed-care networks. The software, Atlas Managed Care from Strategic Mapping, Inc., analyzes client access to provider networks, locates gaps in coverage, and measures a managed-care system's performance against a user-defined set of health-care standards. (For more information on products and vendors, see accompanying sidebars.)

CIGNA used GIS to determine how well the location of the company's providers matched the locations of the prospective client's employees. The GIS was fed a database file that included the locations of as many as 100,000 employees, then automatically matched employee locations to CIGNA provider locations. The GIS produced reports and maps showing exactly where the provider network was strongest and weakest. CIGNA used these maps and reports in proposals to prospective clients to show them how accessible CIGNA providers would be to the client's employees.

(Continued)

(Continued)

"After the program was installed, we increased our efficiency a hundredfold," reports Jennifer Fisk, assistant director of presale strategy and case implementation for CIGNA.

Improved efficiency—along with positive feedback from clients and several initial successes in closing sales using GIS-based network analysis—created a dramatic increase in demand for GIS from other CIGNA groups. Consequently, CIGNA added GIS services in three regional centers and developed similar GIS "hubs" for other divisions that needed to analyze location-sensitive factors.

Marina Pye, then-supervisor of CIGNA's eastern operations support unit, took on the task of implementing GIS for one of CIGNA's sales regions. "Using GIS, our office provides mapping services and analysis for 400 salespeople, in addition to working on CIGNA's health plans and analyzing underwriting issues," she says.

"We began using this GIS software based on the competitive need. Mapping reassured people that if they were to go to managed care, they would have access to the providers and specialists they desired," says Pye. Today, CIGNA's GIS project has grown from a small pilot into a network of regional centers serving approximately 1,000 salespeople nationwide.

Matching Resellers with End Users at Sun Microsystems

Sun Microsystems, Inc., a leading computer workstation company in Mountain View, California, implemented a large-scale marketing information network with a GIS at its heart. Sun's decision to use GIS technology as a marketing tool was driven by the company's need to match value-added resellers (VARs) to end users according to the VARs' expertise and targeted markets.

Sun determined that GIS technology provided the best means to collect and analyze reseller and target customer information. Furthermore, the same GIS tools enabled Sun's channel managers to analyze location-sensitive data relative to individual territories. Sun selected two GIS products developed by Environmental Systems Research Institute (ESRI): ARC/INFO software to perform the geographic information processing and analysis, and ARC/INFO's sister product, ArcView, to provide desktop mapping tools for distributing, evaluating, and displaying reseller information.

Data reduction was vital for implementing Sun's marketing information network, since Sun's application user database contained almost

(Continued)

(Continued)

600,000 records. This user database was first geo-coded, a process wherein nongeographic data, such as names and addresses, are matched with actual map locations. Next, using ArcView, the user database information was distributed to more than 100 workstations throughout the United States for display and analysis. Data for this part of the project came from Computer Intelligence, InfoCorp., G-2 Research, and Geographic Data Technology (GDT), as well as from Sun's internal databases.

Bo Johnson, then Sun's manager of channel marketing and development, elaborated on the channels marketing strategy. "The key to effective channels marketing is to compare local business types with a reseller's target market to ensure that the reseller's strengths are properly focused on localized market need. To accomplish this, we had to first categorize the computing needs of Fortune 1000 companies located in a particular region and examine their capabilities."

Johnson adds: "Consider this scenario: suppose a Sun reseller in one territory specializes in selling systems and services to manufacturing companies. Yet in this same territory, there are also a number of Fortune 1000 companies that need computing products to support financial services, one of Sun's targeted markets. With the help of GIS analysis, we quickly knew that we needed more resellers focusing on the financial services market."

Ed Katibah, a GIS consultant who helped to implement Sun's marketing information network project, explains how GIS turned mountains of data into valuable information. "To give you an idea of some of the data sets' sizes, there are approximately 28,800 Fortune 1000 company sites throughout the United States. Sun has an average of 20 records of descriptive data for each of these sites, yielding approximately 600,000 records of information pertaining to the computing resources and applications of these companies. All of this information was made more readily available through the GIS-supported marketing information network."

Using GIS technology as a marketing tool, Sun Microsystems created an innovative relationship between several information systems and the geographic factors that directly affected its channel marketing. GIS allowed Sun to visualize the importance of location-sensitive data, and now the company is using GIS technology for both tactical and strategic marketing.

Deciding Where to Build New Facilities at GTE

GTE Corporation of Dallas, Texas, deployed desktop mapping tools from MapInfo Corporation as part of a competitive analysis to better

(Continued)

(Continued)

understand how GTE's fiberoptics network facilities were positioned to deliver communications services to users, compared with its competitors' facilities.

By plotting the addresses of its customers against the addresses of competitors' customers, GTE quickly determined the best sites for new facilities to attract and support users. Desktop mapping tools also helped GTE identify potential new business by finding areas without fiber-optic services. The same maps used to determine where to build new network facilities were used to brief management on why network facilities should be expanded. GTE also uses desktop mapping in sales presentations to show prospective customers where network facilities are relative to the customers' businesses.

Quentin Bredeweg, assistant vice president of business analysis, explains GTE's move to use desktop mapping as a marketing tool: "We desperately needed to visualize our data." Before desktop mapping, he says, GTE simply used markers on rental car maps.

Motivating Resellers at Fidelity Investments

Fidelity Investments of Boston, Massachusetts, uses desktop mapping to help resellers of Fidelity's products find the largest concentrations of mutual-fund buyers. As a service to its customers—banks, insurance companies, and brokerage firms that resell mutual-fund products—Fidelity creates maps locating the greatest number of mutual-fund buyers for a particular customer's branch site. Data visualization quickly captures customers' interest and motivates them to sell Fidelity mutual funds.

Using data from Equifax National Decision Systems, Fidelity matches the demographics of major metropolitan areas with the psychographic profiles of households with the greatest propensity to buy mutual funds, then maps the results for use in sales presentations. Some prospective customers were skeptical at first, according to Tom Chapman, manager of marketing databases, but when Fidelity showed them maps that indicated where the greatest number of potential mutual-fund buyers were, they became highly motivated to work with Fidelity.

Chapman describes the advantages of using desktop mapping. "It has helped us become more competitive on two levels: first, by getting banking, insurance, and brokerage firms interested in working with Fidelity instead of a competitor; and secondly, by helping Fidelity customers fill their sales pipeline with highly qualified mutual-fund buyers."

(Continued)

(Continued)

Untapped Resources: The Future of Marketing

The best reason to adopt desktop mapping and GIS is that these tools will help your business become more competitive, provide better customer service, and maximize its resources by more efficiently managing the flood of corporate data. Only 2 percent of all data available today are analyzed, according to the Gartner Group. Desktop mapping and GIS not only reveal the hidden connections between marketing data and geographical factors, but will apply database mining to reveal the wealth of information hidden in your corporate databases. With these tools, you can get the most out of the marketing data you have and discover new information resources you never even knew were there.

Source: Marketing Tools (November/December 1994).

*F*ast *orward to the Real World*

Drowning in Data?

John Miglautsch

Much has been written about how research data can improve your marketing efforts. Yet while everyone appears intent on amassing information, few companies seem to know how to make the most of what they have at any point in the accumulation process. I mentioned "RFM" in a speech at a recent database marketing conference and got blank looks. I asked how many people were unfamiliar with the term, and almost all the hands went up (for the uninitiated, it stands for "Recency, Frequency, Monetary" analysis, which is a method of identifying the most profitable customers on a database).

This remarkable gap between what is being done in the real world and what is being preached from the marketing pulpits has little to do with technological awareness. Prospective clients are asking about "neural/fuzzy logic/chaos theory" while they mail to customers who haven't ordered in ten years.

Part of the problem stems from the insatiable appetite marketing has for the new and exotic; the mindset that says, "If we just compare the correlation of coffee bean prices with the crime rate in New York City, we can extrapolate the net response rate and calculate future lifetime value."

In this article, I would like to examine some of the underlying principles of database marketing, without worrying about technology. Let's step back for a moment and look at what we are trying to accomplish, and perhaps in the process, we'll be able to see the forest for the trees.

Eternal Truth #1: There Are Never Enough Data to Make a Decision.

When I began in direct-marketing consulting in 1981, we would show clients how to modify their computer systems so they could gather marketing information like key codes and average order size. In those days, we made decisions by the seat of the pants because there was little hard data to go on.

Things changed dramatically in the mid-1980s, when clients started asking for help understanding all the data they had accumulated. We typ-

(Continued)

(Continued)

ically couldn't get at the real data, so we asked for totals from the data processing department (that is what it was called before IS and MIS).

Of course, each report came back looking a bit different from what we had expected. We always went through several versions before they understood what we wanted. At the time, I thought it was because there was a language problem between Marketing and MIS. But then I noticed that even when we got what we wanted, the additional information opened new vistas and generated more questions. The new questions suggested new report requests, and the cycle began again. One day I realized that whether we got what we asked for or not, we still seemed to "need" more information.

The problem is not really in the data. The problem is in ourselves. When the time comes to make a decision, we are all a bit timid. Decisions have consequences, which will only occur in the future; and we can't predict the future with 100 percent accuracy. Thus, no matter how much data we've collected, we put off the moment of truth, telling ourselves that if we knew that one additional number, we would be comfortable making the decision.

The fact is that mountains of data can immobilize corporations. Much has been made of the emerging quality movement in America. "You will never control what you do not measure" leads us to conclude that total quality management means measuring everything. Yet companies that win the Malcolm Baldrige Awards typically struggle for years afterward. A colleague who does Quality Management consulting says that they become so fixated on measurement, they often lose sight of their core business.

Therefore, if you think marketing databases are simply about data, you will make expensive mistakes when you build one. One of our clients has about 14 million customers and about 300 million transactions in their mainframe. Another prospective client has 27 million customers and 1 billion transactions. Both came in saying they needed online real-time access to all that information. Another prospective client actually put 11 million customers in a special data warehouse, but it is now so cumbersome that the company can't make sense of it and is looking for consulting help. All these and many other companies are filling disk drives without thinking about what exactly they want to do with the data.

Marketing Databases Are About Making Good Decisions

The quality and flexibility of a database is far more important than the sheer volumes of data. For the moment, the client with the 14 million-name database is working with several smaller databases and finding

(Continued)

(Continued)

that with only a few exceptions, less than 100,000 names works very well for analysis.

Marketing is perhaps justifiably suspicious about settling for less than everything they think they need. For years, their only access to data was through the veil of paper reports. When they finally got crude query tools, they found that much of their detailed data was fundamentally flawed. Because no one had been using or looking at the details, no one realized the problems that were being created. Nearly everyone we work with is surprised by what is discovered in their data.

Unfortunately, such rude awakenings tend to inspire the notion that if not seeing all the data leads to corruption, we must *always* look at all the data. This misses the point of analysis, which is that patterns and trends are easier to spot in a limited and controlled environment. Models are intended to simplify complicated things so decisions can be made.

Besides, historical data will *never* exactly match what you are trying to do in the future. A multitude of variables will have changed. On the whole, the concept of projection still works, but the tighter you try to match past and future, the harder the process becomes . . . and it is very easy to come to the wrong conclusions.

Let's say you want to sell jewelry to your consumer customers. You start by looking at who has bought cosmetics in the past. You use modeling tools to see how these people are different from those who didn't buy. But this only works if you mailed broadly in the past. If you used this trick before and only mailed to people you thought would be likely prospects (let's say you mailed to only women), then you must be careful about what your current model will tell you (past buyers won't, for example, include men, because they weren't selected for previous offers). Ironically, segmentation analysis works best with sloppy clients who have been mailing to everyone in the past.

Given some of the limitations of traditional statistics, users must be able to examine data that does not yet create a trend. With regression, we generally look for correlation (i.e., people who buy Item A are older than people who buy Item B). My stats friends tell me that they will often remove odd data (like the person who ordered $10,000 when the average order size is $100) in order to build more accurate models.

However, some of the best marketing successes have occurred well before the trend became obvious (for example, photo copiers, portable computers, and Federal Express). Understanding the difference between irrelevant static in your data and interesting exceptions that reveal new marketing breakthroughs may require a human brain. There will always be room in database marketing for a good offer and a gut feel. A bad

(Continued)

(Continued)

offer will seldom be saved by analytically finding enough "suckers," and a good offer will have broad-enough appeal to overcome a few bad list choices.

A common misperception is that if there were just enough information, we could mail only to those who are likely to respond. However, to be realistic, *I* don't even know exactly when *I* will buy particular items. If people cannot predict their own behavior, it's unlikely you'll be able to predict it for them, no matter how you fill your database. The bottom line is that we will never achieve 100 percent response rates. We will always need to overpromote (to communicate with people who don't yet know that they want our product) with great marketing offers.

Assessing the Great Middle

We have been talking about some of the areas that database marketing purports to address. Yet without some careful thought, the data technology can often cloud more basic issues. Perhaps this explains the wide gulf between what is being preached and what the parishioners are practicing.

Once we understand some of the limitations of database marketing, we should look at the fundamentals one last time. If the issue is how to promote most efficiently, we should step back and look at what we know without elaborate analysis.

I have clients who mailed successfully for 30 years without using key codes, but they made good decisions. They had good products at fair prices. The fact is even without a marketing database, we know most of the answers already. We can easily divide our customers into three groups: the good, the bad, and the middle. We know we should mail to the hot line (most recent buyers), and we're pretty sure that we don't have to mail to customers who haven't bought for more than a few years.

The only real question is which of those in the middle are good enough to mail. Most of the techniques, be they sophisticated analysis or seat-of-the-pants guesswork, are focused on this great middle. If you have 10,000 customers, your middle is probably only about 4,000. This means that it is far cheaper to mail them all than to spend tens of thousands on elaborate models.

This illustration has used recency (the "R" in "RFM"). You can also look at the number of times a customer orders and how much they have spent ("frequency" and "monetary," or "F" and "M"). But no matter

(Continued)

(Continued)

how many additional variables and sophisticated techniques you add, you are still basically working with the great middle. If you have 20 million customers, this level of sophistication will be very much worthwhile. Otherwise, take your time exploring new (and expensive) analytical silver bullets.

If you are building a marketing database, focus on key data and the crucial questions. Make a list of very specific things you want to answer. You don't need millions of customers to do statistically valid modeling. However, if you want to build models based on what people have actually purchased, you will want to include transactions in your system (so you can select based on product numbers). You must have more than a quick counts system to find the people who have bought a given item. It is probably better to have all of the information on some of your customers than some of the information on all of your customers!

You must have the ability to spot anomalies. This may mean fancy query tools, but for most of us, it means programs that allow us to select customers and look at their related data. Summaries will always cover up the facts, however, so make sure there is a way to look under the covers.

Finally, it is very difficult to anticipate exactly what should be included, so build for maximum flexibility. Look for tools that allow you to interact with your data, build your own reports, etc. Allow the system to do simple things well for a while, then phase in a second set of requirements.

Above all, don't get so wrapped up in pursuing the state of the art that you overlook simple improvements that can be implemented immediately.

I recently ordered merchandise from a telemarketer who made no effort at upsell or cross sell. When I asked about it, I was informed that their computer program was ready but hadn't been completely set up for that. My response: "You just take a big red crayon and write 'THIS WEEK'S SPECIAL IS . . .' and hang it over all the telemarketing tubes." No new LAN, no CD-ROMs, no new software—just a bright red Crayola. The moral of the story: before you start hiring consultants and buying whiz-bang equipment, think long and hard about what you could do with what you have!

Source: Marketing Tools (March/April 1995).

Marketing Research 101

Paula Kephart

Every business has the same goals. We all want to improve customer service, deliver more value to our customers, and find new customers without spending a fortune on marketing. Marketing research can help you reach these goals—or it can be a complete waste of money. It all depends on what you know before you start.

Used wisely, marketing research can tell you why some consumers like your product while others hate it. It can tell you how much of your product is selling at what stores. It can tell you what factors are influencing sales. And marketing research can deliver all of this information in a variety of ways, from a large sampling of consumers to one-on-one interviews. But each type of marketing research is a tool with specific uses. To choose the right research for the job, you need to ask the right questions.

You wouldn't use a shovel to hammer a nail. It would be just as foolhardy to launch a new product based solely on focus-group research. Do you know why?

Today's research methodologies are easier, faster, and more sophisticated than ever before, but figuring out what kind of marketing research is right for your needs may seem overwhelming. Do you need qualitative research or quantitative, and just what is the difference anyway? Is telephone surveying the best way to talk to consumers about your product, or would focus groups be a better approach? Should you do a short-term independent research project or buy into a syndicated or omnibus study?

It's tempting to call a marketing research firm at random and let them make all those decisions for you. But getting the most from your research dollar means knowing from the start what you need and how to use it. You don't need to be a research expert, but you owe it to yourself to become a knowledgeable customer.

Defining the Job

The first step is to define your research objectives, determining what questions you need to answer. You may want to know why your product is not selling, or how consumers will respond to new packaging or a new

(Continued)

(Continued)

price. Your questions will determine whether you need quantitative or qualitative research.

Quantitative research deals with numbers and answers questions about how many, how much, or how often. These surveys generally rely on close-ended questions—questions that can be answered briefly, often with a "yes," a "no," or a number.

Qualitative research deals primarily with the feelings and attitudes that drive behaviors. Open-ended questions, which can't be answered in one word, encourage respondents to describe their feelings, opinions, attitudes, and values.

The next step is to settle on a method of data collection. There are a number of ways to collect both quantitative and qualitative data, and a number of reasons for using one instead of another.

Telephones, mail surveys, diaries, and cash-register scanners are the tools of quantitative research. Mall intercept interviews and focus groups are most appropriate for qualitative research; extended mail and telephone surveys can be used as well. Most marketing research companies specialize in a particular method or technique of data collection, although not exclusively.

Before embarking on a solo research effort, you might want to investigate whether your needs can be met by signing on to a collaborative venture. Syndicated research is a joint effort undertaken by a group of entities that are interested in one particular topic. All parties share in the cost, help to formulate the questions asked, and have access to the results. Omnibus surveys usually cover a wide range of subjects and issues, with participants contracting to add very specific questions that may not be of interest to anyone else involved in the project.

For the purposes of this article, let's assume you've decided to strike out on your own. In hiring a marketing research firm, you'll need to know how much assistance a given firm provides. Full-service companies can help with each step of the project, from defining the objectives and designing the study through collecting the data and interpreting the results. Field services only offer assistance with specific aspects of the project, such as data collection. Most firms, full service or field service, specialize in specific kinds of research, so it pays to shop around for one with experience in your area of interest.

Niches of Expertise

MarketVision Research, Inc. of Cincinnati, Ohio, is a full-service custom research and consulting firm, serving both business-to-business and consumer-focused clients.

(Continued)

(Continued)

MarketVision collects most of its data via telephone surveys, conducted from telephone facilities in Cincinnati, Ohio, and Orlando, Florida. The company also offers mail surveys, focus groups, and one-on-one interviews.

Its clientele is drawn largely from a handful of industries, especially consumer packaged goods, health care, business-to-business, office supplies, and chemical products. This allows MarketVision's staff to become thoroughly familiar with the issues and languages of those industries. "We stick with the categories we are familiar with," says director of client services, Katie Klopfenstein, who calls these categories "niches of expertise."

Mail surveys account for about 20 percent of the company's work. They are used for lengthy surveys and when clients need to gather additional information in order to respond, such as in business-to-business surveys. In terms of access to the respondent, mail surveys are often better suited to business-to-business situations, especially at the executive level. A telephone survey may not get past the secretary screening calls; an attractive, well-designed mail survey is more likely to be passed on to the executive. A disadvantage of mail surveys is that they require a much longer time frame for completion, especially if there are multiple mailings.

MarketVision has also been taking advantage of the new disk-by-mail survey format, which is especially useful in business-to-business surveys. The survey form is copied onto a computer disk, on which the respondent enters answers using his or her own computer. Although disk-by-mail can cost more due to programming expenses, data entry costs are eliminated.

Klopfenstein offers these tips to ensure a good response from mail surveys:

- Design is very important. The cover letter should be attractive and personalized and explain the survey's objectives—why it is being done and why the respondent was chosen. The questionnaire itself should be well laid out with lots of white space and easy-to-follow directions. Crowding questions too closely can make the survey look too complicated and intimidate respondents.

- Offer respondents an incentive to participate, such as a fresh dollar bill included with the questionnaire for consumers or the promise of some feedback from the survey for business-to-business respondents.

- If at first you don't succeed, try again. "Doing multiple stage mailings and remailings will increase response rates," says Klopfenstein.

(Continued)

(Continued)

"We typically like to go for a response rate of 50 percent, and that can take between two and five mailings."

Collecting at the Cash Register

Advances in electronic technology created another tool for quantitative data collection—the scanner used by store cash registers. Information Resources, Inc. (IRI) of Chicago, Illinois, pioneered the scanner method in the late 1970s. Now the company offers two core services—market testing, called BehaviorScan, and ongoing tracking, called InfoScan.

"This type of research is not on a project by project basis," says IRI spokesman Robert Bregenzer, "but rather on a continuous weekly basis. The client contracts for three or five or seven years to receive a continuous flow of data."

This constant stream of information allows the client to micro-market, addressing problems and recognizing opportunities at the individual store level. IRI can supplement the data with on-site assessment of factors influencing product sales, such as displays, in-store advertising, and competitors' advertising.

BehaviorScan provides market testing by tracking purchases made by households recruited for this purpose. This makes it possible to analyze household demographic and purchase patterns and monitor the performance of new products.

IRI recently devised computer software to make analysis of scanner data faster and more manageable and to assist with any stage of the research project. The company also recently began offering census data collection: Instead of gathering information from a sample of stores, IRI now collects data from all the stores in its system. Says Bregenzer, "This represents about 80 percent of the country's total stores. You can draw good conclusions from that amount."

Scanner data cannot predict future sales. "But if you want to know what is happening today," says Bregenzer, "there are no alternatives."

Dear Diary . . .

Diaries provide another means of collecting detailed data on what consumers are buying, but the method takes the process a step further by analyzing consumer behaviors. MRCA Information Services of Stamford, Connecticut, developed this method during World War II to measure the purchasing behaviors of a sample of households over a period of time. Respondents record purchase and use behaviors in diaries at the time

(Continued)

(Continued)

they buy and use the product. The diaries list a range of questions such
as brand, size, price, outlet where purchased, and intended user. This on-
the-spot recording offers big advantages over methods that rely on
respondents' recollections.

The sample of households is called a static panel. MRCA maintains a
12,000 household panel that is representative of the national census in
age, geography, presence of children, and other significant variables.
The same households are used over a year's time, enabling MRCA to
measure even small changes in household purchases and use, and
ensuring a high degree of reliability and validity.

Diaries are especially appropriate for answering questions on brand
penetration and loyalty. Furthermore, says Ken Murphy, senior vice
president of sales and marketing for MRCA, the diary method reveals
what factors influence purchasing behaviors, such as price and advertising, and where purchases are made—supermarkets, warehouse outlets,
drugstores. The method appeals to a wide range of clients in packaged
goods, apparel, home furnishings, financial services, travel, and entertainment.

Another service MRCA offers is the Menu Census. This service measures
consumer food usage right down to the ingredient level, getting at what
people actually eat, rather than what they think they should. This helps
clients avoid what MRCA president/CEO David Learner calls "nutritional
schizophrenia." "This explains why people who do surveys on healthy
foods have dismal failures, because consumers' attitudes don't mesh with
their behaviors," he explains. "It is the discrepancy between attitude and
behavior that is important from the marketing point of view."

Syndicated or Omnibus?

Lou Bender is in the unique position of heading two companies that deal
primarily with syndicated and omnibus studies. As president and chief
operating officer of Mediamark Research, Inc. in New York City, Bender is
actively involved in the company's national syndicated study, which
serves over 700 clients. The study determines the size and composition of
audience to media; as you might expect, its clientele is largely composed
of ad agencies, media, and large manufacturers of products. Says Bender, "Each client gets the same database of survey results, which can be
used to make media decisions, such as where to place their advertising."

The Mediamark study interviews 10,000 adults in their homes twice
a year, providing a total of 20,000 interviews to members of the syndicated study. Respondent samples are drawn from large markets such as

(Continued)

(Continued)

New York City. (Mediamark just finished a survey in Toronto and will include all of Canada next year.)

Respondents answer a range of questions about their media use—the magazines and newspapers they read, what TV, radio stations, and cable networks they tune into, and when. Demographic questions are included. After the interview, respondents complete a questionnaire about use and purchases of different brands, products, and services.

Every six months, the Mediamark study releases survey data to members along with data from the previous six months, so that clients have a year's worth of survey data at any one time. Data are available in printed form, on CD-ROM, or through on-line services. (Mediamark also provides custom research for small or localized magazines. The data from the customized research study can be compared with the national study.) The overall shape of the study varies little from year to year, although clients provide input on which questions to include. Members also keep Mediamark advised of new products being advertised or new television shows being aired.

Syndicated research is a good buy for a small company with a small budget because it's affordable—price is based on the member's size—and it provides a large amount of information that can be analyzed from several different perspectives.

Another advantage of syndicated studies is that all clients have access to the same information to help them work out advertising and media decisions. In addition, trend data can be generated since the same basic questionnaire is used over time.

The disadvantage in participating in a syndicated study of this type, of course, is the extended time frame. If time is of the essence, the omnibus study offers the advantage of speed. OmniTel, a service of Bruskin/Goldring—where Bender is chief executive officer—does 1,000 telephone interviews each weekend. Survey data, along with crosstabulations, are faxed to clients on Monday.

"The difference between omnibus and syndicated research," says Bender, "is that in an omnibus situation, each client gets to ask specific questions in the overall interview, which also includes a set of demo-graphic questions. All the clients share the cost of making the phone call and the demographic questions. And they pay for the specific questions they ask."

Omnibus surveys can use other methods of data collection such as in-home interviews, but these are more costly in terms of time and money. Generally, the telephone interviews take about 20 minutes each. The limited time, however, also limits the number of questions. Computer-

(Continued)

(Continued)

assisted telephone interviewing, often referred to as "CATI" (pronounced "Katie"), speeds the process and allows for instant analysis of data.

Reach Out and Count Someone

Iowa Field Research was started as a data collection center by Grapentine Company, a full-service marketing research and data collection company. Both companies are located in Ankeny, Iowa. Iowa Field Research has focus group facilities and does focus group recruitment and mall intercept interviews, but the majority of its data collection is through telephone surveys.

"The ideal way to collect data for any kind of study is person-to-person interviews," says Terry Grapentine, president of Grapentine Company. "The problem is it's very costly."

Telephone surveys are the next best thing. They are cheaper, faster, and can reach a large number of respondents. Depending on the project, surveys can be carried out overnight or over a weekend. The surveys can collect data for an array of purposes—customer satisfaction, image and positioning, product usage, media and readership surveys—although they are not useful for testing advertising or product concepts.

Grapentine offers the following list of things to look for in telephone data collection services:

- Interviewers should be well-trained and closely monitored;
- Quotas should be established to make sure a representative sample is reached;
- Call-backs should be made to ensure validity and reliability;
- Pretests should be run to make sure respondents understand the questions and their intent.

Standard phone surveys take about 15 minutes; when used for qualitative surveys involving open-ended or brainstorming questions, interviews can take up to 45 minutes. To accommodate respondents' schedules, Iowa Field Research arranges interview appointments, provides an 800 number for respondents to call back, and keeps the facility open extended hours. Computer-assisted interviewing enables their interviewers to log responses directly into computers.

Focus on the Consumer

Focus group interviews provide the richest detail in qualitative research. Although commonly portrayed in the mainstream media as the be-all

(Continued)

(Continued)

and end-all of marketing research, focus groups are actually designed for the initial stage of a research project. They provide a way to explore questions before designing the questionnaire to be used in the larger survey.

"Qualitative research is traditionally exploratory, whereas quantitative is confirmatory," explains Mary Rubin, senior manager of qualitative research at Maritz Marketing Research, Inc. of St. Louis, Missouri. "Qualitative research is an investment. You're investing in your tool [questionnaire]. Before that tool goes out you need to do some research and development."

Focus groups are traditionally used in areas like customer satisfaction, advertising copy testing, and new product development, where there are lots of variables and plenty of room for error.

"The attributes that drive satisfaction with Wal-Mart are different than the attributes that drive satisfaction with Marshall Fields," explains Rubins. "There is no survey I can buy off the shelf to determine customer satisfaction with a particular company—say, Smith Bank; I have to develop a survey by talking to the customers to determine what customers base their satisfaction of banks on, and in particular, Smith Bank."

A focus group ordinarily involves 8 to 12 respondents brought together for about two hours under the direction of a moderator, who facilitates the group's discussion about the research objectives. The moderators themselves are key to the success of any focus group. As such, they must be highly trained, skilled professionals with a thorough understanding of specific industries. Regional, ethnic, and gender differences must also be accommodated in the focus groups in order to ensure that respondents relax and talk freely.

Facilities are equipped with two-way mirrors so that clients and project monitors can watch the focus group in process. Generally, a minimum range of 12 to 24 focus groups will be required to gather enough data to shape the questionnaire. But depending on the project, many more groups can be used.

Maritz does up to 2,000 focus groups a year in facilities located all over the country. "Qualitative research is a hot area now. The industry is booming," says Rubins. "We're doing more qualitative research vis-à-vis our overall business every year. In the past, people were rushing to market without taking the steps to get important information, and they were increasing their risks.

"Survey results are only as good as your initial instrument," she warns. "Statistics can lie if you left out an important variable. We're

(Continued)

(Continued)

gathering data—whether qualitative or quantitative—to minimize the risks for clients making tough [marketing] decisions."

Mall intercept interviews offer another way to talk to consumers face-to-face. While not as in-depth as focus groups, they offer some important benefits. "There are quick turnarounds," says Jerry Carter, vice president and general manager of operations for Consumer Opinion Services in Seattle, Washington. "You have access to a lot of people." And mall intercepts are less costly than door-to-door interviews.

Interviewers are placed in enclosed shopping center malls to "intercept" shoppers. Just which shoppers they intercept depends on the type of consumer the research study wants to reach—if a study is looking for feedback from middle-aged women, for example, interviewers won't stop teenagers. A potentially serious drawback to mall intercepts, incidentally, is that most malls are located in suburbia, making it difficult to get a good mix of ethnic and socioeconomic respondents.

The interviewer then asks some qualifying questions to make sure the shopper does fit the study's profile. If so, then the respondent is asked to participate in a longer interview. These interviews may involve a taste test, a commercial preview, or a product trial. For this reason, most firms specializing in mall intercepts have a room at the mall where interviews take place. Interviews generally last 15 to 18 minutes since respondents are reluctant to take much time away from their shopping. If the interview will take much longer to conduct, the respondent is usually offered an incentive.

Often such projects require interviews in malls in more than one city. This may mean relying on several data collection services, although some companies, including Consumer Opinion Services, have mall locations in several cities.

There will always be those in the business community who make decisions by guess or by gosh, who are comfortable relying on a hunch or instinct; and sometimes the choices they make pay off. The rest of us prefer not to gamble. Whether we've got millions of dollars at stake or just a couple thousand, marketing research can help us minimize risk. Knowing what kind of research is appropriate for the job at hand, we can hire a research service, confident that we've taken the first steps toward action—without charging off in the wrong direction.

Source: Marketing Tools (May 1995).

*F*ast *orward to the Real World*

That's a Good Question

Lynn M. Newman

If you have ever sent what you thought was a "final" questionnaire to a marketing research supplier, only to have it returned to you full of wording changes, deletions, and other editorial comments, you're not alone. Writing a questionnaire does not, at first glance, appear to be a very difficult task: Just figure out what you want to know, and write questions to obtain that information. But although writing questions is easy, writing *good* questions is not.

Typically there are three areas that researchers must consider when writing questions: type of information desired, question structure, and wording.

Type of Information Desired

When you ask people questions, you are usually looking for information pertaining to four areas:

- Attitudes (feelings/views)
- Beliefs (what is true or false)
- Behavior (what do they do)
- Attributes (personal/demographic characteristics)

It is important to understand the differences among these types of information, because it is easy to inadvertently move from one type of information to another when writing and rewording questions. For example, you may start out asking people about their television viewing habits (behavior) and actually end up asking them about their feelings concerning television (attitudes). Remember, a change in wording can trigger a complete turnabout in the kind of information you collect.

Question Structure

Questions can be asked as:

- Open-ended (respondents create their own answers);
- Close-ended questions with a gradation or ordering of responses (respondents pick a response on the continuum);

(Continued)

(Continued)

- Close-ended questions with unordered responses (respondents choose from discrete, unordered responses); or
- Partially closed-ended questions (answer choices are provided, but respondents can add their own).

No one question structure is best. The proper structure depends largely on how the researcher wishes to use the responses.

Wording of Questions

The third area of consideration, and the focus of this article, is the wording of questions. Here are some dos and don'ts when writing questions.

1. **Avoid abbreviations, slang, or uncommon words** that your audience might not understand. For example: *What is your opinion of PPOs?* It is quite possible that everyone does not know that PPO stands for Preferred Provider Organization. If the question targets the general public, the researcher might run into problems. On the other hand, if the question is for physicians or hospital administrators, then the acronym PPO is probably acceptable.

2. **Be specific.** The problem with vague questions is that they generate vague answers. For example: *What is your household income?* As respondents come up with numerous interpretations to this question, they will give all kinds of answers—1994 income before taxes, 1994 income after taxes, 1995 income before taxes, 1995 income after taxes, etc.

   Another example: *How often did you attend sporting events during the past year? (1) Never, (2) Rarely, (3) Occasionally, (4) Regularly.* Again, this question is open for interpretation. People will interpret "sporting event" and the answer list differently—does "regularly" mean weekly, monthly, or what?

3. **On the other hand, don't overdo it.** When questions are too precise, people cannot answer them. They will either refuse or guess. For example: *How many books did you read in 1994?* You need to give them some ranges: *(1) None, (2) 1–10, (3) 11–25, (4) 26–50, (5) More than 50.*

4. **Make sure your questions are easy to answer.** Questions that are too demanding will also lead to refusals or guesses. For example: Please rank the following 20 items in order of importance to you when you are shopping for a new car. You're asking respondents to do a fair amount of calculating. Don't ask people to rank 20 items; have them pick the top 5.

(Continued)

(Continued)

5. **Don't assume too much.** This is a fairly common error, in which the question-writer infers something about people's knowledge, attitudes, or behavior. For example: *Do you tend to agree or disagree with the President's position on gun control?* This question assumes that the respondent is aware that the President has a position on gun control and knows what that position is.

   To avoid this error, the writer must be prepared to do some educating. For example: "The President has recently stated his position on gun control. Are you aware that he has taken a stand on this issue?" If the answer is yes, then continue with: "Please describe in your own words what you understand his position on gun control to be." And, finally: "Do you tend to agree or disagree with his stand?"

6. **Watch out for double questions and questions with double negatives.** Combining questions or using a double negative leads to ambiguous questions and answers. For example: "Do you favor the legalization of marijuana for use in private homes but not in public places?" If this question precisely describes the respondent's position, then a "yes" answer is easily interpreted. But a "no" could mean the respondent favors use in public places but not in private homes, or opposes both, or favors both.

   Similarly, here is an example of a question with a double negative: "Should the police chief not be directly responsible to the mayor?" The question is ambiguous; almost any answer will be even more so.

7. **Check for bias.** A biased question can influence people to respond in a manner that does not accurately reflect their positions. There are several ways in which questions can be prejudiced. One is to imply that respondents *should* have engaged in a certain behavior. For example: "The movie, *The Lion King,* was seen by more people than any other movie this year. Have you seen this movie?" So as not to appear "different," respondents may say yes even though they haven't seen the movie. The question should be: "Have you ever seen the movie *The Lion King?*"

   Another way to bias a question is to have unbalanced answer choices. For example: "Currently our country spends XX billion dollars a year on foreign aid. Do you feel this amount should be (1) Increased, (2) Stay the same, (3) Decreased a little, (4) Decreased somewhat, (5) Decreased a great deal?" This set of responses encourages respondents to select a "decrease" option, since there are three of these and only one increase option.

(Continued)

(Continued)

Pretesting: The Survey Before the Survey

All the rewriting and editing in the world won't guarantee success. However, pretesting is the least expensive way to make sure your questionnaire research project is a success. The primary purpose of a pretest is to make certain that the questionnaire gives the respondent clear, understandable questions that will evoke clear, understandable answers. Pretesting will also help:

- Uncover question sequence problems
- Locate areas where respondents may terminate
- Eliminate and/or add questions
- Determine any recording difficulties
- Refine closed-end categories
- Time the length of the interview
- Improve wording
- Determine clarity of each issue
- Convert open-ends to checklists, if possible

Remember that you are writing for a particular audience and purpose, and for placement next to other questions. As you prepare a questionnaire, fill in the blanks to the five simple questions below:

1) Have you asked the right question?

What do you want to know?

How will you use the answer?

2) Are respondents going to understand the question?

3) Are respondents going to know the answer?

4) Are respondents willing and able to answer?

5) What do the answers mean?

Answering these questions will help ensure that your final draft is indeed final.

Source: Marketing Tools (June 1996).

Fast Forward to the Real World

Understanding Your Customers

Amanda Prus and D. Randall Brandt, Ph.D.

The idea that loyal customers are especially valuable is nothing new to today's business managers. Loyal customers repeatedly purchase products or services. They recommend a company to others. And they stick with a business over time. Loyal customers are worth the special effort it may take to keep them. But how can you provide that special treatment if you don't know your customers and how their loyalty is won—and lost?

Understanding loyalty—what makes your customers loyal and how to measure and understand loyal customers—enables your company to improve customer-driven quality. A customer loyalty index provides management with an easily understood tool that helps focus the organization toward improving satisfaction and retention, for a positive impact on the bottom line.

What Customer Loyalty Is—and Isn't

To better understand the concept of customer loyalty, let's first define what customer loyalty is *not*.

Customer loyalty is *not* customer satisfaction. Satisfaction is a necessary component of loyal or secure customers. However, the mere quality of being satisfied with a company does not necessarily make customers loyal. Just because customers are satisfied with your company today does not mean they will continue to do business with you in the future.

Customer loyalty is *not* a response to trial offers or incentives. If customers suddenly begin buying your product or service, it may be the result of a special offer or incentive and not necessarily a reflection of customer loyalty. These same customers may be just as quick to respond to your competitors' incentives.

Customer loyalty is *not* strong market share. Many businesses mistakenly look at their sales numbers and market share and think, "Those numbers are surrogates for direct measures of customer loyalty. After all, we wouldn't be enjoying high levels of market share if our cus-

(Continued)

(Continued)

tomers didn't love us." However, this may not be true. Many other factors can drive up market share, including poor performance by competitors or pricing issues. And high share doesn't mean low churn (the rate at which existing customers leave you—possibly to patronize your competition—and are replaced by new customers).

Customer loyalty is *not* repeat buying or habitual buying. Many repeat customers may be choosing your products or services because of convenience or habit. However, if they learn about a competitive product that they think may be less expensive or better quality, they may quickly switch to that product. Habitual buyers can defect; loyal customers usually don't.

Now that we know what does *not* constitute customer loyalty, we can talk about what does. Customer loyalty is a composite of a number of qualities. It is driven by customer satisfaction, yet it also involves a commitment on the part of the customer to make a sustained investment in an ongoing relationship with a brand or company. Finally, customer loyalty is reflected by a combination of attitudes and behaviors. These attitudes include:

- The intention to buy again and/or buy additional products or services from the same company.
- A willingness to recommend the company to others.
- A commitment to the company demonstrated by a resistance to switching to a competitor.

Customer behaviors that reflect loyalty include:

- Repeat purchasing of products or services.
- Purchasing more and different products or services from the same company.
- Recommending the company to others.

Any one of these attitudes or behaviors in isolation does not necessarily indicate loyal customers. However, by recognizing how these indicators work together in a measurement system, we can derive an index of customer loyalty, or in a broader sense, customer *security*.

Measuring Customer Loyalty

At Burke Customer Satisfaction Associates, we have developed a Secure Customer Index (SCI) using three major components to measure customer loyalty: overall customer satisfaction, likelihood of repeat busi-

(Continued)

(Continued)

ness, and likelihood to recommend the company to others. Other elements may be included in the index depending upon the industry. However, in our experience, these three components are the core of a meaningful customer loyalty index.

We measure these components by looking at the combined scores of three survey questions. For example, in examining the overall or global satisfaction of restaurant customers, we may ask, "Overall, how satisfied were you with your visit to this restaurant?" To examine their likelihood to recommend: "How likely would you be to recommend this restaurant to a friend or associate?" And finally, to examine the likelihood of repeat purchases, we'd ask, "How likely are you to choose to visit this restaurant again?"

Using these three components, with the appropriate scales for each, secure customers would be defined as those giving the most positive responses across *all three components*. All other customers would be considered vulnerable or at risk of defecting to a competitor. The degrees of vulnerability or risk also can be determined from responses to these questions.

When we interpret a company's SCI, we typically compare it to other relevant SCI scores, such as the company's SCI score in past years, the SCI scores of competitors, and the SCI scores of "best-in-class" companies. While a company should always strive for higher scores, understanding how "good" or "bad" a given score might be is best done in comparative terms.

Customer Loyalty and Market Performance

Increasingly, we are able to link customer satisfaction and customer loyalty to bottom-line benefits. By examining customer behaviors over time and comparing them to SCI scores, we see a strong connection between secure customers and repeat purchasing of products or services.

For example, we examined the relationship between customer satisfaction survey data and repeat purchasing levels in the computer industry. Secure customers in this industry were *twice* as likely to renew contracts than were vulnerable customers. Secure customers also were twice as likely as vulnerable customers to expand their business with their primary vendor.

As we've continued to look at cases across customer and industry types, we've found other compelling illustrations that show a connection

(Continued)

(Continued)

between the index scores and financial or market performance. These findings demonstrate the value of examining index scores not only across an industry but also over time within the same company to determine changes within the proportion of secure customers.

Competition, Customers, and Surveys

As with any measurement, a customer loyalty index may be influenced by additional factors depending on the industry, market characteristics, customer characteristics, or research methods. These factors should be considered when interpreting the meaning of any loyalty index.

Industries with more than one provider of services tend to produce higher customer satisfaction scores than industries with limited choices. For example, the cable television industry, which in many markets still tends to be monopolistic, generally has lower customer satisfaction scores in comparison to other industries. The notion that competition breeds more opportunities clearly affects customer satisfaction as well.

A second factor that may contribute indirectly to a customer loyalty index score is the type of market being examined. In specialty markets where the product is tailored or customized for the customer, loyalty index scores tend to be higher than general or noncustomized markets. For example, index scores for customers of a specialized software or network configuration would likely be higher than scores for customers of an airline.

The type of customers being measured also may influence the index scores. For example, business-to-business customers may score differently than general consumers. Again, the type of industry involved also will influence the type of customers being examined.

Finally, the data collection method may influence the customer's response. Researchers have long recognized that the different methods used to collect information, such as live interviews, mail surveys, and telephone interviews, may produce varying results.

Recognizing these factors is important not only in collecting information but also in interpreting an index. Learning how to minimize or correct these influences will enhance the validity or true "reading" of a customer loyalty index.

Using Data to Evaluate Your Own Efforts

Businesses committed to customer-driven quality must integrate the voice of the customer into their business operations. A customer loyalty

(Continued)

(Continued)

index provides actionable information by demonstrating the ratio of secure customers to vulnerable customers. An index acts as a baseline or yardstick for management to create goals for the organization, and helps to focus efforts for continuous improvement over time. And as changes and initiatives are implemented in the organization, the index's score may be monitored as a way of evaluating initiatives.

Using a customer loyalty index helps companies better understand their customers. By listening to customers, implementing change, and continuously monitoring the results, companies can focus their improvement efforts with the goal of winning and keeping customers.

Source: Marketing Tools (July/August 1995).

*F*ast *F*orward to the Real World

The Sales Behind the Scowl

Gary Hren

Can a customer who complains be your best customer? That might be difficult to believe when an irate customer yells at a service rep, or when you get a nasty letter about a product or service. Even though these dissatisfied customers appear to be nothing but trouble, they may be your company's most valuable asset.

A recent national study of 1,179 department store shoppers conducted by Burke CSA revealed that the customer most likely to complain also may be one of the store's most loyal patrons. Moreover, the complainers also are those most likely to expect that their problems with a department store will be resolved to their satisfaction.

Understanding how to capture and then use information provided by concerned customers can help a company improve its service. Equally important, service recovery—the ability to respond quickly to problems by improving overall processes and systems—is directly correlated with the overall satisfaction and loyalty of a company's customers.

Capitalizing on Customer Concerns

By capturing customer feedback, responding to complaints, and recognizing the value of customer feedback, companies can capitalize on complaining customers and improve their overall customer satisfaction level. Understanding several principles can help companies capitalize on customer concerns:

1. **Recognize that your customers are a rich source of information.** There is significant value in each person's concern, however loudly that person may complain. It is important to treat a complainer as a source of information—not as a disgruntled loudmouth you wish would go away. All personnel should receive training on uncovering the true source of a problem and getting as many specifics as possible, while showing the customer that feedback, even if negative, is still very valuable to the company.

(Continued)

(Continued)

2. **Make sure customers complain to your company, not to other customers.** Dissatisfied customers are more likely to speak poorly of a company than satisfied customers are to speak highly of a company. Burke has found that customers whose problems are resolved to their satisfaction will tell approximately 5 to 8 people about their positive experience; those whose problems were not satisfactorily resolved will tell approximately 10 to 16 people about the negative experience. Those with complaints need a vehicle to voice their concerns to the company. If they do not have that opportunity, they will stop using the company's services or products, and/or they will tell others about their problems, making more people skeptical about the company. Even companies with limited resources can offer a simple complaint collection method, such as comment cards or publicizing a store manager's phone number, to listen to and evaluate customer complaints.

3. **Treat each complaint genuinely.** Beyond creating a system to collect feedback, a company must treat each customer who responds in a positive manner, regardless of the complaint. For example, I recently visited a restaurant with friends where I was unhappy with the quality of the food and the service. When the manager asked how we were enjoying our meal, I told him my honest impressions. He responded with what he felt to be an appropriate solution—to pay for our meal. However, his sarcasm and insincerity made me realize he couldn't care less that we were dissatisfied. And because of his response, not only do I no longer dine there, but I have told numerous friends of my experience.

4. **Recognize that many customers want to give you a second chance.** Customers with concerns offer companies an opportunity to "do it right the second time." The Burke study of department-store customers revealed that three-fourths of the respondents either definitely or probably would report a problem directly to store management. Of these potential complainers, three-fourths expected that they would reach satisfactory resolution with the store. Significantly, those who said they would complain were more likely to be the most frequent shoppers—54 percent of those who shop every two to three weeks versus only 45 percent of those who shop once or twice a year.

Creating a Feedback System

How can a company capture this information to improve on customer concerns and avoid "second" or even "third chance" situations? One way

(Continued)

(Continued)

is to develop an easy-to-use feedback system that credits the customer for providing information and gives your company enough information to solve problems.

Creating a system that allows both the customers to share concerns and the company to pro-actively seek feedback is best. Regardless of a company's size or customer satisfaction research resources, one of the most important rules to remember is to establish as many "listening posts," or feedback collection sites, as possible to gather a complete perspective of customer satisfaction.

For example, one of Burke CSA's clients, a delivery service company, has developed a method to capture concerns that includes collection through account executives, drivers, a telephone center, and a help manager whose specific job is to assist the customers. The combination of data allows the company to assess the true problems faced by customers. This is important because it helps companies prioritize "real" problems and target key areas for improvement, versus company-wide changes to what may have been a one-time problem.

Several types of systems can be combined to provide a more complete picture of your customers' satisfaction. These range from a simple qualitative "log" of customer complaints to an in-depth qualitative survey. Some examples of feedback systems include:

- **Front-line collection.** The people in the company closest to the customers naturally receive the most customer feedback. A system can be created whereby field representatives, salespeople, account executives, and the like can easily pass information along to others in the company.

- **In-bound customer lines.** In-bound feedback can be achieved through 1-800-numbers established for customer response. Consumer products companies often use this method, printing toll-free numbers on their product packages. Customers speak with service representatives who log concerns, which then become part of an overall database of customer feedback.

- **Baseline surveys.** These types of surveys determine what is important to customers and how the problems they are experiencing affect their willingness to be a satisfied customer.

- **Outbound surveys.** For an outbound survey, a company lists 20 or so problems that customers have identified and asks others if they have experienced the same problems. This type of survey is completed on a regular basis to learn the ongoing incidence as

(Continued)

(Continued)

well as the impact of these problems on customer retention and loyalty.

Respond, Remedy, Remember, Review

Responding to feedback or complaints requires two steps: correcting the problem, then using the complaint information to evaluate an overall process, product, or service.

First and foremost, it is crucial that when a customer complains, the company responds. The first step must be the act of service recovery— doing what is necessary to correct the problem and please the customer. There is nothing worse than listening to a customer's complaint and then not responding. In essence, the company has asked for customer feedback and then ignored their suggestions. Studies show that the mere act of recovery, or correcting the problem to a customer's satisfaction, will make a customer more loyal.

Secondly, the company must look at the complaint in the larger context of the way the company does business. Complaint data can be overwhelming, especially when using information from several listening posts. To make sense out of the data, develop criteria to identify the true problems. One way to do this is to prioritize the data based on incidence and impact. Looking at the number and type of complaints helps determine which concerns are most important and must be addressed immediately. In other words, the company can separate the "vital few" crucial problems from the "trivial many" complaints.

Again, a company can refine the process of prioritizing incidence and impact by using more than one collection system. For example, Burke CSA looks at a company's primary data collection method, such as a survey, to begin the process. Then Burke uses another piece of data, such as in-bound calls, to check and modify its conclusions.

The delivery service company mentioned previously uses this method of collecting data from various sources and prioritizing improvements in order to respond quickly and appropriately to problems. And it works—the survey that Burke CSA completed for this client confirmed that people who have had a problem that was resolved to their satisfaction are more satisfied and loyal than those who never had a problem.

Bearing that in mind, companies that want to improve their overall customer satisfaction need to follow three important principles:

(Continued)

(Continued)

1. **Provide a vehicle for customers to voice concerns.** This may be as simple as empowering front-line personnel to take down complaints or providing comment cards in a waiting area.

2. **Recover.** Once a customer complains, it is vital that the problem is corrected to the customer's satisfaction.

3. **Use all customer feedback to evaluate processes.** Using information from several sources will provide a more complete picture of a company's strengths and weaknesses.

All businesses recognize the value of a happy customer. However, when a company steps back and looks at the information that complaining customers provide, it can see the importance of responding to complaining customers and using their information to make positive changes. Listening to all customers—including the disparaging ones—will help companies improve customer satisfaction, loyalty, and ultimately, a company's bottom-line success.

Source: Marketing Tools (March/April 1996).

Fast Forward to the Real World

Learning about Lists

Lorrie MacKain

Every company that sells products or services has a list—a roster of customers or inquirers that have had contact or done business with that company. One company might use its list to maintain contact with the people on it. Another organization may have decided that direct mail isn't a suitable marketing medium for its goods. Either way, a set of customer names and addresses is considered a mailing list, and it has real value in the list rental marketplace. Even a company that decides not to mail to its own list can allow it to be rented, or exchange it for a list compiled by another company. And unless that company is prepared to learn (and finance) a whole new set of skills, it will probably require the services of a list manager and/or list broker.

Veteran direct mailers will find this fairly elementary stuff. But the direct-marketing industry is experiencing an influx of newcomers, who bring with them a mixed bag of confusion and misunderstanding. Let us presume that a given company is using direct mail as an advertising and selling medium, has a decent-sized mailing list of customers, uses the list to up-sell and re-sell these customers, and furthermore, wants to capture ancillary income from renting the list to other direct marketers. Should the company use a list manager? A list broker? What is the difference between these two functionaries, and how do they work with their clients?

The List Manager

A list management company contracts with a client who owns a list and wants to take advantage of the revenue that renting the list can generate. A list manager's primary function is to market that list to two key groups—the list brokerage community and the direct mailer who will ultimately rent the list—and to handle all the rental arrangements on the list owner's end. Standard list management services usually include the invoicing and collecting for each and every rental transaction, and the reporting and payment of receivables due the list owner, usually on a monthly or quarterly basis. List managers should also be able to demonstrate how they will exercise fiduciary responsibility over revenue created

(Continued)

(Continued)

and aging receivables; how they will advertise the list; and, more important, how they will protect the list (and list owner) from misuse.

Let's say you have compiled a substantial list of customers, and you're interested in turning it into a revenue-producing vehicle. The first thing you should know is that every list is not a profit center waiting to be tapped. A good mailing list has certain characteristics that make it work well for other mailers.

To begin with, the source of the names is very important. The names with the highest market value are those of people who responded to a direct-mail offer ("proven responders"). Space-sourced names—people who requested more information after seeing an ad in a magazine, for example—are next in quality. Then come lists of individuals who responded to a survey and offered specific information that marked them as targets for certain offers. In nearly all cases, the list should have more than 20,000 names, and you should be able to add new ones on a continuing basis.

If you serve a very tight, vertical market, or your customer list is quite small, you needn't abandon the idea of renting it—but you probably should not seek a list management company, because it wouldn't make economic sense. Instead, you can advertise the availability of your list in the trade journals that serve the vertical marketplace targeted.

If you decide that it does make sense to hire a list manager, and you have a candidate in mind, your first task is to look at the type of trade periodicals he or she usually advertises in, and to examine the style of his or her ads. You should also approach a number of brokerage companies to make sure that the manager is promoting vigorously to all of the account executives in the firm, and that the account executives are pleased with the response time and accuracy of information flow between manager and broker. The list management company itself should submit a marketing plan that will indicate how much revenue it believes a given list can produce, and how to go about reaching those projections.

The list manager will want to become the exclusive rental agent for your list, and will charge around 10 percent of the gross revenue from rentals—probably less money than you would spend advertising, promoting, order processing, billing, collecting, and generally riding herd on the list rental business.

The List Broker

As demonstrated earlier in this article, a list can be generated from space advertising and other media, as well as through direct-mail mar-

(Continued)

(Continued)

keting. If these methods have yielded an extensive, highly responsive list, you may not need the services of a list broker. However, if your marketing plan is heavily dependent on direct mail, it is probably wise to work with at least one list broker to ensure the best results.

At the risk of oversimplifying, it's sometimes easiest to describe a list broker's role by comparing it to that of a stock broker. Good stock brokers become intimate with the needs and objectives of their customers, and the resources a given client wants to devote to a "project." At that point, a stock broker can recommend a group of stocks that the client should invest in. In preparing the recommendation, the stock broker can select from any listing on the stock exchange.

Likewise, a list broker preparing a recommendation for a client-mailer has over 20,000 lists to choose from. And much like the stock broker, the more your list expert knows about your project, the better equipped he or she will be to suggest lists that will produce successful mailings. The broker should be trusted enough to be given "inside information" about your current campaign, past projects, future projections, and just about anything pertinent to the advertising and marketing of the product or service involved. After all, the fate of the whole campaign hangs on the performance of the lists selected to be mailed.

That last thought really can't be overstated. The best product, properly priced, packaged superbly, and accompanied by copy that describes it with utmost taste and irresistibility will fail miserably as a direct-mail offer if it is sent to an unqualified or blatantly inappropriate audience. The list selection process is critical to the success (or failure) of any direct-mail project, and is probably the single most important component of the campaign.

There are a number of ways to "rate" a list broker according to that individual's or company's expertise. Here are a few of the attributes to look for when choosing a list broker:

- A great deal of knowledge and experience in the categorical product group being marketed;

- Working knowledge of your competition and the impact your competition might have on the project at hand;

- Good negotiating skills and an understanding of your future plans, so the best possible terms can be agreed on for continuations;

- A very competent support staff, who will be readily available to ensure good tracking and smooth overall production and delivery of lists;

- An ability to provide in-depth information regarding lists, including their makeup, future growth, and other facets that have even the

(Continued)

(Continued)

smallest bearing on their performance. Who has used the lists being recommended? Which of these mailer-users have come back to re-use the lists?

To summarize, the list manager contracts with list owners to become their list rental agent. The manager sells to the brokerage community and occasionally directly to the mailer-user. The list broker serves the mailer-user, ferreting out lists that will hit the desired target audience and produce high response rates, and thus profitable mailing campaigns.

Deciding whether or not to use a list broker is a much simpler matter than deciding whether to hire a list manager. To begin with, a broker's services don't cost you a cent—brokers make their money by being commissioned by the list owner (usually through a list manager) for recommending and ultimately ordering the list on your behalf. The broker's responsibility is to devise a list schedule, arrange testing of untried lists, negotiate best "deals" with the list manager, order lists, track the on-time and accurate delivery of the lists, and, after the mailing, help you analyze response and profitability.

Choosing a broker (or brokers) depends on individual circumstances. Brokers tend to become product- or niche-oriented. For instance, one type of broker may specialize in lists for sweepstakes-driven offers. The marketing department at American Family Publishers (Ed McMahon, et al.) would seek out brokers who had a lot of experience with lists that had been proven winners for sweeps marketers. Women's apparel catalogs, computer magazines, book clubs, general merchandise catalogs, business-to-business marketers—all of these categories, and many more, are served by brokers with specific experience and knowledge in their respective fields.

Earlier, we recounted many of the basic qualifications that a broker must have to thrive in this very competitive market. Finding someone who meets these criteria should be fairly simple. Finding someone who meets your specific needs may be another matter. Bear in mind that brokers do work on commission. If your plan calls for the mailing of 10,000 names a year, you probably won't get a ton of service from a prominent list broker.

The list business is rather complex, but it can serve its many constituencies well. The list owner can receive substantial revenue through renting the list to outside users; the list manager profits by successfully marketing the list; the list broker prospers by having mailer-clients trust in his or her judgment and ability to provide the services required; the mailer wins by having qualified brokers guide a campaign toward the desired target audience. The mailer's success in turn brings together new direct-mail-sold names and addresses, creating new lists—and the cycle starts all over again.

Source: Marketing Tools (June 1996).

CHAPTER 6

Action Marketing

Managers divide markets into segments in order to meet more directly the needs of their customers. This is basically the definition of *target marketing*. Whether most markets will be divided as completely as the one-to-one gurus contend remains to be seen, but the computer's power to supply more customer information in greater detail will clearly increase in the near future. Clearly, too, the broad lines of division we've already discussed—demographic, geographic, and psychographic—will themselves be subdivided again and again. It is an exaggeration to say that marketers can know everything about their customers' buying habits, but it's not beyond the realm of possibility. In this section we will explore the ways marketers divide and subdivide their markets in order to steer their products more directly into their customers' hands.

AGGREGATION

Before we begin slicing it, let's look at the whole pie. Henry Ford's oft-quoted statement that Model T drivers "can have any color they want as long as it's black" carries a couple of implications about his product and his market. Though the Tin Lizzie was not literally alone in the market, Ford's revolutionary production methods had made his automobile, and his alone, accessible to the mass market, to the average American. Producing only one color was one among many means of cost cutting that made this possible. Also, the automobile itself was enough of a novelty that its buyers didn't care about color or style.

In today's parlance, Ford saw his customers as an aggregation. Under this approach (also known as *undifferentiated marketing*), the market is not divided into segments, but taken as a whole, and a single marketing program can be used to sell the product to all customers. By definition, market aggregation will not please every customer, but it will please enough of them.

However, technological change fuels change in other areas, and even Henry Ford was not impervious to it. Other producers, notably Chevrolet, copied his assembly-line method and before long were able to offer competitively priced automobiles of equal quality in more modern styles—and colors. This development, historians relate, led to titanic battles between Henry and his son Edsel.

Edsel argued that Ford Motor Company would steadily lose market share to Chevrolet and others if it didn't respond to the competition. But since Henry had had the market to himself—except for a sliver of the population for whom price was no object—he refused even to recognize the existence of market share. But time and technology proved Edsel correct. Market aggregation was no longer applicable for the simple reason that the market had ceased to be a single mass. Obviously, in today's auto industry, no producer would dream of aggregating the market.

This is not to say, however, that market aggregation is obsolete today. Consider such items as sewing needles, rubber bands, and paper clips—customers perceive little difference between one producer and another. And where it is applicable, aggregation is cost-efficient, since only one product is produced and only one marketing plan is necessary to sell it. However, no one today owns an aggregate market free of competition.

Since market aggregation cannot please all customers, producers are vulnerable to competition. To combat their vulnerability, "aggregationists" seek to establish the perception that theirs is superior to the competitors' product, often whether it is or not. To so position their product requires heavy promotion, and the risk to the producer is significant because heavy promotion obviates one of the advantages of aggregation, namely, simplified promotion strategy. The rewards of succeeding are also great—if the marketer can capture a large enough chunk of the total market.

Xerox did so for a time, when it was the only game in town, and as we've said, its precipitous decline in market share resulted from its tacit assumption that its customers would remain an aggregate. As a more precise example of market aggregation, consider laundry bleach. Chemically, bleach is pretty much bleach, one brand the same as the next. However, "Clorox" and "bleach" are almost synonymous, just as "Xerox" and "to copy" were synonymous. Clorox, more expensive than the adjacent brand on the supermarket shelf, owns the lion's share of the market because its producer has spent big money on promotion to separate its brand name from those of its competitors.

If aggregation lies at one end of the spectrum and one-to-one marketing lies at the other, there is in the real world a lot of room between the two into which fall strategies such as *segmentation, targeting,* and *positioning.*

SEGMENTATION

As the word suggests, segmentation strategies break the aggregate market into smaller, in some ways homogeneous, parts, with the aim to match and market your product to those customers most likely to want it.

Though single-product producers use segmentation strategies, they are most applicable to multiproduct producers. Segmentation is more costly than aggregation for the multiline producer who makes different products for different segments, because the strategy sacrifices some of the cost savings of mass production. Furthermore, the producer must spend money for research that will tell it how best to segment its market. Sometimes sales to one segment will cut into sales for another segment.

Some time ago, Arizona Company began bottling iced tea. First it was generic iced tea; then Arizona began to expand its line by adding various flavors. Most recently, Arizona added green tea with ginseng, and at this writing it is promoting the green tea through billboard-style advertising. Even if Arizona used the same bottle and cap for all the teas in its line, it still had to produce separate labels (they are all elaborately designed) for each new flavor, and a certain amount of money had to be allocated for advertising and promotion. Say, however, that you are a loyal Arizona tea customer who discovered and liked the original generic tea but then switched to its green tea. If enough customers make that switch, sales of the original product will suffer. What is Arizona to do? Should it drop the less profitable lines, thereby incurring losses on research and packaging?

TO SEGMENT OR NOT TO SEGMENT?

Segmentation, remember, is a strategy that must be actively implemented. Managers *decide* to implement it. Managers might, of course, decide not to implement the strategy because of increased costs or for other sound business reasons. As we mentioned earlier, if you make rubber bands or paper clips, there isn't much point in implementing expensive segmentation. If you are an independent construction contractor, you might try to serve the entire local market if it is small, but you might, in areas where building is more active, want to tailor your work, say, to the carriage trade, who want their kitchens meticulously remodeled to the highest standards. In that case, you might turn down a job to build a storage shed for a small farmer.

But what general criteria do you use to decide whether or not to segment, regardless of the market you serve? To answer that broad question, marketing pundits suggest that you ask yourself the following five questions:

1. *Can the market be identified and measured?* The story of marketing is filled with examples of intuitive successes. "You could never produce the Mazda Miata solely from marketing research," states Peter Senge. "It required a leap of imagination to see what the customer *might* want."[1] As a rule, however, intuition should not be the driving impulse behind your decision to segment. You should be able to identify a group of potential customers with shared characteristics. Remember, information is not in short supply today.

2. *Is the segment large enough to be profitable?* If segmentation strategies were free of costs to the producer, you might well go ahead and give it a try, but of course they are not free. The potential sales volume must be large enough to make the expenditure feasible. Coecles Harbor Marine in Shelter Island, New York, has begun producing a large (38-foot) motorboat intended for day trips. It costs something in the neighborhood of a quarter of a million dollars. The segment of the boating market ready to pay that kind of money for a limited-purpose boat is minuscule. However, its producers need to sell only several boats a year to turn a profit. The producers might have elected to offer a less pricey boat, but they concluded that other segments of the market were heavy with competition, so they decided to sell fewer units to a tiny but high-end wedge of the motorboat market.

3. *Is the market reachable?* To be successful, segmentation requires communication between sellers and buyers; in other words, some form of promotion. For example, Hiam and Schewe point to inexpensive digital watches. How do you talk to the customers for such a product if they don't read the same magazines, belong to the same organizations, or otherwise share some characteristic—other than wanting to know what time it is without having to buy a Rolex? In this case, some form of direct marketing might be the ticket.

If you make goggle-style eyeglasses for near-sighted people who play contact sports, you might be able to communicate with your customers via subscription lists to magazines about contact sports or, less directly, you might choose to advertise in those magazines.

4. *Is the segment responsive?* Again, this is a matter of measuring cost against potential return. Chances are, if you can identify and measure your segment, you will have some idea whether or not you can expect it to buy your product.

5. *Is the market stable?* Developing a marketing plan not only takes money, it takes time. Long, baggy shorts are popular—at this writing—among teenage boys. Marketing clothes for this segment is a tricky business, because unpredictable trends and fads sweep the market. Long, baggy shorts, for instance, were adapted from styles favored by skateboarders. Today, the simultaneity and pervasiveness of mass culture cause fads to develop and pass very quickly. Other markets are more stable, but they all change, and the lead time necessary to develop a marketing plan must always be considered in the strategy.

BASES FOR SEGMENTATION

Sometimes marketers pull creative, original ideas out of the hatful of variables, but traditionally markets get segmented along the lines of the variables we spoke of in Chapter 5, such as sex, age, marital status, race, and family, and these are commonly called *demographic variables. Socioeconomic variables* such as occupation, income, and education also affect buying behavior and so make reasonable market segments. Some marketing texts refer to these as *descriptive variables.* However we categorize them, these variables are useful to the marketer because they can be measured.

The traditional divisions of labor within the family are preindustrial—perhaps prehistoric—in origin: The husband left home to perform some heavy labor while the wife maintained the home, and the children helped out as their ages allowed. While this broad profile still predominates, its edges have splintered. Women work outside the home, and they buy cars and homes; men shop and care for children; single-parent households have proliferated, and so have same-sex couples living as a family, with or without children. These changes affect buying behavior, and they can all be tracked through demographic information sources.

Here are two examples of how changing gender roles can impact marketing. Recreational running changed the shoe market radically. At the outset of the jogging craze, men led the way, and shoemakers expanded their lines of running shoes for men. After a while, sales flattened, so marketers directed their efforts toward women, adapting shoe-style shapes and sizes to fit them.

Similarly, Williams-Sonoma, marketers of cookware by mail order, recognized that 15 percent of its customers were men. The company bought mailing lists from men's magazines, such as *GQ* and *Esquire*, that fit its profile.

Geographic variables can also influence your marketing approach. This is a big country, and people differ from region to region. For example, New Englanders annually eat more ice cream, 23.1 quarts per capita, than people in other regions. The 33 percent of the population that live in the South account for 48 percent of the nation's tea consumption and 21 percent of the wine consumption. The 22 percent of the population that live in New England drink 19 percent of the tea and 30 percent of the wine.[2]

Thomas Moore, in his article "Different Folks, Different Strokes,"[3] points out that S. C. Johnson, makers of Raid pesticides, markets a roach killer in urban areas and a flea killer in the Southeast. "Since the program began last year, Raid has increased its market share in 16 of 18 regions and its overall piece of the $450 million-a-year U.S. insecticide market by five percentage points."

BEHAVIORAL BASES FOR SEGMENTATION

Though somewhat harder to measure than descriptive variables, behavioral variables "determine," whereas descriptive variables merely "qualify." In other words, just because a consumer is a member of a particular group doesn't mean he or she will behave according to the characteristics of that group by buying the same things other members buy. Personal watercraft (Jet Skis and the like) constitute the fastest-growing segment of the boating market. Young, single men are the most common consumers of personal watercraft, but that doesn't mean the majority of young, single men will buy one.

User status is used by marketers to distinguish types of behavioral buyers. There are nonusers, ex-users, and first-time users, and each requires a different kind of marketing strategy. User status involves identifying heavy users and light users in forming a marketing plan. Here the so-called 80-20 principle comes into play. Twenty percent of the market accounts for 80 percent of sales. The 80-20 principle is not universal, but it is particularly useful to marketers because the heavy users are easy to identify by using such means as credit-card slips and syndicated services.

Benefit segmentation concentrates on the primary benefit the consumer seeks, the assumption being that

EXAMPLES OF PRODUCT USAGE SEGMENTATION

Product	Light Half 1962[a]	Light Half 1982[b]	Heavy Half 1962[a]	Heavy Half 1982[b]	Nonusers 1962[a]	Nonusers 1982[b]
Soaps and detergents	19%	25%	80%	75%	2%	6%
Toilet tissue	26	29	74	71	2	5
Shampoo	19	21	81	79	18	6
Paper towels	17	25	83	75	34	10
Margarine	17	23	83	77	11	12
RTE cereals	13	20	87	80	4	14
Cake mixes	15	17	85	83	27	26
Frozen orange juice	11	16	89	84	28	32
Sausage	16	18	84	82	3	31
Cola	10	17	90	83	22	33
Hair fixative	12	19	88	81	54	47
Beer	12	13	88	87	67	59
Lemon and lime drink	9	13	91	87	42	61
Dog food	13	19	87	81	67	70
Hair tonic	13	25	87	75	52	78
Bourbon	11	5	89	95	59	80

[a]Chicago Tribune Panel Data.
[b]Simmons Study of Media and Markets.
Source: Victor J. Cook, Jr., and William A. Mindak, "A Search for Constants: The 'Heavy User' Revisited!" Journal of Consumer Marketing, 1, spring 1984, p. 80.

benefit differences are the most basic explanation for the existence of market segments.

Lifestyle segmentation, sometimes called *psychographic segmentation,* seeks to categorize consumers on the basis of their *activities, interests,* and *opinions.* Joseph T. Plummer, in his January 1974 article "The Concept and Application of Lifestyle Segmentation" for *Journal of Marketing,* breaks down the three categories as follows:

1. *Activities:* Work, hobbies, vacations, entertainment, membership, shopping, sports

2. *Interests:* Family, home, job, community, recreation, fashion, food, media, achievements

3. *Opinions:* Themselves, social issues, politics, business, economics, education, products, future, culture

KEY CONCEPT Segmentation divides the market into distinct groups with different needs, behavior, or other characteristics that might need separate marketing approaches. Segmentation increases costs to the producer, but "aims" the product directly at those most likely to buy it.

SEGMENTATION AS A PROCESS

Conventional marketing wisdom holds that there are five steps in the segmentation process:

1. *Determine the market.* The benefits to the consumers usually determine the marketing methods and mix.

2. *Set segmentation variables.* As we've said, the purpose of fixing variables is to identify the unfulfilled wants and needs of a particular group and then plan how to meet those needs.

3. *Profile the segment.* Most marketers begin with demographic and geographic variables, then narrow these to demonstrable buyer behavior.

4. *Target the segment.* Here the marketer must determine the best fit between the company's resources and capabilities, its competition in the market, and the size of the segment toward which it will market the product. The largest segment doesn't always offer the best opportunity, because it is often already well served. Here a certain amount of creativity can be mated with market research to find a neglected segment or one in which competition is weak or unsatisfying to the customer.

5. *Design a marketing plan.* This final step is the plan of action by which customer needs will be satisfied. It is based on the input discussed in items 1 through 4.

MARKET TARGETING

The lines between *segmentation, targeting,* and *positioning* as a matter of definition tend to blur because targeting and positioning can be seen as part of the segmentation process. But let's make the distinction on this broad basis: Segmentation identifies the slice of the market the producer might address; targeting actively addresses the consumer needs of that segment.

Targeting is sometimes referred to as *niche marketing* or *micromarketing.* Arm & Hammer is far and away the best-known producer of baking soda, and for over a century it has dominated the market. Most people in this country would be able to identify the yellow box and the logo—the arm with the bulging bicep wielding a weighty sledgehammer—even if the brand name were removed from the label.

For decades, Church & Dwight, the producers of Arm & Hammer, sold their product—sodium bicarbonate—to everyone from bakers to fire-extinguisher manufacturers. But by the early 1970s, Church & Dwight targeted the growing segment of environmentally conscious consumers by offering a laundry detergent free of phosphates. It now accounts for about 33 percent of the company's sales. Church & Dwight then coupled this shrewd piece of marketing with a toothpaste and a household cleaner directed toward the same general segment.

Few companies have such a versatile product and huge brand-name awareness, but that doesn't detract from the creative targeting by Church & Dwight marketers. Constantly searching for new niche markets, the company produced spin-off products, including a feed supplement for dairy cows, an environmentally friendly blasting material to replace the dangerous use of sand for removing paint and grime, and an industrial cleanser called Armakleen that does the job without chlorofluorocarbons. And if you peer into the reaches of almost any American refrigerator, you'll find an open box of Arm & Hammer baking soda used as a safe, neutral deodorizer.[4]

PRODUCT POSITIONING

Positioning veers into the region of promotion in that it relates to the consumer's perception of a product, but perception is not precisely the same as image. Product positioning seeks to establish a reference point in relation to the competition. Marketers attempt to simplify a product through positioning. Volvos are safe. Avis tries harder because it's number two. One shampoo builds body, another fights grease. Coke is *it*.

Often a product is positioned on the basis of its *attributes* or *features*. One beer has "full body," another is "low in calories." American Express emphasizes its prestige, while VISA stresses the number of outlets that accept it. BMW bills itself as "the ultimate driving machine." Ford says "Quality Is Job One."

A product may be positioned around the *benefits* to the consumer. Remember the beer ad built around the argument "less filling" versus "tastes great!" Diet soft drinks proliferated on the basis of benefit to the customer.

The relationship between *price* and *quality* is another way strategically to position your product. High price signals quality. Rolex watches, BMWs, and Hinkley sailboats are perceived as high-quality products. They promote themselves as such, and people buy them not only because they are excellent but because they project a certain image. Thus it would be unwise for Rolex to market a cheap digital watch; to do so would blur its position in the market.

Specific use is another way to position a product. Few athletic-shoe manufacturers make only one kind of shoe (i.e., baseball or soccer), but they position products within their lines in relation to specific sports. Gatorade is positioned specifically as a beverage to replace electrolytes for active athletes; few people drink

Gatorade, say, with lunch as they would Coke or Pepsi. To market Gatorade as a general-use beverage would dilute its position.

When *positioning* a product *against its competitor,* marketers must make direct reference to that competitor. A clear example of this is Avis's "We're number two. We try harder." When an auto manufacturer says that its vehicle offers all the same qualities as a Mercedes for $20,000 less, it is positioning its car against the competitor.

Some marketers try to position their products *in relation to other kinds of products.* Makers of certain kinds of health foods such as granola try to position their products so as to compete with other kinds of cookies and snack foods by contending that granola bars taste as good as those others but that they have the added advantage of being better for you.

STEPS TOWARD DEVELOPING A POSITIONING STRATEGY

Like so much of marketing today, positioning, whether for a new product or the repositioning of an old one, is dependent on market research. That said, there are seven steps for identifying an appropriate market position:

1. *Determine the market.*   As we've said, a product satisfies a customer's want or need, but some products satisfy more than one want or need. Therefore, step 1 is to determine just which wants or needs your product might satisfy.

2. *Identify the competition.*   It is important to identify both primary and secondary competitors. Take so-called designer water, such as Perrier, Evian, or Poland Springs. If you are in the business of bottling water, your primary competitors are other water bottlers. But you will also have secondary competitors, those whose products speak to the same core benefit—in this case, to satisfy thirst These competitors would be producers of soft drinks, fruit juice, even Gatorade and other "sports drinks."

3. *Determine how consumers evaluate options.*   Here research comes to the fore. You must understand what customers look for in a product. To continue the beverage example, are health concerns primary or are customers interested in sweet drinks? The answers will affect your positioning moves.

4. *Learn how customers perceive your competitors.* Related to step 3, this step determines to some extent where not to position your product. There is little point in positioning a product in an area already rich in competition.

Southwest, the Story of an Airline That Knows Its Place— and Loves It

The year 1992 was a dark one for the U.S. airline industry, with losses totaling $3 billion. Southwest Airlines, however, made $91 million in 1992. How did that happen? To paraphrase that adage about restaurants: positioning, positioning, positioning.

Southwest is exclusively a short-haul, no-frills carrier; its average flight time just under one hour; average one-way fare, $58. Short-haul rates on the major carriers are notoriously high. Southwest's competitors charge $250 for a flight from Louisville to Chicago. Southwest charges $49 for a one-way trip between those two cities, and when Southwest scheduled that flight, passenger traffic increased from 8,000 a week to 26,000. Southwest made it cheaper to fly between Louisville and Chicago than to drive or take a bus.

Southwest calls itself the "love" airline—it was founded, in 1972, at Love Field in Dallas, Texas. Its customers return the feeling. In 1992 and 1993, Southwest rated first in customer satisfaction over all the other carriers in the country. The Department of Transportation concurred, awarding Southwest the coveted Triple Crown for best on-time service, best baggage handling, and best customer service.

Southwest has posted a quarter century of year-in, year-out profitability by taking routes that major carriers couldn't or wouldn't cover and by affording customers impeccable, if no-frills, service. Southwest coupled its shrewd positioning with some creative and funny promotion, making a joke of no-frills flying. During gate delays, ticket agents have offered prizes to the customers with the largest holes in their socks. Flight attendants have been known to announce, "Please pass all plastic cups to the center aisle so that we can wash them for the next group of passengers." When Northwest Airlines ran an ad claiming to be number one in customer satisfaction, Southwest responded, "After lengthy deliberation at the highest level, and extensive consultation with our legal department, we have arrived at a response to Northwest Airlines' claim to be number one in customer satisfaction. 'Liar, liar, pants on fire.' "

Short-haul passengers have for years felt ignored by the major airlines, and with good reason. Southwest positioned itself to fill those passengers' needs, and it did so with witty self-deprecation. Perhaps the "love airline" has found a recipe for success.[5]

5. *Identify gaps in positions.* Step 4 will reveal gaps in competition. It might be that competitors have missed lucrative positions you could fill. However, your research might show that there are sound reasons why no one has filled the gap. Perhaps costs are too high or the unserved customer segment is too small to prove profitable.

6. *Execute the positioning strategy.* Promotion is the crux of a positioning strategy. After you have selected your target market, you must design a promotion plan that conveys all appropriate information about your product to the determined target market. Your price must also be consistent with the product's benefits to and the characteristics of the customers you hope to win.

7. *Monitor the position.* Remember that nothing remains unchanged for long, in nature or in marketing. Therefore, you will find it in your interests to monitor developments to be sure that you've attained your intended position.

*F*ast *F*orward to the Real World

A Learning Experience

Carole Hedden

A leading mail-order business has taken an innovative approach to ensuring that every employee is part of its marketing effort. Using research, the marketing organization developed a personality for each of its five customer segments, putting a face to the myriad factoids that go into knowing each customer as a person. Every employee knows those five customer profiles intimately. When they pick up the phone to answer a call, they try to determine which of the five they are speaking with and how they can best help him or her.

Last January, *Marketing Tools* covered the rudiments of writing a marketing plan ("The Very Model of a Modern Marketing Plan"). In May, we gave more specific instructions on how to describe your business ("Build a Better Image"). This month, we'll focus on how to turn research you have already gathered into an analysis of the market and your company's position in that market—and how that information can be shared throughout your organization.

We want to stress the participatory nature of this undertaking. Information about a company's position in the market, its customers, its competition, and its goals, cannot be locked up in a filing cabinet in the executive suite. By sharing the information, you've given employees a rationale for their actions, better enabling them to act on behalf of your business and your customers. Information about customers enables any business to better meet their needs. Sharing that information helps the entire organization work to meet those needs.

The emphasis in this article is on your role in showing how the data fit together to create a seamless execution of the strategy. Under this scenario, marketers become knowledge brokers, sharing data and research in a way that helps an entire organization learn about the customer and the challenges that lie ahead. It's a critical step between the planning models of yesteryear and those that go beyond short-term financial results.

Responding to this new reality requires an integrated plan that coworkers learn, understand, and see a way to influence. As one charged with implementing that plan, you need to know who these peo-

(Continued)

(Continued)

ple are, how they receive information, the best learning environment, and who they need to teach them. Armed with knowledge about your coworkers, you can make sure that they can relate to information from their own position within the company. You can set in motion a planning process that helps yours become a learning organization, breathing life into a strategy document.

There is no one model for the best way to do this, but we're proposing a system that shows a stream of thought, from data to strategy to action.

Making a Business Bloom

To illustrate our model, let's say you own a floral design business. You have already identified your business's strengths, limitations, and distinguishing features. You have also looked at information concerning the competition, current and potential customers, and the environmental factors that would affect you in the coming years. These four areas combined allow us to set goals and formulate strategies and tactics designed to help us achieve those goals.

The flow of this road map provides a lot of information, but it also provides a logical sequence that makes sense and results in knowledge, as opposed to mere numbers. Your own, real-life plan will provide information such as pricing structures, the stage of your product in the life cycle, the dollar value of the market, etc.

Note that even in this very simple model, there are actions for people throughout the organization. For instance, the weekly design review is more a quality initiative than one for marketing. Snow-removal problems and flooding reflect on your image, but negotiating with the city council to solve these problems is a job for your company's government relations or legal department. Identifying necessary workshops or training usually ends up on the desk of the personnel or human resources manager.

What's important is that everyone in the organization realizes how these efforts flow together to form the backbone of your relationship with the customer. It's a relationship that needs the care and attention of everyone, not just the marketing department.

Source: Marketing Tools (July/August 1996).

Sources of Marketing Information*

PRIVATE SOURCES

A. C. NIELSEN

Keywords: buying behavior; market research; retailing

Elliot Bloom, Vice President,
Public Relations & Advertising
150 N. Martingale Road
Schaumburg, IL 60173-2076

Phone: 708/605-5881
Fax: 708/605-2570
E-mail: ebloom@nielsen.com

A. C. Nielsen provides a wide range of services that help consumer packaged-goods manufacturers and retailers screen, plan, test, and evaluate individual brands and marketing programs. The company provides manufacturers and retailers with comprehensive insights on sales volume, shares, trends, pricing, promotions, distribution, and inventory levels. Nielsen also offers a full range of scanner-based services, from comprehensive national analyses to local markets and individual household buying patterns.

ABOUT WOMEN, INC.

Keywords: consulting; market research; women

Michelle LeBrasseur,
Marketing Services Manager
33 Broad Street
Boston, MA 02109

Phone: 617/723-4337
Fax: 617/723-7107

About Women, Inc. reports exclusively on the women's marketplace. It provides compiled market research in formats ranging from a monthly business-to-business newsletter to topical reports to customized marketing consulting. Each issue of *Marketing to Women* provides 15 to 20 executive summaries taken from major

*Excerpted from *Marketing Know-How* by Peter Francese (Ithaca, N.Y.: American Demographics Books, 1996).

research studies on the women's market. Topics covered include demographics, advertising, buying behaviors and influences, consumer behaviors and influences, consumer attitudes, media preferences, gender gap, health, technology, and more.

ADVANCED MARKETING SOLUTIONS, INC.

Keywords: analytical services; computer services; statistical software

Emil D. Morales, Vice President,
Custom Applications
One Corporate Drive, Suite 506
Shelton, CT 06484

Phone: 203/925-3038
Fax: 203/925-3009

Advanced Marketing Solutions, Inc., a subsidiary of NFO Research, offers a full range of Windows-based software. Its Expert Report Systems produce graphic and narrative reports of business information and research data. The AMS SmartSystem Suite is designed to address the needs of marketing professionals engaged in the analysis and output of concept tests, product tests, or tracking studies.

ADVERTISING RESEARCH FOUNDATION

Keywords: advertising research; market research; media research

Carol A. White,
Office Services Manager
641 Lexington Avenue
New York, NY 10011

Phone: 212/751-5656
Fax: 212/319-5265

The Advertising Research Foundation (ARF) is the only organization whose principal mission is to improve the practice of advertising, marketing, and media research in pursuit of more effective marketing and advertising communications. ARF conducts research projects ranging from assessing the validity of research measures to pinpointing the contribution of advertising in a specific situation. It maintains a highly active and continuing program of conferences and workshops. ARF constantly develops and distributes new guidelines, criteria, position papers, and other publications of value to the industry. ARF's membership includes major advertisers, advertising agencies, media, research firms, educational institutions, and other industry associations.

AMERICAN BUSINESS INFORMATION, INC.

Keywords: business to business; database marketing; market research; sales and marketing

Tony Sgroi
5711 S. 86th Circle
Omaha, NE 68127

Phone: 402/593-4593
Fax: 402/331-6881
E-mail: online@abii.com

American Business Information, Inc. provides business lists and company profiles for more than 11 million businesses. Selection is based on type of business and size of business for any geographic segment in the U.S. and Canada. Information is available online and is updated monthly.

AMERICAN MARKETING ASSOCIATION
Keywords: market research

Pat Goodrich, Director,
AMA Marketing Research Division
250 S. Wacker Drive
Chicago, IL 60606-5819

Phone: 800/262-1150
Fax: 312/648-5625
E-mail: http://www.ama.org

The American Marketing Association (AMA) is a professional society of marketers with nearly 50,000 members in 92 countries. The AMA assists in personal and professional career development among marketing professionals and advances the science and ethical practice of all marketing disciplines.

The AMA conducts seminars, workshops, and more than 25 national conferences across the country on topics such as attitude research, behavior research, and applied research methods. Its quarterly *Journal of Marketing Research* covers the latest marketing research techniques, methods, and applications. The quarterly *Marketing Research: A Magazine of Management and Applications* covers legislative and regulatory issues, management tools, research trends, and new technology. The AMA also published the results of a joint study conducted by the AMA and the Advertising Research Foundation on the marketing research profession.

CLARITAS, INC.
Keywords: consumer segmentation; database marketing; demographics; desktop mapping/GIS; local and market information; market research; projections

Kathleen Dugan,
Public Relations Officer
1525 Wilson Boulevard, Suite 1000
Arlington, VA 22209

Phone: 703/812-2700
or 800/284-4868
Fax: 703/812-2701

Claritas develops national target marketing databases and software systems designed to meet the marketing needs of various consumer industries. Claritas, an information firm of VNU Marketing Information Services, Inc., has five offices in the U.S.

The company's Compass package is a PC-based targeting system for product development and profiling, site location, strategic planning, media planning, and direct marketing. The system combines and analyzes clients' customer information files, cartographic data, syndicated surveys, demographic indicators, and Claritas's PRIZM and P$YCLE segmentation systems. Compass links directly to several GIS systems and is available in a Windows platform with mapping, data retrieval, and analysis functions. PRIZM classifies U.S. households into 62 neighborhood types.

Claritas offers several products specifically for the financial services industry. P$YCLE is a segmentation system, and LifeP$YCLE is an insurance consumer database. Claritas also offers The Market Audit database, an annual consumer survey of financial services.

Claritas also produces annual demographic estimates and five-year projections for small geographic units. The firm taps 1,600 local sources to annually update its small-area data.

CONFERENCE BOARD (THE)
Keywords: consumer confidence; consumer spending

845 Third Avenue　　　　　Phone: 212/759-0900
New York, NY 10022-6601　　Fax: 212/980-7014

The Conference Board is a nonprofit membership organization whose Consumer Research Center conducts ongoing analysis of demographic, social, and economic changes in the consumer market and of consumer spending. The monthly *Consumer Confidence Survey* newsletter reports the results of a nationally representative survey of 5,000 households. The newsletter also reports regional data and buying intentions for high-ticket items. *The Consumer Market Watch* newsletter carries current income, employment, expenditure, and price data. The Consumer Market Guide, which is updated continuously, is a statistical compendium of consumer data. The center provides annual updates of consumer spending patterns based on the government's Consumer Expenditure Survey. It also produces crosstabulations of households and income from the Census Bureau's annual demographic file of the Current Population Survey.

DATABASE MARKETING RESOURCE SERVICES, INC.
Keywords: consulting; database marketing; market research

Bernice Grossman, President　　Phone: 212/465-0814
333 Seventh Avenue, 20th Floor　Fax: 212/465-8877
New York, NY 10001　　　　　E-mail: dmrsbtg@aol.com

Database Marketing Resource Services, Inc. (DMRS) is an independent consultancy specializing in the design and development of marketing databases. It assists marketers in the vendor selection process as well as filling the project-facilitator position during marketing database projects. DMRS offers marketing database consulting for operational needs assessment and RFP development and administration; technical administration and systems integration; vendor evaluation, selection, contract review, and outsourcing; due diligence for mergers/acquisitions; expert witness testimony; research, analysis, and modeling; and workshops and seminars.

DECISIONMARK CORPORATION

Keywords: attitudes and opinions; business to business; demographics; desktop mapping/GIS; mailing lists; statistical software

Sarah Caldwell,
Marketing Representative   Phone: 800-365-7629
200 Second Avenue SE, Suite 300   Fax: 319/365-5694
Cedar Rapids, IA 52401-1214

Decisionmark's Proximity software has information mapping, analysis, and presentation capabilities. The product includes more than 800 population, housing, economic, and agricultural census attributes at the state, county, five-digit zip code and/or census block group level, plus current-year estimates and five-year projections for more than 20 key census attributes at the state and county level. Proximity includes a Data Resource Catalog featuring the leading compilers of consumer and business lists, demographics, psychographics, cartographic data, and specialty databases that may be used within Proximity. Data come map-, graph-, and table-ready. All data come with an installation program so users do not require assistance to access data.

DIRECT MARKETING ASSOCIATION, INC.

Keywords: database marketing

1120 Avenue of the Americas   Phone: 212/768-7277 x1155
New York, NY 10036-6700   Fax: 212/768-4546

The Direct Marketing Association (DMA) offers members online services and publications through its Library and Resource Center. Its seminars, conferences, and special-interest councils are places for meeting and learning from fellow professionals. DMA addresses direct-marketing concerns in the marketplace, in the media, and in government.

EQUIFAX NATIONAL DECISION SYSTEMS

Keywords: business to business; census data; consumer segmentation; demographics; desktop mapping/GIS; local and market information

5375 Mira Sorrento Place, Suite 400   Phone: 800/866-6520
San Diego, CA 92121   Fax: 619/550-5800

Equifax National Decision Systems offers more than 60 marketing databases; industry-focused expertise; and computer technology for data access, analysis, planning, and targeting. MicroVision is a consumer segmentation and targeting system. Infomark for Windows is a desktop PC system for market analysis, planning, and targeting that provides immediate, unlimited access to any or all of the company's information resources. Sparta is a PC-based software and data package that provides access to a number of business applications, including site evaluation, trade area analysis, CRA analysis, and market optimization. On-CD is a CD-ROM product line providing census demographics, consumer, and business data for places to the census-tract level.

GENESYS SAMPLING SYSTEMS

Keywords: demographics; geocoding; market research; survey samples

Amy W. Starer, Vice President   Phone: 215/653-7100
565 Virginia Drive   Fax: 215/653-7114
Fort Washington, PA 19034

GENESYS Sampling Systems is a full-service research sample provider. In addition to custom samples, it offers the GENESYS Sampling System, including the GENESYS database, a compilation of geodemographic information organized on the basis of telephone area code/exchange combinations. For each of approximately 37,000 area code/exchanges, the GENESYS database provides demographic estimates, PRIZM cluster codes, and geographic designations down to the census-tract level. It can be used for imputing demographic variables for incomplete survey data, appending geographic codes for data analysis, and creating geodemographic profiles from a variety of data sources including ANI, warranty card, or customer database information.

HISPANIC MARKET CONNECTIONS, INC.

Keywords: California; Hispanics; Latin America; New York

M. Isabel Valdes, President   Phone: 415/965-3859
5150 El Camino Real, Suite D-11   Fax: 415/965-3874
Los Altos, CA 94022

Hispanic Market Connections, Inc. (HMC) offers Hispanic cultural and marketing expertise to corporations, nonprofits, and government agencies. To describe and measure the Hispanic market, HMC has developed and tested Hispanic market-specific qualitative and quantitative research tools and methodologies. It conducts annual syndicated studies in New York, Chicago, and southern and northern California. HMC also offers marketing and research consulting services in all Latin American countries.

J. D. POWER & ASSOCIATES

Keywords: automotive; customer satisfaction; financial services; international; market research; sales and marketing

Steve Goodall, Senior Partner
30401 Agoura Rd
Agoura Hills, CA 91301

Phone: 818/889-6330
Fax: 818/889-3719
E-mail: jdpa@aol.com

J. D. Power & Associates is an international market research firm that measures and analyzes consumer opinions and behaviors including customer satisfaction. The firm conducts syndicated and proprietary studies in the telecommunications, automotive, office products, airline, and financial services industries. The firm is headquartered in Agoura Hills, California, with branch offices in Detroit; Westport, Connecticut: Torrance, California; Toronto; Tokyo; and London.

LANGER ASSOCIATES, INC.

Keywords: focus groups; lifestyles; market research; trends

Judith Langer, President
19 West 44th Street
New York, NY 10036

Phone: 212/391-0350
Fax: 212/391-0357

Langer Associates, Inc. specializes in qualitative studies of social and marketing issues. The firm conducts focus groups, personal and telephone depth interviews, and offers consulting services on trends. The *Langer Report* is a syndicated newsletter on changing values and lifestyles. TrendSpotter studies identify emerging trends.

LEXIS-NEXIS

Keywords: attitudes and opinions; business to business; online; trends

Tom McElroy, Market Manager
9443 Springboro Pike
Miamisburg, OH 45342

Phone: 800/227-9597 x5365
Fax: 513/865-1780
E-mail: thomas.mcelroy@lexis-nexis.com

LEXIS-NEXIS provides NEXIS, a premier database containing more than 4,000 sources of national and international news, financial, industry, and marketing information. Because of the continuity of database design, researchers can use similar search logic in a wide variety of databases. Highlights include the Roper Center's Public Opinion Poll dating back to 1935, several consumer trends publications, and Lexis-Nexis's Predicasts. The new Market Quick & Easy product helps marketing professionals easily find information essential to their work-competitors' marketing strategies, industry forecasts, brand and product category analysis, pricing information, new-product introductions, and more.

MARITZ MARKETING RESEARCH INC.

Keywords: customer satisfaction; international; market research

Phil Wiseman, Marketing Director
1297 North Highway Drive
Fenton, MO 63099

Phone: 800/446-1690
Fax: 314/827-8605
E-mail: wisemapl@maritz.com

Maritz Marketing Research is a nationwide firm that conducts custom and syndicated studies in the U.S. and abroad. It specializes in customer satisfaction measurement and offers full-service research in key areas: qualitative, tactical (tracking; attitude, trial, and usage, etc.), and strategic (product positioning, market segmentation, etc.).

MEDIAMARK RESEARCH, INC.

Keywords: buying behavior; consumer segmentation; market research; media research

Ken Wollenberg, Senior Vice President,
Sales and Marketing
708 Third Avenue
New York, NY 10017

Phone: 212/599-0444
Fax: 212/682-6284
E-mail: info@mediamark.com

Mediamark Research, Inc. conducts an annual syndicated survey of 20,000 adults in the 48 continental states, collecting data on demographic and socioeconomic characteristics, media usage, and purchase behavior. Data are available in printed reports and online. MEMRI is a PC-based system that allows custom analysis of survey data. MRI also combines its media and product data with all four U.S. geodemographic (cluster) systems for lifestyle analysis at the local level.

METROMAIL

Keywords: database marketing; demographics; housing and real estate; lifestyles; mailing lists

Julie Springer, Marketing Analyst
360 E. 22nd Street
Lombard, IL 60148

Phone: 708/932-2627
Fax: 708/620-3014
E-mail: jspring@interaccess.com

Metromail provides direct-marketing products and services, including targeted demographic and psychographic lists, list enhancement, database, modeling, and mail-production services. Its National Consumer Data Base (NCDB) provides household and individual demographic information for more than 142 million individuals. Metromail offers specialty lifestyle business and realty lists, including families with children, new movers, and new homeowners. Metromail also compiles BehaviorBank, a 28-million-name database of psychographic and lifestyle information.

POPULATION COUNCIL (THE)
Keywords: academic research; demographics; health care

Sandra Waldman, Director,
Office of Public Information
One Dag Hammarskjold Plaza
New York, NY 10017

Phone: 212/339-0500
Fax: 212/755-6052
E-mail: publnfo@popcouncil.org
or www: http://www.popcouncil.org

The Population Council, an international nonprofit, nongovernmental organization established in 1952, conducts research on three fronts—biomedicine, social science, and public health—to improve people's reproductive health, safely reduce unwanted pregnancies, and clarify the causes and consequences of population growth. The council participates in a uniquely wide scope of activities in these areas ranging from molecular biology to demography, contraceptive development, and on-site analyses of family planning programs and clinical trials. The council publishes and disseminates a wide range of written materials to varied audiences, including two peer-reviewed journals, newsletters, working papers, conference proceedings, guideline for research, pamphlets, and project summaries.

POPULATION INFORMATION PROGRAM, CENTER FOR COMMUNICATIONS PROGRAM, JOHNS HOPKINS UNIVERSITY
Keywords: academic research; demographics; health care; international

Elizabeth Duverlie,
Assistant to the Director
111 Market Place, Suite 310
Baltimore, MD 21202

Phone: 410/659-6300
Fax: 410/659-6266

The Population Information Program (PIP) provides up-to-date and extensive information on a broad range of family planning, population, and related health issues. As the publishing and research arm of the Center for Communications Programs (CCP), PIP operates the

computerized POPLINE database, containing more than
225,000 citations and abstracts of scientific articles,
reports, books, and papers (published and unpub-
lished) in all languages. Topics include family-planning
technology and programs, fertility, population law and
policy, demography, AIDS and other STDs, maternal
and child health, primary health-care communication,
and population and environment issues. Information is
searchable by subject, author, country, year of publication, and other data fields. It is available online from
the U.S. National Library of Medicine, by mail from PIP,
and on compact disc. POPLINE also publishes a User's
Guide to POPLINE Keywords, POPLINE on Disc, and
POPLINE CD-ROM User's Manual.

ROPER CENTER FOR PUBLIC OPINION RESEARCH (THE)
Keywords: attitudes and opinions;
elections; trends

Lois Timms-Ferrara   Phone: 203/486-4440
P.O. Box 440   Fax: 203/486-6308
Storrs, CT 06268-0440

The Roper Center maintains a record of publicly
released polls and surveys for the U.S. and a growing
collection of data compiled outside the U.S. The center's holdings are historic—containing data from as
early as 1936—and contemporary. It disseminates this
material in paper and electronic form to academic
social scientists, government researchers, and policy
professionals.

TRW TARGET MARKETING SERVICES
Keywords: affluent market; automotive; computer
services; database marketing; ethnic markets;
financial services; housing and real
estate; mailing lists

Raelyn Wade, Sales Director   Phone: 214/390-5229
701 TRW Parkway   Fax: 214/390-5195
Allen, TX 75013

TRW Target Marketing Services, a business unit of TRW
Information Systems and Services based in Allen,
Texas, provides information services to the direct marketing, financial services, real estate, and automotive
industries. It helps marketers locate consumers most
likely to respond to offers. Its PerformanceData System
(PDS) allows marketers to reach 183 million consumers
in 98 million households nationwide. The PDS is compiled from consumer names and addresses from TRW's
consumer credit database, public record information
and data from questionnaires, publications, direct mail,

real estate deed recordings, birth records, tax assessor files, telephone White Pages, and other sources. TRW list selections include the Consumer Database, Highly Affluent Database, Ethnic Markets, New Movers, Home-ownersPlus Smart Targeting Tools, Credit Card Markets, and Buyers' Response. TRW also offers radius marketing capabilities and behavior-based segmentation tools. The company provides database marketing services, including data enhancement, address cleaning, National Change of Address (NCOA)* file processing, merge/purge and postal qualification services. *TRW Inc. is a nonexclusive licensee of the U.S. Postal Service.*

U.S. TRAVEL DATA CENTER (RESEARCH DEPARTMENT OF THE TRAVEL INDUSTRY ASSOCIATION OF AMERICA)

Keywords: travel and tourism

Suzanne D. Cook, Ph.D.,
Senior Vice President, Research   Phone: 202/408-1832
1100 New York Avenue, NW, Suite 450   Fax: 202/408-1255
Washington, DC 20005-3934

The U.S. Travel Data Center provides U.S. domestic travel volume and trip characteristics based on a national monthly survey of 1,500 U.S. resident adults. The National Travel Survey covers travel in the past month, purpose of trip, mode of transportation, other members of the household traveling, as well as basic demographic information.

FEDERAL GOVERNMENT SOURCES

BUREAU OF ECONOMIC ANALYSIS

Public Information Office   Phone: 202/606-9900
U.S. Department of Commerce
1441 L Street, NW
Washington, DC 20230   E-mail: REIS.REMD@BEA.DOC.GOV

The Bureau of Economic Analysis (BEA) provides the only ongoing annual measure of economic activity at regional and local levels, as well as national and international economic analysis. It examines principal sources of personal income, including transfer payments and rental income, dividend and interest income, wages and salaries, and the industries that supply them. The BEA also produces an important economic indicator—per capita personal income.

BEA data differ from those of the Census Bureau in that the latter surveys people to learn their income, while the BEA works down from the macrolevel, determining the total personal income of a county or state. For more information, see the "User's Guide to BEA Information," which appears each year in the January issue of the Survey of Current Business (see below). The publication is available free from BEA's Public Information Office.

Telephone Contacts

Public Information Office,	202/606-9900
Economic Projections, State and Metropolitan Areas, George Downey	606-5341
Personal Income and Employment, State, MSA and County Data Requests, Regional Economic Information Staff	606-5360

What You Can Get from the Bureau of Economic Analysis

Survey of Current Business

This monthly publication provides four valuable series of income data:

1. Quarterly estimates of personal income for states appear in the February, May, September, and November issues.

2. Preliminary annual estimates of personal income and disposable personal income for states appear in the May issue; revised estimates appear in September.

Federal Justice Statistics

Provides data on the movement of accused offenders through the federal criminal process, beginning with the number of suspects investigated, prosecution, adjudication, sentencing of defendants, and concluding with the types and durations of sanctions received and served.

BUREAU OF LABOR STATISTICS

Veola Kittrell	Phone: 202/606-7828
2 Massachusetts Avenue, NE	E-mail: stats.bls.gov/blshome.html
Washington, DC 20212	

The BLS is known for employment and unemployment information, but it also provides some of the best consumer spending data around.

Many of the statistics that people need to assess what is going on in the economy—trends in prices, earning, employment, unemployment, consumer spending, wages, and productivity—come from the Bureau of Labor Statistics. The following reports are free and may be obtained from the Office of Inquiries and Correspondence, U.S. Bureau of Labor Statistics, 2 Massachusetts Avenue, NE, Room 2860, Washington,

DC 20212; telephone 202/606-7828: Major Programs of
the Bureau of Labor Statistics describes each of the
agency's activities in detail and lists relevant publications; BLS Update is a quarterly publication that lists all
new publications and tells how to get them; and Telephone Contacts for Data Users lists names and telephone numbers of all subject-matter specialists.

What You Can Get from the Bureau of Labor Statistics

Employment and Unemployment Statistics

The Bureau of Labor Statistics analyzes and publishes
data from the monthly Current Population Survey (CPS)
on the labor force, employment, unemployment, and
persons not in the labor force. Studies based on CPS
data cover a broad range of topics, including analyses
of the nation's overall labor market situation, as well as
special worker groups such as minorities, women,
school-age youth, older workers, disabled veterans,
persons living in poverty, and displaced workers.

The bureau also collects, analyzes, and publishes
detailed industry data on employment, wages, hours,
and earnings of workers on payrolls of nonfarm business establishments. It publishes monthly estimates of
state and local unemployment for use by federal agencies in allocating funds as required by various federal
laws. In addition, the bureau provides current data on
the occupational employment of most industries for
economic analysis, vocational guidance, and education
planning. Data collection and preparation are carried
out under federal-state cooperative programs by state
agencies using methods and procedures prescribed by
the bureau.

Program Information
Business Establishment List, Michael Searson	202/606-6469
Employment and Earnings, Gloria P. Green	606-6373
Employment and Wages (ES 202), Staff	606-6567
Data Diskettes and Tapes, Staff	606-6567

Employment Situation
News Release, Staff	606-6378 or 606-6373
Recorded Messages, 24-Hour Hotline	606-7828

Establishment Survey Employment, Hours, Earnings
National Data, Staff	606-6555
Benchmarks, Patricia Getz	606-6521
Data Diskettes, David Hiles	606-6551
Real Earnings-News Release, David Hiles	606-6551
State and Area Data, Kenneth Shipp	606-6559
Data Diskettes, Guy Podgornik	606-6559

| Foreign Direct Investment Data, Staff | 606-6568 |
| Occupational Employment Statistics Survey, Staff | 606-6569 |

National Labor Force Data:	606-6378
Concepts and Definitions, Staff	606-6373
Employment and Unemployment Trends, Staff	606-6378
Machine-Readable Data and Diskettes, Gloria P. Green	606-6373
Microdata Tapes, Rowena Johnson	606-6345

Occupational Data

| Current Population Survey, Staff | 606-6378 |
| Occupational Mobility, Lawrence Leith | 606-6378 |

State and Area Labor Force Data

| Demographic Characteristics, Edna Biederman | 606-6392 |
| Data Diskettes and Tapes, Jessie Marcus | 606-6392 |

Weekly and Annual Earnings

Current Population Survey, Staff 606-6378

Special Topics

Absences from Work, Staff	606-6378
Contingent Workers, Staff	606-6378
Discouraged Workers, Harvey Hamel	606-6378
Displaced Workers, Jennifer Gardner	606-6378
Educational Attainment, Staff	606-6378
Flextime and Shift Work, Staff	606-6378
Home-Based Work, William Deming	606-6378
Job Tenure, Joseph Meisenheimer	606-6378
Longitudinal Data/Gross Flows, Francis Horvath	606-6345
Marital and Family Characteristics, Howard Hayghe	606-6378
Mass Layoff Statistics, Lewis Siegel	606-6404
Minimum Wage Data, Steven Haugen	606-6378
Current and Historical Data, Information staff	606-5886
Annual Survey of Occupation Injuries, Ethel Jackson	606-6179
Data Disk, Staff	606-6179
Data Tapes, Staff	606-6179
Census of Fatal Occupational Injuries, Guy Toscano	606-6165
Data Disk, Blaine Derstine	606-6175

Industry Injuries and Illnesses Estimates and Incidence

| Rates, Staff | 202/606-6180 |
| Characteristics, Elyce Biddle | 606-6170 |

Employment Projections

The bureau develops and publishes long-term economic projections. These are based upon certain specific assumptions that lead to projections of aggregate labor force, potential gross domestic product, industrial output, and employment by industry and occupational detail. These projections provide a comprehensive and integrated framework for analyzing the implications of likely economic growth trends for the national economy and employment in specific industries and occupations. Occupational projections and descriptive information are developed for use in career guidance and educational planning. Bureau projections are based upon extensive analysis of current and past economic and employment relationships and on special occupational studies. This work provides the basis for a variety of reports on employment needs generated by major categories of expenditures such as defense, health care, and infrastructure.

Current and Historical Data, Information staff   202/606-5886

Data Tapes and Disk
Industry-Occuption Matrix, Delores Turner   606-5730
   Input-Output and Employment Requirements, Art Andreassen   606-5689
   Industry Output and Employment Time Series, James Franklin 606-5709

Special Topics
Industry-Occupation Matrix, Delores Turner   606-5730
Occupational Outlook Handbook, Michael Pilot   606-5703
Occupational Outlook Quarterly, Neale Baxter   606-5691

Projections
Economic Growth and Industry, Charles Bowman   606-5702
Economic, Norman Saunders   606-5723
Final Demand, Betty Su   606-5729
Industry Employment, James Franklin   606-5709
Intermediate Demand, Art Andreassen   606-5689
Labor Force, Howard Fullerton   606-5711
Occupational, Neal Rosenthal   606-5701

BUREAU OF THE CENSUS

Customer Service   Phone: 301/457-4100
Data User Services Division   E-mail: http://www.census.gov
Washington, DC 20233

Frequently Called Numbers (Use area code 301 unless otherwise noted)
Census Customer Services (Data product and
ordering information for computer tapes,
CD-ROMs, microfiche, and some publications)   457-4100
FAX (general information)   457-4714
(orders only)   457-3842
TDD   457-4611
Agriculture Information   800/523-3215
Business Information   800/541-8345
Census-BEA Bulletin Board   457-2310
Census Job Information (Recording)   457-4449
Census Personnel Locator   457-4608
Congressional Affairs   457-2171
Data Centers (DUSD)   457-1305
FastFax (DUSD)   900/555-2FAX

Foreign Trade Information	457-3041/2311
Internet (General Information)—(DUSD)	457-1242
Library	457-2511
Population Information	457-2422/2435 (TTY)
Public Information Office (Press)	457-2794
Technical Support (CD-ROM Products)	457-1324

Census Regional Offices (information services, data product information)

Regional Office Liaison—FLD	457-2032
Atlanta	404-730-3833/3964 (TDD)
Boston	617-424-0510/0565 (TDD)
Charlotte	704-344-6144/6548 (TDD)
Chicago	708-562-1740/1791 (TDD)
Dallas	214-767-7105/7181 (TDD)
Denver	303-969-7750/6769 (TDD)
Detroit	313-259-1875/5169 (TDD)
Kansas City	913-551-6711/5839 (TDD)
Los Angeles	818-904-6339/6249 (TDD)
New York	212-264-4730/3863 (TDD)
Philadelphia	215-597-8313/8864 (TDD)
Seattle	206-728-5314/5321 (TDD)

Key to Office Abbreviations

AGFS—Agriculture & Financial Statistics Division
CAO—Congressional Affairs Office
DMD—Decennial Management Division
DPD—Data Preparation Division
DSD—Demographic Surveys Division
DSMD—Demographic Statistical Methods Division
DSSD—Decennial Statistical Studies Division
DUSD—Data User Services Division
EPCD—Economic Planning & Coordination Division
ESMPD—Economic Statistical Methods & Programming Division
FLD—Field Division
FTD—Foreign Trade Division
GEO—Geography Division
GOVS—Governments Division
HHES—Housing & Housing Economic Statistics Division
MCD—Manufacturing and Construction Division
PIO—Public Information Office
POP—Population Division
PPDO—Program & Policy Development Office
SRD—Statistical Research Division
SVSD—Services Division
TCO—Telecommunications Office
TMO—CASIC Technologies Management Office
2KS—Year 2000 Research and Development Staff

Other Key Contacts

1990 Census Tabulations and Publications—	
U.S.: Gloria Porter (DMD)	457-4019
Puerto Rico and Outlying Areas: Lourdes Flaim (DMD)	457-4023
1992 Economic Census—Paul Zeisset/Robert Marske (EPCD)	457-4151

2000 Census Plans—Catherine Keeley (DIR)	457-4036
Bulletin Board (Technical assistance)—DUSD	457-1242
CENDATA (Online service)—DUSD	457-1214
Census & You (newsletter)—Neil Tillman (DUSD)	457-1221
Census Catalog—John McCall (DUSD)	457-1221
Census History—Les Solomon (DUSD)	457-1167
Census Records (Age search)—DPD	812-285-5314
Conferences/Exhibits—Joanne Dickinson (DUSD)	457-1191
Confidentiality and Privacy—Jerry Gates (PPDO)	457-2516
County and City, State and Metropolitan Area Data Books—	
Wanda Cevis (DUSD)	457-1166
Economic Studies—Arnold Reznek (CES)	457-1856
Education Support—Dorothy Jackson (DUSD)	457-1210
FastFax (General Information)—DUSD	457-1242
Freedom of Information Act—Gary Austin (PPDO)	457-2532
Historical Statistics—DUSD	457-1166
Legislation—Thomas Jones (PPDO)	457-2512
Litigation—Nick Birnbaum (PPDO)	457-2490
Microdata Files—Carmen Campbell (DUSD)	457-1139
Monthly Product Announcement (Newsletter)—	
Mary Kilbride (DUSD)	457-1221
Statistical Abstract—Glenn King (DUSD)	457-1171
Statistical Briefs—Robert Bernstein (DUSD)	457-1221
Statistical Research—C. Easley Hoy (SRD)	457-4978
User Training—DUSD	457-1210

Internet

Census—BEA Bulletin Board (Telnet)	cenbbs.census.gov
Gopher	gopher gopher.census.gov
FTP	ftp.census.gov
World Wide Web	http://www.census.gov

NATIONAL TECHNICAL INFORMATION SERVICE (NTIS)

Stuart M. Weisman, Product Manager
5285 Port Royal Road
Springfield, VA 22161

Phone: 703/487-4650
Fax: 703/321-8547
E-mail: orders@ntis.fedworld.gov
or telnet to fedworld.gov

As information becomes an important business resource, establishments are tapping into NTIS's treasury of information products and services. For 50 years, NTIS, as part of the U.S. Department of Commerce, has served as the nation's clearinghouse for business and management studies, training tools, computer and telecommunications standards, international market reports, mail lists, and much more.

For an introduction to the vast array of publications and electronic products available from NTIS, call or write for its free 1995–96 Catalog of Products and Services, PR-827. For a sampling of the most recent research and statistical information available in the business fields, ask for the free Business Highlights,

PR-985. For free information available by fax, call 703/487-4142. For free dial-up and Internet access to information available at NTIS, connect to the FedWorld Information Network either by modem at 703/321-3339 or by Internet:telnet to fedworld.gov. For File Transfer Protocol services, connect to ftp.fedworld.gov; for World Wide Web services, point your browser to http://www.fedworld.gov. The FedWorld help desk can be reached at 703/487-4608.

STATISTICS OF INCOME DIVISION, U.S. INTERNAL REVENUE SERVICE

John Kozielec,
Sandra Byberg, Statisticians
CP:R:S, P.O. Box 2608
Washington, DC 20013-2608

Phone: 202/874-0410
Fax: 202/874-0964
E-mail: electronic bulletin board
202/874-9574 or
http://www.irs.ustreas.gov

IRS data are useful for more than tax and income information. They can be used to examine migration and population trends between censuses. Income-by-income source, tax deductions, and tax exemptions are all reported by marital status of the taxpayer. Researchers can infer household composition based on marital status and the number of exemptions claimed. Exemption data can also be used in making population inferences for years between censuses; researchers can also obtain exemption data from matched tax returns for adjacent years to track annual migration by county and state, based on changes in mailing address.

What You Can Get from the Internal Revenue Service

Statistics of Income (SOI) Bulletin

This quarterly report publishes the most current, preliminary statistics based on individual income tax returns. Selected income and tax data are also shown by state by size of taxpayer income. For some years, the Bulletin also provides estimates of the personal wealth of the nation's top wealthholders derived from estate tax returns, by age, sex, and marital status. SOI Bulletin (Publication 1136) is available for $26 per year from the Superintendent of Documents, Government Printing Office, P.O. Box 371954, Pittsburgh, PA 15250-1954; telephone 202/512-1800 or fax 202/512-2250.

Statistics of Income—Individual Income Tax Returns

This annual report presents the final statistics for a given income year. It includes data (at the national level only) on income sources, tax deductions, personal exemptions, and income tax, in considerably more detail than that offered by the preliminary estimates presented in the SOI Bulletin. The data are presented by several classifications, including taxpayer marital state and size of income. Statistics of Income (Publication 1304) can be purchased for $14, also from the Superintendent of Documents, Government Printing Office, P.O. Box 371954, Pittsburgh, PA 15250-1954; telephone 202/512-1800 or fax 202/512-2250.

Individual Income Tax Return File

The microdata available in the public-use tapes often provide more detailed information than the printed publication, based on the same sample used for the final statistics. However, some data are edited to protect the identity of individual taxpayers. Individuals can buy annual files from the IRS for $2,150.

Migration Data

IRS sells summaries of migration patterns, presenting origins and destinations, by county and state, based on year-to-year changes in taxpayer addresses. Income data for migrants are also available for the most recent year. Prices vary.

County Income Data

IRS sells county-level income tables showing types of income, number of returns, and personal exemptions. Data are also summarized by state. Prices vary.

STATE AND LOCAL SOURCES:

Usually located in the capitals, each state has a Data Center, supplying information about business and economic research, as well as information about labor, health, and education.

NOTES

INTRODUCTION

1. Philip Kotler and Gary Armstrong, *Principles of Marketing* (Englewood Cliffs, N.J.: Prentice Hall, 1996).
2. Ibid., pp. 20–21.

CHAPTER 1

1. Brian Dumaine, "The Bureaucracy Busters," *Fortune* (June 7, 1991), pp. 36–50.
2. Theodore Levitt, "How Do You Follow an Act Like Bud?," *Business Week* (May 2, 1988).
3. William Taylor, "The Business of Innovation: An Interview with Paul Cook," *Harvard Business Review* (March/April 1990), pp. 97–106.
4. Alexander Hiam and Charles D. Schewe, *The Portable MBA in Marketing* (New York: John Wiley & Sons, 1994), p. 245.
5. Ibid., p. 245.
6. Howard Schlossberg, quoting Peter Senge, "Author: Consumers Just Can't Wait to Be Satisfied," *Marketing News* (February 4, 1991), p. 13.
7. Hiam and Schewe, p. 255.
8. Ibid., p. 284.
9. Ibid., p. 284.
10. Ibid., p. 285.

CHAPTER 2

1. Philip K. Y. Young and John J. McAuley, *The Portable MBA in Economics* (New York: John Wiley & Sons, 1994), pp. 185–186.
2. Henry Ford, *My Life and Work* (New York: Doubleday Page & Co., 1923), pp. 146–147.
3. Hiam and Schewe, pp. 311–312.

4. Frederick L. Webster, *The New Portable MBA* (New York: John Wiley & Sons, 1994), p. 145.

5. Ibid., pp. 145–146.

CHAPTER 3

1. Kaoru Ishikawa, *What Is Total Quality Control? The Japanese Way* (Englewood Cliffs, N.J.: Prentice Hall, 1985), p. 32.

2. James Brian Quinn, Thomas L. Doorley, and Penny C. Paquette, "Beyond Products: Service-Based Strategy," *Harvard Business Review* (March/April 1990), pp. 58–68.

3. Philip Kotler and Gary Armstrong, *Principles of Marketing* (Englewood Cliffs, N.J.: Prentice Hall, 1996).

CHAPTER 4

1. James C. Schroer, "Ad Spending: Growing Market Share," *Harvard Business Review* (January/February 1990), pp. 44–48.

2. Hiam and Schewe, p. 363.

3. Mark Landler, "Consumers Are Getting Mad, Mad, Mad, Mad at Mad. Ave.," *Business Week* (April 30, 1990), pp. 70–72.

4. Hiam and Schewe, p. 364.

5. Ibid., pp. 375–377.

6. *Marketing Definitions: A Glossary of Marketing Terms.* (Chicago, 1960), p. 20.

7. Edward Nash, *Direct Marketing* (New York: McGraw-Hill, 1995), p. 4.

8. Rebecca Piinta, "The TV Beast," *American Demographics* (May 1993), pp. 34–42.

9. Peter Bieler, *This Business Has Legs* (New York: John Wiley & Sons, 1996).

CHAPTER 5

1. Martha F. Riche, "Psychographics for the 1990s," *American Demographics* (July 1989), pp. 25–31.

2. Hiam and Schewe, p. 185.

3. Don Peppers and Martha Rogers, *The One-to-One Future* (New York: Doubleday, 1993).

4. Ibid., p. 5.

5. Garth Hallberg, *All Consumers Are Not Created Equal* (New York: John Wiley & Sons, 1995), p. 28.

6. Peppers and Rogers, p. 52.

7. Ibid., p. 59.

8. Hallberg, p. 10.

CHAPTER 6

1. Peter Senge, "The Leaders' New Work: Building Learning Organizations," *Sloan Management Review* (fall 1990), pp. 7–23.

2. Hiam and Schewe, p. 210.

3. Thomas Moore, "Different Folks, Different Strokes," *Fortune* (September 16, 1985), p. 65.

4. James P. Meagher, "Church & Dwight: It Scores Big with the Brand-Name Pull of Arm & Hammer," *Barron's* (December 10, 1990), pp. 49–50; Peter Nulty, "Church & Dwight: No Product Is Too Dull to Shine," *Fortune* (July 27, 1992); Kotler & Armstrong, p. 253.

5. Charles Butter, *Sales & Marketing Management* (August 1993); Jennifer Lawrence, *Advertising Age* (November 8, 1993); Kenneth Labich, *Fortune* (May 2, 1994); Philip Kotler and Gary Armstrong, *Principles of Marketing* (Upper Saddle River, N.J.: Prentice Hall, 1996).

administered vertical marketing system   A vertical marketing system in which one member is informally designated as captain.

advertising   Any impersonal form of communication about ideas, goods, or services that is paid for by an identified sponsor.

advertising campaign   A set of messages with a single theme that is repeatedly conveyed to the target audience over an extended period.

advertising platform   The issues and product benefits that a marketer wishes to convey in an advertising message.

advertising target market   The specific audience toward which an advertising message is aimed.

advertising theme   The parts of an advertising message that are repeated throughout the campaign.

affective component (of an attitude)   The emotional feeling of favorableness or unfavorableness that results from a person's evaluation of an object.

agent   A wholesaling intermediary that does not take title to merchandise but serves primarily to bring buyers and sellers together and facilitate exchanges.

area sample   A probability sample in which respondents are chosen at random from a complete list of the population in a specific geographic area.

augmented product   An expected product that has been enhanced by a set of benefits that consumers do not expect or that exceed their expectations.

bait-and-switch pricing   A pricing strategy in which a product is given a low price in order to lure customers into a store, where an attempt is made to persuade them to buy a more expensive model or product.

The Glossary has been excerpted from *The Portable MBA in Marketing* by Alexander Hiam and Charles D. Schewe (New York: John Wiley & Sons, 1992).

barometric techniques Forecasting techniques that use analyses of past trends to predict the future.

basing-point pricing A geographic pricing policy in which the seller designates one or more geographic locations from which the rate that a buyer will be charged is calculated.

brand A name, term, symbol, design, or combination of these elements that is intended to identify the goods or services of one seller or group of sellers and differentiate them from those of competitors.

brand competitor An organization that competes with others to satisfy consumers' demand for a specific product.

brand extension A new product category that is given the brand name of an existing category.

brand mark The portion of a brand that consists of a symbol, design, or distinctive coloring or lettering.

break-even pricing An approach to pricing in which the price of a unit of the product is set high enough to cover the variable costs of producing that unit as well as the fixed costs of producing the product.

broker A wholesaling intermediary whose primary function is to supply market information and establish contacts in order to facilitate sales for clients.

business definition The way an organization answers the questions, "What business are we in?" and "What business *should* we be in?"

buying center All the individuals and groups participating in the buying process that have interdependent goals and share common risks.

cash-and-carry wholesaler A limited-service wholesaler that sells on a cash-only basis and does not provide delivery.

cash cow A strategic business unit (SBU) that has a higher market share than its competitors and is in a low-growth market.

cash discount A discount that is offered to buyers who pay their bills within a stated period.

cash flow The flow of cash into a company; maintaining a steady cash flow is sometimes used as a pricing objective.

causal studies Research in which the cause-and-effect relationships between various phenomena are explored.

channel captain A channel member that is able to influence the behavior of the other members of the channel.

channel management The activities involved in anticipating and understanding the sources of channel conflict and trying to eliminate or minimize them.

channel of distribution The route taken by a product and its title as it moves from the resource procurer through the producer to the ultimate consumer.

cognitive component (of an attitude) A person's evaluation of the characteristics of an object.

cognitive dissonance The state of anxiety or uneasiness that follows a purchase decision and creates a need for reassurance that the decision was the best one.

combination store A type of superstore that places emphasis on nonfood items and on services.

commission merchant An agent that performs selling functions for manufacturers, normally on a one-time basis.

common carrier A transportation company that transports products on a specified schedule and according to regulations and standards established by government regulatory agencies.

common costs Costs that must be allocated among two or more functional areas.

competitive advantage Differential access to resources (such as distribution channels, expertise, or technology) that can give a firm cost and quality advantages compared to its competitors.

concentrated strategy A media scheduling strategy in which the marketer limits its advertising to specified periods.

concentration strategy A marketing strategy that aims at a single market segment.

conclusive stage The stage of the research process in which the researchers develop a plan for collecting data, implement the plan, and provide the resulting information to decision makers.

consolidated metropolitan statistical area (CMSA) A population unit that contains a major metropolitan area and has a total population of more than 1 million.

consumer In the exchange process, the person who uses a product.

consumer market A market in which goods and services are actually used up.

consumer panel A variation of the mail survey in which respondents are given some form of remuneration for participating in an ongoing study by filling out a series of questionnaires or keeping detailed records of their behavior.

continuity strategy A media scheduling strategy in which advertisements are spread out over the entire period of the campaign.

continuous improvement Frequent incremental improvements driven primarily by customer requirements and competitor actions. Requires active organizational learning.

contract carrier A transportation company that agrees to transport a specified number of shipments to specific destinations for an estimated price.

contractual vertical marketing system A vertical marketing system in which channel members draw up a legal agreement that specifies the rights and responsibilities of each party.

contribution margin technique An approach to cost analysis that ignores nontraceable common costs.

control The process of monitoring action programs, analyzing performance results, and, if necessary, taking corrective action.

convenience products Inexpensive, frequently purchased goods and services that consumers want to buy with the least possible effort.

convenience sample A nonprobability sample in which respondents are selected to suit the convenience of the researchers.

cooperative organization A retail organization that consists of a set of independent retailers that combine their resources to maintain their own wholesaling operation.

core competency A constellation of closely related areas of expertise that, combined, give a firm a long-term advantage over competing firms.

corporate culture A set of values that create a distinct pattern that is reflected in all of an organization's activities.

corporate mission A statement of an organization's overall goals, usually broadly defined and difficult to measure objectively.

corporate vertical marketing system A vertical marketing system in which one member gains control through ownership of both production and distribution systems.

cost per thousand The dollar cost of an advertisement per 1,000 readers or viewers.

cost-plus pricing An approach to pricing in which the list price is determined by adding a reasonable profit to the cost per unit.

cross elasticity of demand A situation in which a change in the price of a product affects sales of another product.

cue An environmental stimulus that is perceived as a signal for action.

culture A set of values, ideas, attitudes, and other meaningful symbols created by human beings to shape human behavior and the artifacts of that behavior as they are transmitted from one generation to the next.

cumulative quantity discount A quantity discount that is applied to a buyer's total purchases over a set period.

customary pricing A pricing strategy in which the marketer maintains a traditional price level.

custom research firm A research firm that assists a marketer in designing a study, collecting information, and preparing a report.

data bank The component of a marketing information system (MIS) that stores raw data that come in from both the external environment and internal records.

dealer brand A brand that is created and owned by an intermediary.

decider In the exchange process, the person who chooses an alternative that will satisfy a want or need.

decoding The process whereby a receiver extracts meaning from a transmitted message.

delphi technique A forecasting technique in which a panel of experts is asked to assign rankings and probabilities to various factors that may influence future events.

demand The composite desire for particular products as measured by how consumers choose to allocate their resources among different products in a given market.

demarketing A marketing tool whose objective is to persuade consumers to use less of a product while maintaining the same level of satisfaction.

demographics Statistics about a population, such as sex, age, marital status, birthrate, mortality rate, education, income, and occupation.

derived demand Demand that is dependent on the demand for another product.

descriptive label A label that explains the important characteristics or benefits of a product.

descriptive studies Research that focuses on demographic information about markets and their composition.

determining (behavioral) variables A set of variables that determine whether a consumer is a member of a particular market segment.

difference threshold The smallest change in the intensity of a stimulus that can be noticed.

differentiated marketing A marketing strategy that aims at several market segments, varying the marketing mix for each segment.

direct costs Costs that can be assigned to a specific functional area.

direct marketing   An approach to marketing that uses one or more advertising media to effect a measurable response.

discretionary income   The amount of disposable income that is left over after spending on essentials such as food, shelter, and clothing.

display unit   The component of an MIS that permits the user to communicate with the system.

distinctive competencies   Activities that a firm can perform better than other firms.

distribution   The process of making sure that a product is available when and where it is desired.

distribution center   A storage facility that takes orders and delivers products.

dog   An SBU that has a low relative market share and is in a low-growth market.

drive   A strong motivating tendency that arouses an organism toward a particular type of behavior; see also **motive.**

drop shipper   A limited-service wholesaler that sells goods but does not stock, handle, or deliver them.

dumping   A situation in which a product is sold at a lower price in a foreign market than in a domestic one, or at a price below the cost of production.

early adopters   Consumers who buy a product early in its life cycle and influence other people to buy it.

early majority   Consumers who wait and watch others before adopting a new product.

economic order quantity   The optimum quantity of a product to order at a given time.

economies of scale   The savings that result when fixed costs are spread over more units of a product.

effective demand   The combination of desire to buy and ability to buy.

80-20 rule   A term used to refer to the fact that a large percentage of a company's sales and profits may come from a relatively small percentage of its customers or products.

elastic demand   A situation in which a percentage change in price brings about a greater percentage change in quantity sold.

encoding   The process whereby a source translates a message into words and signs that can be transmitted, received, and understood by the receiver.

Engel's law   A set of statements concerning the proportional changes in expenditures that accompany increases in family income.

environment   A set of forces external to the organization that the marketer may be able to influence but cannot control.

evaluator In the exchange process, an individual who provides feedback on a chosen product's ability to satisfy.

even pricing A form of psychological pricing in which the price is an even number.

evoked set The set of alternatives that come immediately to mind when a consumer seeks a solution to a problem.

exchange An exchange occurs when two or more individuals, groups, or organizations give to each other something of value in order to receive something else of value. Each party to the exchange must want to exchange; must believe that what is received is more valuable than what is given up; and must be able to communicate with the other parties.

exclusive dealing A method of control over distribution in which the manufacturer forbids dealers to carry competitors' products.

exclusive distribution An approach to distribution in which the number of intermediaries is limited to one for each geographic territory.

exempt carrier A company that is exempt from state and federal transportation regulations.

expected product A generic product plus a set of features that meet additional expectations of consumers.

experience curve A graphic representation of the effect of experience on the per-unit cost of producing a product.

experiment A research method in which the effect of a particular variable is measured by making changes in the conditions experienced by a test group with respect to the variable and comparing the results with those of a control group that did not experience the change.

exploratory stage The stage of the research process in which the problem is defined, objectives are set, and possible solutions are explored.

express warranty A statement that specifies the exact conditions under which a manufacturer is responsible for a product's performance.

extended family A nuclear family plus aunts, uncles, grandparents, and in-laws.

extensive distribution An approach to distribution that seeks the widest possible geographic coverage.

family of orientation The family into which a person is born.

family of procreation The family that a person establishes through marriage.

feedback Information that tells an organization's managers about the performance of each marketing program.

fixed-cost contribution The portion of a selling price that is left over after variable costs have been accounted for.

flexible-price policy A pricing policy in which the marketer offers the same products and quantities to different customers at different prices, depending on their bargaining power and other factors.

flighting strategy A media scheduling strategy in which there is heavy advertising during some parts of the campaign and no advertising in between.

FOB pricing A geographic pricing policy in which buyers pay transportation costs from the point at which they take title to the product.

focus group A form of personal interview in which a group of 8 to 12 people are brought together to offer their views on an issue, idea, or product.

form competitor An organization that competes with others to satisfy consumers' wants or needs within a specific class of products or services.

form utility The satisfaction that buyers receive from the physical characteristics of a product (e.g., its shape, function, or style).

franchise A legal contractual relationship between a supplier and one or more independent retailers. The franchisee gains an established brand name and operating assistance, while the franchiser gains financial remuneration as well as some control over how the business is run.

freight absorption A geographic pricing policy in which the seller charges the same freight rate as the competitor located nearest to the buyer.

freight forwarder A transportation company that pools many small shipments to take advantage of lower rates, passing some of the savings on to the shippers.

frequency The average number of times that the average prospect will be exposed to a specific advertisement in a specified period.

full-cost approach An approach to cost analysis that takes both direct and common costs into consideration.

full-service wholesaler A merchant wholesaler that performs a full range of services for its customers.

functional account An accounting category that reflects the purpose for which money is spent.

functional satisfaction The satisfaction received from the tangible or functional features of a product.

generic competitor An organization that competes with others to satisfy consumers' wants or needs within a general category of products or services.

generic name   A brand name that has become associated with a product category rather than with a particular brand.

generic product   A set of tangible or intangible attributes that are assembled into an identifiable form.

globalization   The tendency for markets to expand across national boundaries, leading to increasing competition among firms from different nations and a growing dependence on diverse, multinational, and multicultural customer bases.

governmental market   A set of federal, state, county, or local agencies that buy goods and services for use in meeting social needs.

gross rating points   The reach of an advertisement multiplied by its frequency.

horizontal conflict   Conflict that occurs between channel members at the same level of the distribution channel.

horizontal cooperative advertising   Advertising in which marketers at the same level in the distribution system advertise jointly.

horizontal market   A market that is made up of a broad spectrum of industries.

horizontal price fixing   A form of price fixing in which marketers at the same level of the distribution system get together and decide the price at which all of them will sell the product.

ideal self-image   Our mental picture of ourselves as we would like to be.

implementation   The actual execution of a strategic plan.

implied warranty   A legal promise that a product will serve the purpose for which it is intended, whether stated by the manufacturer or not.

impressions   The total number of exposures to a specific advertisement in a specified period.

impulse items   Convenience products that are purchased not because of planning but because of a strongly felt need.

independent retailer   A retailer that owns a single outlet that is not affiliated with any other retail outlet.

industrial distributor   An independently owned operation that buys, stocks, and sells industrial products.

inelastic demand   A situation in which a percentage change in price brings about a smaller percentage change in quantity sold.

influencer   In the exchange process, an individual who provides information about how a want or need may be satisfied.

initiator   In the exchange process, the person who first recognizes an unsatisfied want or need.

innovators Consumers who are ready and willing to adopt a new idea.

institutional advertising Advertising that develops and maintains a favorable image for a particular industry or company.

interactive MIS A computer-based marketing information system that allows managers to communicate directly with the system.

intermediary An independent or corporate-owned business that helps move products from the producer to the ultimate consumer.

intermediate market A set of wholesalers and retailers that buy goods from others and resell them.

intrapreneurship An approach to new-product development in which a small team of employees is set apart from the rest of the organization and freed from ordinary bureaucratic requirements long enough to develop a particular product.

joint demand Demand for two products that are complementary.

judgment sampling Nonprobability sampling in which respondents are selected on the basis of criteria that the researchers believe will result in a group that is representative of the population being surveyed.

jury of executive opinion A forecasting technique in which executives from various departments of the company are asked to estimate market potential and sales and then try to reach a consensus.

just-in-time purchasing An approach to inventory management in which products are bought in small quantities to reduce inventory carrying costs and obtain delivery just in time for use.

laggards Consumers who are strongly oriented toward the past and very suspicious of new concepts; they are the last to adopt a new product.

late majority Consumers who are committed to familiar ways of doing things and skeptical of new ideas.

lead The name of any individual or organization that may be a potential customer.

leveling A cognitive process in which the information retained becomes shorter and more concise.

limited-line retailer A retailer that offers only one or a few lines of related merchandise.

limited-service wholesaler A merchant wholesaler that performs a limited number of services for its customers.

line extension A new variety of a basic product.

list price The initial price of a product; also termed the *base price.*

loss leader A product that is given a lower than normal price in order to attract customers to a store.

macromarketing Bringing about exchanges between individuals and/or groups so as to provide satisfaction of a society's wants and needs.

macrosegmentation A process in which an industrial market is divided into segments based on types of buying organizations.

major innovation An item that has never been sold by any other organization.

manufacturer's brand A brand that is owned and marketed by the manufacturer that produces it.

marginal cost The cost of producing one more unit than the most recent unit produced.

market A group of people with unsatisfied wants and needs who are willing to exchange and have the ability to buy.

market aggregation A marketing strategy that uses a single marketing program to offer the same product to all consumers.

market atomization A marketing strategy that treats each individual consumer as a unique market segment.

market breakdown technique A forecasting technique in which the sales forecast for a large unit is broken down into forecasts for smaller units.

market buildup technique A forecasting technique in which information on a few specific market segments is aggregated to arrive at a total sales forecast.

marketing audit A comprehensive, systematic, independent, and periodic examination of an organization's marketing environment, objectives, strategies, and activities.

marketing concept The management philosophy that recognizes that the consumer should be the focal point of all activity within an organization.

marketing control chart A chart that combines trend analysis with the performance standards set by the organization.

marketing decision support system A coordinated collection of data, models, analytic tools, and computing power by which an organization gathers information from the environment and turns it into a basis for action.

marketing information system (MIS) A set of procedures and methods for regular, planned collection, analysis, and presentation of marketing information.

marketing intelligence system Within a marketing information system, the set of activities whose purpose is to monitor the external environment for emerging trends or events.

marketing mix   The combination of activities involving product, price, place, and promotion that a firm undertakes in order to provide satisfaction to consumers in a given market.

marketing research   A systematic, objective approach to the development and provision of information for decision making regarding a specific marketing problem.

market segment   A group of buyers within a market who have relatively similar wants and needs.

market segmentation   A marketing strategy in which a large, heterogeneous market is broken down into small, more homogeneous segments and a separate marketing program is developed for each segment.

market share   The total number of units of a product (or their dollar value) expressed as a percentage of the total number of units sold by all competitors in a given market.

market-share analysis   A forecasting technique in which it is assumed that the firm's market share will remain constant and sales forecasts for the firm are based on forecasts for the industry.

matrix organization   An organizational structure in which projects are assigned to task forces made up of people drawn from various functional departments.

mean   The sum of all the numbers in a set of scores divided by the number of scores.

median   In a list of numbers, the number above which half of the numbers in the list fall and below which the other half fall.

merchant middleman   An intermediary that takes title to the products it distributes.

merchant wholesaler   A wholesaling intermediary that is an independently owned business and takes title to the goods it sells.

message   An idea that is to be conveyed from a source to a receiver.

message channel   A vehicle for delivering a message.

micromarketing   Strategically managing human and organizational exchange relationships so as to provide socially responsible want and need satisfaction throughout the world while achieving the marketer's objectives.

microsegmentation   A process in which industrial market segments are subdivided on the basis of characteristics of the buying center and individual participants.

minor innovation   A product that was not previously sold by the company but has been marketed by some other company.

mode In a set of data, the number that occurs most frequently.

model bank The component of an MIS that contains mathematical marketing models that show relationships among various marketing activities, environmental forces, and desired outcomes.

modification Any adjustment of an existing product's style, color, or model; any product improvement; or a brand change.

modified rebuy A purchasing situation in which the organization has bought the good or service before, but some aspect of the situation has changed.

monopolistic competition A competitive situation in which there are many buyers and sellers, imperfect market information, some barriers to entry, and differentiated products.

monopoly A competitive situation in which there is only one seller of a product and entry to the market is restricted.

motive A need or want that is activated by a particular stimulus and initiates behavior toward some goal.

multinational corporation (MNC) A corporation that operates in more than one country and makes all of its decisions within a global framework.

nationalization A situation in which a national government becomes involved in the ownership or management of a business organization.

natural account An accounting category that reflects how money is actually spent.

new-task purchase A purchasing situation in which the organization is making the purchase for the first time.

noise Any distraction that interferes with the effectiveness of a communication.

noncumulative quantity discount A quantity discount that is offered on each sale made to a particular buyer.

nonprobability sampling A sampling technique in which respondents are selected partly on the basis of researchers' judgment.

nontraceable costs Common costs that are assigned to functional areas on an arbitrary basis.

norms Rules that tell the members of a particular cultural group what behavior is correct in certain situations.

observational approach A research method in which researchers observe people's behavior and record what they see but avoid direct interaction.

odd pricing A form of psychological pricing in which the price is an odd number or a number just below a round number.

off-price store   A discount store that buys manufacturers' overruns and end-of-season goods at below-wholesale prices and resells them at prices significantly lower than the regular department store price.

oligopoly   A competitive situation in which a few firms account for a large percentage of the industry's sales and in which there are substantial barriers to entry.

one-price policy   A pricing policy in which the marketer assigns a price to the product and sells it at that price to all customers who purchase the same quantity of the product under the same conditions.

open dating   A form of labeling in which consumers are informed of the expected shelf life of a product.

opportunity   An unsatisfied want or need that arises from a change in the organization's environment.

organization   All the activities involved in getting ready to carry out a strategic plan.

organizational learning   The process whereby individuals within an organization learn as a group and apply that learning to their work. Traditionally thought to vary with amount of experience (as measured, for example, by number of units produced), but increasingly seen as an independent variable that can be managed as a source of competitive advantage.

organizational structure   A set of relationships among individuals with different responsibilities.

original equipment manufacturer (OEM)   An organization that purchases industrial goods to incorporate into other products.

others self-image   Our mental picture of ourselves as we believe others see us.

packaging   All activities that are related to designing and producing the container or wrapper for a product.

penetration   A pricing strategy in which the initial price is set at a low level in order to generate the greatest possible demand for the product.

perception   The process by which a person attaches meaning to the various stimuli he or she senses.

perfect competition   A competitive situation in which there are many buyers and sellers, perfect market information, few or no barriers to entry, and homogeneous products.

personal selling   Person-to-person communication in which the receiver provides immediate feedback to the source's message.

phantom freight   A term used to refer to the difference between the true freight cost and the cost charged to the buyer in situations in which the buyer is charged an amount greater than the actual cost.

physical distribution   All the activities that provide for the efficient flow of raw materials, in-process inventory, and finished goods from the point of procurement to the ultimate consumer.

physical obsolescence   Obsolescence that results when products are built to last only a limited time.

piggyback service   A transportation service in which loaded trucks are taken directly onto railroad flatcars.

place utility   The satisfaction that buyers receive from having a product available at the appropriate place.

planned obsolescence   A product management strategy in which a marketer forces a product in its line to become outdated, thereby increasing replacement sales.

planning   The process of predicting future events and using those predictions to set courses of action that will achieve the organization's goals.

point-of-purchase promotion   A sales promotion technique that consists of locating an attention-getting device at the place of actual purchase.

positioning   A process in which a marketer communicates with consumers to establish a distinct place for its product or brand in their minds.

possession utility   The satisfaction that buyers receive from having the right to use or own a product.

postponed obsolescence   Obsolescence that occurs when technological improvements are available but are not introduced until the demand for existing products declines.

premium   A product that is offered free or at less than the regular price in order to induce the consumer to buy another product.

price   That which the buyer gives up in exchange for something that provides satisfaction.

price lining   A pricing strategy in which prices are used to sort products into "lines" based on an attribute such as quality, prestige, or style.

price-off   A price reduction that is used to induce trial or increase usage of a product.

primary data   Data that are collected specifically for use in a particular research project.

primary demand   Market demand for a product class rather than a particular brand.

primary demand advertising   Advertising in which the marketer attempts to create awareness of and provide information about a type of product.

primary group   A group that is small and intimate enough so that all of its members can communicate with one another face-to-face.

private carrier   A company that owns the goods it transports.

probability sampling   A sampling technique in which all members of the population being surveyed have a known chance of being included in the sample.

producer market   A set of buyers that purchase goods and services and use them to make other products.

product   A combination of functional and psychological features that provides form utility; the entire set of benefits that are offered in an exchange, including goods, services, ideas, people, places, and organizations.

product differentiation   A marketing strategy that uses promotion and other marketing activities to get consumers to perceive a product as different from and better than those of competitors.

product life cycle   A sequence of stages in the marketing of a product that begins with commercialization and ends with removal from the market.

product line   Within a company's product mix, a broad group of products that are similar in terms of use or characteristics.

product mix   The various products that a company offers to consumers.

product portfolio   A company's product mix viewed from a strategic perspective; a set of products or brands that are at different stages in the product life cycle.

product relaunch   A product management strategy that focuses on finding new markets and untapped market segments, new product uses, and ways to stimulate increased use of a product by existing customers.

program evaluation and review technique (PERT)   An implementation technique that uses detailed flowcharts showing which tasks can be carried out only after certain other tasks have been completed and which tasks can be done simultaneously.

promotion   Any technique that persuasively communicates favorable information about a seller's product to potential buyers; includes advertising, personal selling, sales promotion, and public relations.

promotional discount   A discount that is offered to intermediaries as compensation for carrying out promotional activities.

prospecting   The process of locating and classifying potential buyers of a product.

psychological pricing A pricing strategy in which the product is given a price that is psychologically appealing to consumers.

psychological satisfaction The satisfaction received from the intangible benefits of a product, such as a feeling of self-worth.

publicity Any message about an organization that is communicated through the mass media but is not paid for by the organization.

public relations A promotional activity that aims to communicate a favorable image of a product or its marketer and to promote goodwill.

public warehouse A warehouse that is owned by an independent contractor, which rents space to users.

pull strategy A promotional strategy in which each channel member attempts to persuade the next member in the system to handle and promote the product.

pulsing strategy A media scheduling strategy in which a continuous campaign is combined with short bursts of heavier advertising.

push strategy A promotional strategy in which the producer uses mass promotion to stimulate demand in the consumer market, thereby causing intermediaries to want to carry the product.

qualifying (descriptive) variables A set of variables that allow or qualify an individual to be a member of a particular market segment.

quality control The traditional approach to quality in which problems are detected after manufacturing and an effort is made to remove substandard products before shipping to customers.

quantity discount A discount offered to buyers who purchase larger than normal quantities of the product.

question mark An SBU that has a low relative market share and is in a high-growth market.

quota sampling A form of judgment sampling in which the population is divided into subgroups on the basis of one or more characteristics and a specified proportion of respondents are chosen from each subgroup.

rack jobber A limited-service wholesaler that supplies nonfood products to supermarkets, grocery stores, and drug retailers.

reach The percentage of total prospects that are exposed to a specific advertisement in a specified period.

real self-image Our mental picture of ourselves as we think we really are.

receiver The audience that is the target of a message.

recruiting The activity of locating skilled people and inducing them to apply for employment.

reference group Any set of people that influences an individual's attitudes or behavior.

reinforcement The extent to which satisfaction is derived from a response to an aroused need.

relative market share An organization's or SBU's market share divided by that of its largest competitor.

repatriation The transfer of profits to a parent firm from an affiliate in a foreign country.

research design An overall plan for conducting a research project, including the choice of the method that will be used to achieve the goals of the research.

response Whatever occurs as a reaction to an aroused need.

retailer An intermediary who sells products primarily to ultimate consumers.

retailing All activities undertaken by intermediaries whose primary function is to sell goods and services to ultimate consumers.

retention The extent to which one remembers what one has learned.

reverse elasticity A situation in which anticipation of a steady increase (decrease) in price causes buyers to make more (fewer) purchases of a product.

role expectations The rights, privileges, duties, and responsibilities that are associated with a particular role.

role theory An approach to the study of group influence that recognizes that people conduct their lives by playing many roles, each of which is accompanied by a certain range of acceptable behaviors.

rollout An approach to new-product introduction in which the product is launched in a series of geographic areas over an extended period.

sales-potential forecast A forecast of total potential sales for the firm for a specific time period.

sales promotion The array of techniques that marketers use to stimulate immediate purchase.

sales-variance analysis A method of data analysis in which data on actual sales are compared with quantitative sales objectives.

sample A group of respondents who are representative of the population being surveyed.

sampling Giving free samples of a product to consumers or offering a trial size at a very low cost.

scenario analysis A forecasting technique in which researchers develop a subjective picture of several possible futures by identifying cause-and-effect relationships and following them to their logical conclusions.

scientific method   A research process that involves the development of a hypothesis that can be confirmed, modified, or rejected on the basis of information gathered by objective means.

scrambled merchandising   The practice of carrying any product line, however dissimilar from other lines carried, as long as it yields a profit.

secondary group   A large group whose members have a shared goal but do not engage in face-to-face communication.

secondary source   Data that have been collected for a purpose other than the research project in question.

selective demand   Demand for a particular brand.

selective-demand advertising   Advertising in which the marketer attempts to create awareness of and provide information about a specific brand.

selective distribution   An approach to distribution that involves the use of a limited set of outlets in a given territory.

self-liquidating premium   A premium for which the buyer pays all or part of the cost.

selling agent   An agent who handles the entire marketing function for a manufacturer.

sensory thresholds   The upper and lower limits on the ability of human sensory processes to perceive increases or decreases in the intensity of a stimulus.

sharpening   A cognitive process in which the information retained becomes more vivid and important than the event itself.

shippers' cooperative   A group of shippers that pool shipments of similar items in order to benefit from lower freight rates.

shopping-mall intercept   A form of personal interview in which respondents are approached or intercepted as they pass a particular spot in a shopping mall.

shopping products   Goods and services about which consumers will seek information before making a purchase.

simple random sampling   Probability sampling in which respondents are chosen at random from a complete list of the members of the population.

simple trend analysis   A forecasting technique in which managers review historical data and use the rates of change to project future trends.

single-line wholesaler   A full-service wholesaler that carries only one or two product lines but offers considerable depth in each.

skimming A pricing strategy in which the initial price is set at a high level with the goal of selling the product to people who want it and are willing to pay a high price for it.

slice-of-life advertising Advertising that portrays consumers in realistic situations that are consistent with consumers' perceptions of their own lifestyles.

social class A relatively permanent and homogeneous category of people within a society. The members of a class have similar values, lifestyles, interests, and behavior.

socialization The process by which we learn the values and norms of our culture.

sorting A process in which products are brought together at one location and then divided up and moved in smaller quantities to locations closer to the ultimate buyers.

specialty-line retailer A limited-line retailer that carries only one or two product lines, but offers substantial depth and expertise in those lines.

specialty-line supplier A research firm that specializes in one aspect of the marketing research process.

specialty-line wholesaler A full-service wholesaler that carries a limited number of products for customers with specialized needs.

specialty products Goods and services for which there are no acceptable substitutes in the consumer's mind.

specialty store A retail outlet for which customers develop a strong preference based on the assortment of products offered, the service, or the store's reputation.

spokesperson The person who delivers the message in a testimonial.

standard metropolitan statistical area (SMSA) The Census Bureau's standard urban population unit. An area is classified as an SMSA if it contains a city with a population of at least 50,000 or an urbanized area of 50,000 with a total metropolitan population of at least 100,000.

staple items Convenience products that consumers plan to buy.

star An SBU that has a high growth rate and a high relative market share.

statistical bank The component of an MIS that offers statistical techniques to be used in analyzing data.

statistical process control The use of statistical analysis (usually by line employees) to measure and manage specific work processes. Commonly used in total quality programs.

straight rebuy A purchasing situation in which the organization has bought the good or service before and is likely to reorder from the same vendor.

strategic business unit (SBU) One or more products, brands, divisions, or market segments that have something in common, such as the same distribution system. Each SBU has its own mission, its own set of competitors, and its own strategic plan.

strategic information scanning system A formal structure of people, equipment, and procedures to obtain and manage information to support strategic decision making.

strategic market planning The managerial process of developing and implementing a match between market opportunities and the resources of the firm.

strategic plan A long-term plan covering a period of three, five, or sometimes ten years.

strategic planning The process of developing a long-range plan that is designed to match the organization's strengths and weaknesses with the threats and opportunities in its environment.

stratified random sampling Probability sampling in which the total population is divided into subgroups, or *strata,* and a random sample is chosen from each subgroup.

structured question A question that limits respondents to a specific set of replies.

style obsolescence Obsolescence that occurs when the physical appearance of a product is changed to make existing versions seem out of date.

subculture A smaller cultural group within a society that reflects geographic, religious, or ethnic differences.

superstore A combination of a general-merchandise discount operation and a supermarket.

survey approach A research method in which researchers use personal interviews, telephone interviews, or mailed questionnaires to question a group of people directly.

syndicated service A research firm that periodically compiles specific types of data for sale to marketers.

tactical plan A short-term plan that specifies the activities necessary to carry out a strategic plan.

target marketing A process in which the marketer evaluates a number of market segments, decides which one or ones to serve, and develops and implements a unique marketing mix for the targeted segment(s).

target return on investment An amount of income equivalent to a certain percentage of the firm's investment; this amount is set as a goal to be achieved through pricing.

target return pricing   An approach to pricing in which the marketer seeks to obtain a predetermined percentage return on the capital used to produce and distribute the product.

tariff   A tax on imported goods.

technological obsolescence   Obsolescence that results when technological improvements are made in a product.

telemarketing   The sale of goods and services by telephone.

testimonial   An advertising message that is presented by someone who is viewed as an expert on the subject.

test marketing   The controlled introduction of a new product to carefully selected markets for the purpose of testing market acceptance and predicting future sales of the product in that region.

threat   An unfavorable trend or situation that could prevent the organization from satisfying a want or need.

time utility   The satisfaction that buyers receive from having a product available at the appropriate time.

total fixed costs   Costs that ordinarily do not change over time, no matter what quantity of output is produced.

total quality program   The most common rubric for Japanese-inspired efforts to build quality into a product or service as it is produced or performed. Quality may be defined as closeness of fit to specifications, customer needs, or (in the most sophisticated programs) fit to latent customer needs. Total quality programs require the active involvement of the line workers themselves, which generally is best achieved via a radical change in corporate culture led by the chief executive.

total variable costs   Costs that fluctuate, depending on the quantity of output produced.

traceable costs   Common costs that can be assigned to two or more specific functional areas.

trade deficit   The amount by which a nation's total imports exceed its total exports.

trade discount   A discount that is offered to intermediaries as compensation for carrying out various marketing activities.

trademark   A brand that is given legal protection because it has been appropriated exclusively by one marketer.

trading down   A product management strategy in which a marketer that is known for selling high-priced products offers lower-priced products.

trading up   A product management strategy in which a marketer that is known for selling low-priced products offers higher-priced products.

transaction   An exchange between two or more parties.

transfer pricing   Raising the price of a product shipped to a foreign affiliate in order to increase the amount of profit transferred from the affiliate to the parent firm.

trial   The consumer's initial purchase and use of a product or brand.

truck wholesaler   A limited-service wholesaler that specializes in selling and delivery services.

true prospect   A lead that can benefit from the use of the product, can afford to buy it, and has the authority to do so.

tying agreement   A method of control over distribution in which the producer forces the dealer to buy additional products in order to secure one highly desired product.

uniform delivered pricing   A geographic pricing policy in which the seller offers the same delivered price to all buyers, regardless of their location and the actual freight expense.

unitary demand   A situation in which a percentage change in price brings about an equal percentage change in quantity sold.

unit pricing   A form of pricing in which the price of the package is accompanied by the price of the product in terms of some standard measure of quantity.

unsought products   Goods and services for which consumers have no felt need.

unstructured question   A question that allows respondents to answer as they wish and does not limit the length of responses.

value-added tax   A tax that is levied on the value added each time a product is sold to another member of the distribution channel.

values   The deeply held beliefs and attitudes of the members of a particular society.

variety store   A retailer that offers a wide assortment of low-priced items.

vertical conflict   Conflict that occurs between channel members at different levels of the distribution system.

vertical cooperative advertising   Advertising in which marketers at different levels in the distribution system advertise jointly.

vertical market   A market that consists of a single industry.

vertical marketing system   A distribution channel whose members are integrated into a single organization.

vertical price fixing   A form of price fixing in which marketers at different levels of the distribution system get together to set retail prices.

voluntary chain   A retail organization that consists of a set of independent retailers that agree to buy most of their merchandise through a single wholesaler.

warehouse club   A no-frills, cash-and-carry discount store that operates in a poor location; to shop there, the customer must become a member and pay dues.

warehouse showroom   A discount store that follows a strategy based on low overhead and high turnover; customers pay cash and must transport the merchandise themselves.

warehouse store   A no-frills supermarket that stocks a wide variety of food and nonfood items and sells them at lower prices than the typical supermarket price.

warranty   A manufacturer's promise that a product will serve the purpose for which it is intended.

wearout   The tendency of consumer response to a sales promotion to diminish over time.

wholesaler   An intermediary that distributes products primarily to commercial or professional users.

wholesaling   All of the activities provided by wholesaling intermediaries involved in selling merchandise to retailers; to industrial, institutional, farm, and professional businesses; or to other types of wholesaling intermediaries.

wholesaling intermediary   Any firm that engages primarily in wholesaling activities.

workload approach   An approach to sales-force design in which the size of the sales force is determined by dividing the total workload in hours by the number of selling hours available from each salesperson.

zero-based budgeting   An approach to budgeting in which each part of the organization must justify each item in its budget before it will be granted the funds it needs.

zone pricing   A geographic pricing policy in which the seller divides a geographic area into zones and charges each buyer in a given zone the base price plus the standard freight rate for that zone.